EDGE OF THE KNIFE

Edge of
THE KNIFE

POLICE VIOLENCE
in the Americas

PAUL CHEVIGNY

THE NEW PRESS
NEW YORK

278

Library of Congress Catalog Card Number 95-70651
ISBN 1-56584-183-2

Published in the United States by The New Press, New York
Distributed by W. W. Norton & Company, Inc., New York

Established in 1990 as a major alternative to the large, commercial publishing houses,
The New Press is the first full-scale nonprofit American book publisher
outside of the university presses. The Press is operated editorially in the public interest,
rather than for private gain; it is committed to publishing in innovative ways
works of educational, cultural, and community value that, despite their intellectual merits,
might not normally be commercially viable. The New Press's editorial offices
are located at the City University of New York.

Book design by Charles Nix

Production management by Kim Waymer
Printed in the United States of America

95 96 97 98   9 8 7 6 5 4 3 2 1

This book is for
Bell,
still the best detective.

The police are to the government as the edge is to the knife.
— DAVID BAYLEY

CONTENTS

PREFACE

Twenty-five years ago, when I was working on *Police Power: Police Abuses in New York City*,[1] this book would have been all but impossible to write. Brazil and Argentina were in the grip of military interventions that were to lead to bloody dictatorships lasting into the 1980s; information would soon be so hard to obtain that it was difficult even to separate military from police actions. In the Caribbean, the police problems in Jamaica described later in this book had just begun to take shape. In Mexico, police abuses were hidden under the facade of respectability created by government dominance of politics and the press.

In the United States, we were still groping for an understanding of police violence in our own cities, a problem dragged into the light by the social upheavals of the sixties. In *Police Power*, I drew from the cases in New York City a set of dynamics for police abuse, one of them that defiance of police orders would provoke a sanction from the police, perhaps violence, but at least an arrest. Another was that the police would put together a story, consistent with legal requirements, to account for any sanction they imposed. Thus anyone who defied the police—especially if he was part of an outcast group, like hippies or blacks, the very existence of which was a sort of defiance—was likely to be roughed up, and then charged with disturbing the peace and resisting arrest. I began to refer to those petty crimes as "cover charges."

Simple enough. I learned of similar patterns, in succeeding years, from cities all over the United States; the police habit of charging the people they beat up with standardized crimes even got the name of a mock crime: "contempt of cop." But I did not imagine—could not then imagine—that a comparison with other societies in the Americas was possible. I was not to see how general the pattern was of police reaction to defiance of their orders, or how violent it could be, until 1986 when Americas Watch invited me to help investigate police violence, along with other human rights violations, in Jamaica. I was reluctant at first; I thought it was hard enough to understand the dynamics of violence in, say, Brooklyn, let alone try to understand them in a Caribbean island. When I saw the figures of the hundreds killed by the police, collected from newspaper stories by the Jamaica Council for Human Rights, I was no better persuaded that I would understand the problem; but I was galvanized to learn at least a little of what was happening on the island. Deadly force was being used not only to punish defiance of the police, but also to punish such defiance of the law as carrying a gun. And stories of "shoot-outs" were concocted to make the police violence legitimate.

On another investigative mission for Americas Watch to São Paulo and Rio de Janeiro the next year, we found a similar but even larger problem of police violence against poor people in the streets and coercion of suspects in the station houses. I began to think we might be seeing a pattern in Latin American and Caribbean cities of repression of the poor through extrajudicial violence in the name of law enforcement.

I was not alone in that speculation. As the dictatorships in South America disintegrated in the 1980s, criminologists in the region were able to look into the problem of violence that was not outright "political"—at least in the partisan sense—but was instead part of routine crime and police work. Eugenio Raúl Zaffaroni, from Buenos Aires, and Eliane Junqueira, from Rio de Janeiro, assembled scholars from more than ten Latin American countries to collect data on homicides, including killings by police. In Salvador, Bahia, in 1988, at the conference "Mortes anunciadas: A (des)proteção da vida na America Latina" (Deaths foretold: The (non)protection of life in Latin America), the investigators reported their findings. While the figures for traffic fatalities and homicides in general could sometimes be obtained from official sources, the data for killings by police were not released, and sometimes not even collected by governments (as indeed they often were not in the United States until recently). The statistics for killings by police had been culled laboriously from newspaper stories, using methods developed by the Centro de Estudios Legales y Sociales, a human rights center in Buenos Aires. In the end, the reports by no means made out any simple pattern of massive police violence in Latin American cities, even in cases where the cities were overwhelmed by poverty-stricken migrants crowding into squatter settlements. While the number of killings counted in São Paulo was enormous, for example, the number counted in other cities, such as Mexico City, was comparatively small. The question hung in the air as to how the discrepancies were to be explained—by failings in the news reports or in some other way. In this book, I have tried to find explanations that will link at least the cities I myself have studied—Mexico City, Buenos Aires, São Paulo, and, for purposes of comparison, Rio de Janeiro. Jamaica is included because, although its culture is quite different, it is illuminating for precisely that reason, in view of the fact that the problems of police violence in Jamaica are parallel to those in some Latin American cities. Thus I have tried to join the study of human rights abuses with an understanding of the cultures to see why, in day-to-day encounters with authority, human rights are protected or violated.

I saw no useful way to compare such violence, especially torture and the abuse of deadly force, with police abuses in U.S. cities, until after the Rodney King beating in 1991. Although that was not literally an abuse of deadly force, it was a summary punishment of defiance—a vehicle pursuit—by near-deadly violence. And the investigations it pulled in its train uncovered a pattern of such punishments, ultimately including many abuses of deadly force. Those investigations raised the question whether in some cities in the United States, through means that are analogous to those used in cities elsewhere in the Americas, the police are using violence as a means of repression and social control.

In *Los Angeles: Capital of the Third World*, published just before the Rodney King incident, David Rieff tells us that many middle-class people in Los Angeles, confronted with a flood of migrants from the Third World, most of them poor, envision personal security in the city in the image of *Blade Runner*, a film in which the police of the city of the future have the job of liquidating renegade robots who have taken on the appearance and personality of human beings.

> It has become such a commonplace that Kevin Starr, in his epilogue to the "L.A. 2000" report, did not even feel the need to explain its origin when he warned of "the *Blade Runner* scenario: the fusion of individual cultures into a demotic polyglotism ominous with unresolved hostilities." At a dinner in Beverly Hills, I heard a liberal actor, well known for his benefactions to various community groups in L.A., tell his dinner companions that as far as he was concerned, the situation was hopeless. "You might as well face it," he said. "It will be *Blade Runner*."[2]

There are cities in the Americas where, at times, *Blade Runner* very nearly describes practical policing in the streets. The question is: What can keep us from that scenario, either in the United States or anywhere else in the Americas? That question concerns the creation or preservation of institutions of accountability for officials and, more broadly, the preservation of the political and cultural values that have protected us from unbridled official violence. This book says a little about how such institutions and values can be strengthened or created; it says much more about how fragile and yet essential those institutions are.

ACKNOWLEDGMENTS

Because this book is based on investigations over a very long period, my thanks are due to dozens of people, in myriad ways. Those mentioned here are only the most important of those upon whom I have drawn for knowledge and advice. In some cases I have not cited specific names, especially for people from government organizations, because I believed that those who had helped me probably (or definitely) would not want to be mentioned here. It must be said, nevertheless, that the help of many people from government and nongovernmental organizations has been essential. It is just not the case that an eager law professor from New York can pretend to go to a city, in the United States much less in Latin America or the Caribbean, and expect to pick up data and background about police violence; the work requires cooperation and years of digging by people who have long lived there.

For the work in New York City, I had assistance from Joel Berger, Leslie Cornfeld, Myron Beldock, Karen Dippold and Melvin Wulf, Arthur Eisenberg, Barbara Mehlsack, James Meyerson, Paul Shneyer, Jeremy Travis, and a number of very able people at the New York City Police Department.

In Los Angeles, I thank Paul and Diane Asselin, Merrick Bobb and Julio Thompson, Karol Heppe, Paul Hoffman, Ellen Lutz, Hugh Manes, Kevin Reed, Ramona Ripston, Stanley Sheinbaum and Stephen Yagman, and the staff of the American Civil Liberties Union of Southern California as well as officials of the City of Los Angeles, including members of the Los Angeles Police Department. For the work on the United States, generally, I must thank Fred Lawrence, Flint Taylor, and the American Civil Liberties Union, especially Gene Guerrero.

For Buenos Aires, I relied on Luis Brunatti, Alejandro Carrio, Alejandro Garro, Eugenio Raúl Zaffaroni, Alicia Oliveira, Enrique Sdrech, Maria del Carmen Verdú and Daniel Straga, Marta Vedio, Leon Zimmerman, Jeffrey Gracer and the wonderful people of the Centro de Estudios Legales y Sociales, including Emilio Mignone, Octavio Carsen, and Daniel Frontalini, as well as judges, administrators, and police officials. The investigation would have been impossible without the knowledge and organizing ability of Patricia Pittman.

In Brazil, I must thank Maria Helena Alves, Audrey Baker, Caco Barcellos, Nilo Batista, Marcos Bretas, James Brooke, Col. Carlo Magno Nazarethe Cerqueira and his able staff, Teresa Caldeira, Franco Caneva Junior, Beatriz Castelo, Joan Dassin, Claudia Fanucchi Neto, Jairo Fonseca, Michael Hall, James Holston, Eliane Junqueira, Russell Karp, Vera Malaguti, Angelica Mello, Guaracy Mingardi, Maria Teresa Assis Moura, Dacio Nitrini, Michael Mary Nolan, Padre Agostinho, Ben Penglase, Julia Preston, Robert Shirley, Mario Simas, Stella Kuhlmann Vieira, and several organizations, including the Centro Santo Dias, the Teotonio Vilela Commission, and the Bar Association in São Paulo. Most particularly I must thank the Center for the Study of Violence at the University of São Paulo, its directors Paulo Sergio Pinheiro and Sergio Adorno, and its extremely able staff. At the risk of slighting others, I single out Sandra Carvalho, Nancy Cardia, Malak Poppovic, and Oscar Vieira and his father José Osvaldo, who have been enormously helpful. I have also been helped by many police, both civil and military, and by other officials, especially judges.

Among those who gave invaluable help with the work in Jamaica were Harold Crooks, Claudienne Edwards, Roy Fairclough, E. George Green, Anthony Harriott, John Maxwell, Nancy Northup, Donald Robotham, Richard Small, Lois Whitman, Brian Wilson, and many government officials, including, especially, K. D. Knight. Always indispensable is the Jamaica Council for Human Rights, where Florizelle O'Connor and Dennis Daly are the mainstays of my projects.

In the work on Mexico City, I was aided by Lucy Conger, Amalia García, Claudio Lomnitz, Ellen Lutz, Gracia Moheno, Elena Poniatowska, José Reveles, the staff at the Comisión de Defensa y Promoción de Derechos Humanos, and by many government officials, including Manuel Camacho Solís, then the mayor of Mexico City, and René Monterrubio, then the chief of the preventive police, as well by as the very able and helpful staff at the Comisión Nacional de Derechos Humanos.

My debt to Human Rights Watch is greater than I can convey here. In many ways, this is the Watch committees' book, as much as it is mine, although of course I take complete responsibility for the work in it. The research outside the United States was conducted either as a project for the organization or with its close cooperation. The original idea of studying the problem of police violence under democratic governments in the Americas was one I developed through my work for Human Rights Watch. Although the entire staff has always been very supportive, I must thank particularly Aryeh Neier, now with the Soros Foundation, Ken Roth, and Juan Mendez, as well as those mentioned above in connection with particular countries. My wife, Bell, who was cowriter and researcher in most of the investigations, was indispensable to the work in a thousand ways.

Among those who have helped me in investigating or conceptualizing the problems in the book are Martha Huggins, David Garland, Louise Shelley, Jerome Skolnick and James Fyfe, Hans Toch, Sam Walker, and again Paulo Sergio Pinheiro and Teresa Caldeira. The participants in the conference "Mortes anunciadas: A (des)proteção da vida na America Latina" (Deaths foretold: The (non)protection of life in Latin America) in Salvador, Bahia, in 1988, enabled me to think broadly about police violence in the Americas.

I thank New York University—especially its law school where I teach—for its continuing support. I received valuable criticism and interest from the NYU Law and Society Colloquium as well as from the Fortunoff Colloquium under James Jacobs, and from Tony Amsterdam. My research assistants, Christian Johnson and Michael Alcamo, investigated significant background problems in the United States. The work received financial support from the Filomen D'Agostino and Max E. Greenberg Research Fund at NYU Law School, as well as from the Foundation for the Support of Research of the State of São Paulo (FAPESP). I thank the editors of *Criminal Law Forum* for publishing my early thoughts on some of the information from Jamaica, São Paulo, and Buenos Aires.

Finally, I thank my old friend and editor, André Schiffrin, and the very able staff at The New Press.

INTRODUCTION

Until recently, urban policing has been all-pervasive and at the same time nearly invisible as a political force. Policing for the purpose of outright control of opposition to the government is visible enough. It is obvious that such "high" policing, as it is sometimes called,[3] affects the world of politics, and we pay corresponding attention to it; the most dramatic stories about human rights have been about the arrest and detention of dissenters, their harassment and sometimes death at the hands of the state, usually through the police. But we hardly ever think of ordinary day-to-day policing as having the same importance, at least in the places where we live.

We read the headlines or watch television about crimes, their victims, and their perpetrators; and we hear also about police violence and corruption. But for the most part we take the incidents one by one, almost as anecdotes. The police are part of the urban environment, like the perennially smoggy air; we have been slow to see them as actors in politics and history.

Part of the reason is that ordinary policing in fact was traditionally "low" in the minds of the public as well as of many scholars. Policing is a "tainted occupation," as Egon Bittner put it, because it is connected to violence and crime, and because it is almost exclusively work with the poor. The body of crimes, the "common crimes," that the police are mostly asked to enforce, are those most identified with the lower classes; to a striking extent, crimes committed by professional people, like tax-evasion and regulatory offenses, are investigated by administrative agencies and other bodies that are separate from ordinary police.[4] Similarly, almost all street work by police, when they stop people who are supposed to be suspicious, or intervene in an altercation, is conducted among poor people. The style of police work controls and subordinates those with whom the work is done. Almost by definition, the lives of ordinary people, from the lower middle class up, are not a matter for the police. For such a person to fall into a situation where the police have to intervene is always somewhat degrading, a sign that the person has lost control of his life, has at least for the moment fallen below his class. In recent years, the class division has been further exaggerated in some middle-class enclaves, where the residents will hardly ever see a city policeman; the ordinary patrol work is done by private security guards, and the city police are relegated to the neighborhoods outside the enclaves.

The police not only "keep order," they also "reproduce order," to borrow the felicitous phrase of Richard Ericson, both in investigation and preventive policing.[5] When the police decide to stop an expensive car because it is out of place in a poor neighborhood or because the driver is of the "wrong" race or class, they are reading the car and its driver as "out of order." The police put such people in their proper places, letting them know that they do not meet the standards of the respectable. Police departments, furthermore, reflect the social assumptions of the larger society in their own bureaucratic organization and relations between superiors and policemen. It is characteristic of departments in the United States, for example, that they are "integrated" by rank; almost every superior has to have served at the lowest rank. In other societies, such as Brazil, for example, police are trained specifically to be officers or in the lower ranks.

While ordinary police work has never ceased to be a tainted occupation, in the last thirty years historians and political scientists, as well as the citizenry generally, have begun to think of it as important. The urban rebellions in the United States in the sixties brought home for us, in conflict and columns of smoke, the realization that the police are political actors. Histories of police departments as well as broader studies of urban violence have shown that the police participated in a long process of pacification of urban populations and suppression of crime that is still not fully understood.[6] And as the fear of crime has become a dominant issue, the way the police work on the streets as well as in investigation has assumed greater importance.

The Comparative Study of Urban Police

If the work of the police does help to reproduce the order of society, then a comparison of the ways in which the work is done should open a window on what sort of order is perceived in different societies, both by the police and the poor, who are usually the objects of police action. Police work, however, does not reflect the order of society like a mirror; in a modern society, policing allows for enormous discretion. The police may enforce status distinctions or try to minimize them in the interests of reducing conflict; they may impose them through an "order" (in a slightly different sense) that ranges from that of an autocratic military to an impersonal "legal" order. In reproducing order, the police have the power to represent it as well, and, through interpreting, to influence it, at least at the margins. Since the sixties, for example, the use of deadly force by the police in the United States has declined precipitously; it is clear that the new management practices of the departments have brought about the decrease in shootings. Although police chiefs undoubtedly acted in response to pressure from minority groups and the threat of civil unrest, they could have resisted that pressure as they had done for decades before.[7] While the order reproduced by the police is "real," it is also what they make it.

So we cannot pretend in any simple way to "read" the social order through police work; we must bring some understanding of the order to the interpretation of the work, to see how the police have shaped their work to accommodate the order, and how they have in turn tried to shape it. In the chapters that follow, I have provided descriptions of the social and political worlds within which the police operate, so that we can understand how the police have interpreted those worlds while reproducing them— for example, through the use of violence as a way of controlling people, or through controlling the use of violence.

In this book I compare the problems of police violence in urban areas in North and South America: in Los Angeles and New York City in the United States; in São Paulo, Brazil, with some incidental comparisons to Rio de Janeiro; Buenos Aires,

Argentina; the island of Jamaica, especially Kingston; and the Federal District that is the heart of Mexico City. I have compared cities, or in some cases urban areas such as Los Angeles County or metropolitan São Paulo, rather than larger political units, because police are often organized on a local basis, either through the province or state or city, and because problems with the police arise on a local rather than a nationwide basis. Although I draw upon the historical background, especially for the United States, I have chiefly studied these cities during the last decade, during a time when their parent countries all had (at least nominally) democratic elections and a free press, while at the same time they faced serious problems of crime, which provoked outcries for repressive police action. The police departments in all the cities claim to be engaged in ordinary law enforcement, chiefly against common crimes; these are not situations like that of Haiti until 1994, in which the police were, like the military, engaged in the violent repression of a rebellious citizenry. There are some resemblances among the societies, characteristic of the New World. They have faced problems of immigration—forced or voluntary—rapid urbanization and industrialization, and the aftereffects of colonialism, including slavery or peonage.

It goes without saying that all of the societies are different from one another. Although Brazil, like the United States, is enormous, decentralized, and ethnically and economically diverse, it has been ridden by debt and traditions of hierarchy to a degree that the United States has not; and the level of police violence in São Paulo, for example, has been many times greater than in North American cities. The development of many of the huge cities of Latin America and the Caribbean has been different in character from the development of cities in the United States; the latter did not act to the same extent as a catch-basin for masses of the landless and often jobless poor. Nevertheless, the insights gleaned from the comparison of these societies enable us to limit the range of possible explanations for official violence. If we are inclined, looking at Brazil and Argentina, to suppose that police violence is due primarily to a

"Luso-Iberian" tradition, for example, we are reminded that police violence in the very British ex-colony of Jamaica is extremely high, while in Mexico City it seems more nearly to be under control. Similarly, we might attribute arbitrary and violent police habits to the weak democratic traditions and the recurrent dictatorships in Argentina and Brazil; although that explanation has some force, as we shall see in later chapters, its power is limited by the example of Jamaica, again, which suggests that other social factors are important.

In recent years, as the base of jobs has changed in U.S. cities, and as they have been flooded with new waves of in-migration, their resemblance to the cities to the south of them has grown. The fear of crime has become a governing political issue in the United States as well as in Brazil, Jamaica, and Argentina. In a rhetoric that is close to universal, politicians and the public complain that the courts are not tough enough on criminals and that better ways have to be found to deter crime and incapacitate criminals. Everywhere there is discussion about whether defendants have "too many" rights and whether the assertion of rights ought to be, or can be limited in the interests of the safety of others. There is talk of a "war on crime" and often a corresponding conception of the police as the combatants. The political clamor does not die down even when the crime rate appears to drop, because there is no agreement about why it drops and because the fear of crime is a ready way to mobilize the public behind the government. The words translate, however, into different policies and different levels of official violence in the six places; those differences, when cast in similar words, tell us something about the acceptance of violence and the importance of rights in the different cultures.

VIOLENCE AND THE POLICE

Much of the problem in understanding the work of the police lies in the fact that what they do, and what they should do, when they are "doing their job," is always contested. The term *police* was originally synonymous with all the internal governance of the state, including keeping order. As Blackstone said, "Public police...mean[s] the due regulation and domestic order of the Kingdom, whereby the individuals of the state, like members of a well governed family, are bound to conform their general behavior to the rules of propriety, good neighborhood and good manners, and to be decent, industrious and inoffensive in their respective stations."[8]

Crime is by definition "out of order," and in recent decades police in the Americas have emphasized the suppression of crime as central to their work. Nevertheless, the old usage of the word *police* has not entirely passed away; we vacillate in our demands on the police to do one part or another of the primordial job of "policing." In some systems, for example in Brazil and Mexico, the job of investigating crimes is viewed as a function of the courts, and the detective job is completely separated from the jobs of prevention and order maintenance; but that division of labor does not resolve the problems of conflicting demands on the police. We still expect some branch of the police to control crowds, to intervene in domestic disputes, to check on suspicious persons, and to perform an ever-changing list of services to help those who seem too ill or intoxicated to help themselves. To paraphrase James Q. Wilson, we fluctuate between expecting our police to be watchmen, servants, or law-enforcement officers;[9] sometimes we also expect them to be an army. In contemporary parlance, we want the police to maintain or even improve the "quality of life" in the cities. Thus the nature of the job is contested not only for historical or linguistic reasons, but more for political reasons, because we do not agree what it is that the police ought to do or because we want to conceal from ourselves what it is that we ask them to do.

The order that is policed is of course not "natural"; it must be maintained. Whatever aspect of the police role is emphasized, whether it involves checking on people who appear to be out of place, trying to push them out of places where they do not seem to belong, responding to reports of crime, or any of the other jobs under the vague umbrella of "police," it implies that the police have to be willing, in the last analysis, to threaten force and to back the threat with action if necessary. In the formulation of Egon Bittner, "The role of the police is best understood as a mechanism for the distribution of non-negotiably coercive force employed in accordance with the dictates of an intuitive grasp of situational emergencies."[10]

Thus the police are chief players in a political drama that is always a tense one for us in liberal democracies: the balance between violence and order. The threat (and the occasional application) of violence is a strong impulse in the criminal law. The threat of punishment is supposed to deter crime, while the actual imposition of punishment is supposed to deter and to "right the balance"; in both ways, punishment is supposed to strengthen the sense of order. Outside that legal context, even though the notion of "order" is much broader than the law of crimes, we have been uneasy, especially in the United States, about the application of force.

Nevertheless, we recognize that violence is used directly to control people and impose order. It is a recurrent theme in the chapters that follow, as it has been in other literature on police,[11] that defiance of the police, whether in a full-fledged car chase or simply in a refusal to move off a street corner, is very likely to provoke punishment from the police, because defiance of them is tantamount to defiance of order. But the level of violence the police will use varies all the way from merely arresting a defiant person to shooting him or to torturing reluctant witnesses to give up information. Controlling the level of violence is the essential problem of human rights in ordinary police work.

Police Violence and Human Rights

Torture and deadly force illustrate a signal characteristic of official violence: it is a means of distancing oneself from the victim. Although an instrumental excuse commonly given for torture is that it is used to obtain information, it has other functions. All students of torture have remarked on the fact that it dehumanizes the victim for the torturer;[12] torture makes the victim a suffering subject, deprived of the will to speak or keep silent. At the same time that it is a kind of annihilation of the victim, it is also an expression of complete control over him; it "puts him in his place," in a radical way. It is not difficult to understand the temptation to use torture against ideological and political enemies; it degrades them to the "animals" and "enemies" of the established order that they are imagined to be, and it negates the power of their ideology by negating them as people.

Although torture is one of the most profound and dramatic examples, all violence used by officials against the relatively defenseless expresses the distancing and control function. As Spierenburg reminds us, "In common parlance, the term 'punishment' is never used unless the person upon whom the penalty is inflicted is clearly subordinate to the one imposing the penal act."[13] All police brutality, including beatings such as the famous clubbing of Rodney King in Los Angeles, shares this relation of subordination; it is apparent in the police practice of forcing the person to lie on the ground, and in the degrading remarks about King recorded in the police communications. The use of deadly force, except when the officer acts in defense of himself or another, is a limiting case, like torture—the officer makes a nothing out of the victim he kills. He tells society through the shooting that the victim's life is worth less than the assertion of authority and control.

By the same token, it is rare and risky for the police to try to subordinate those who are not subordinate, to use degrading violence against people who are middle or upper class or who are not from a minority. It causes a scandal when the police make a mistake and summarily punish a middle-class person, supposing him to be poor, or when they take the risk of torturing a middle-class victim in an effort to get information. In the ancient world, a free citizen (that is, not an enemy or a stranger) was generally not "torturable," a tradition that has come down to us with great clarity in the cases studied here. One of the things that makes politically repressive regimes so peculiarly terrifying is that they breach this tradition—they make dissenters into "enemies" to be subjected to degrading violence, regardless of their status or class.

Torture and the abuse of deadly force are violations of international human rights law. The Code of Conduct for Law Enforcement Officials, adopted by the United Nations General Assembly in 1979, provides that "firearms should not be used except when a suspected offender offers armed resistance or otherwise jeopardizes the lives of others and less extreme measures are not sufficient to restrain or apprehend the suspected offender." In 1990, in the Basic Principles on the Use of Force or Firearms by Law Enforcement Officials, the U.N. Congress on the Prevention of Crime and Treatment of Offenders stated the law more strongly: "Law enforcement officials shall not use firearms against persons except in self-defence or defence of others against the imminent threat of death or serious injury, to prevent the perpetration of a particularly serious crime involving grave threat to life, to arrest a person presenting such a danger and resisting their authority, or to prevent his or her escape, and only when less extreme means are insufficient to achieve these objectives. In any event, intentional lethal use of firearms may only be made when strictly unavoidable in order to protect life." The Covenant on Civil and Political Rights, to which all the countries involved in this study are parties, provides that "No one shall be arbitrarily deprived of his life," as well as that "No one shall be subjected to torture or to cruel, inhuman or degrading treatment or punishment." The Convention against Torture and Other Cruel, Inhuman or Degrading Treatment or Punishment, which the countries have also approved, requires the parties to punish and prevent acts of torture.[14] It is these standards that ultimately make it possible to compare the six cities; none of them can claim that its culture is so different from the others that it cannot be held to the same standard.

International law recognizes that other forms of degrading punishment, including much police brutality, are on a continuum with the extremes of torture and deadly force. The Code of Conduct for Law Enforcement Officials provides that "Law enforcement officials may use force only when strictly necessary," and the Convention on Torture defines *torture* as any infliction by an official of "severe pain or suffering, whether physical or mental," even if the pain is inflicted for punishment rather than to obtain information. In general, however, I use the term *torture* in the more restricted way in which it is commonly used, to refer to the calculated use of violence to extract information. I have concentrated on torture in this sense and on deadly force, particularly in the chapters on Latin America and Jamaica, in order to isolate the most serious human rights violations. I have tried to determine the circumstances in which they are committed, in order to relate them to the characteristics of the societies and thus to see how they might be controlled. Nevertheless, I do discuss less serious forms of violence, particularly in the United States, where torture to obtain information has largely passed away and the more serious abuses are not so common.[15]

In comparing the cities, I have not found it possible to quantify the use of "torture,"[16] any more than it is possible to give a count of other, lesser types of police brutality. Torture is usually secret; its physical effects may disappear, furthermore, and the victim may have good reason not to report it. Nevertheless, in Brazil, Mexico, and Argentina, the use of torture has been so notorious that even when the government makes some pro forma denial that it is prevalent, it is not necessary to use any quantitative means to establish its existence; in confidential talks, many officials will admit it.

In describing the use of deadly force, on the other hand, I have tried to suggest how prevalent it is on a comparative basis.[17] Thus I have, where I could, obtained a count of the number of killings by the police, much more reliable in some cities than in others. In São Paulo, in Jamaica, and in cities in the United States, we sometimes have official tallies, which may be incomplete but are in any case almost certainly not too low. In Buenos Aires and for earlier years in Jamaica, we have tallies drawn laboriously from newspaper accounts; these are almost certainly incomplete but can be used at least as a minimum count. I have tried to put these figures into context by considering the size of the police forces, as well as by comparing, by city, the number of killings by police with the number of police killed and by comparing the number killed with the number wounded by police, where such figures are available (São Paulo, Jamaica, and U.S. cities). Wherever it is possible, I also compare killings by police with homicides in general. These three last ratios, civilians killed to police killed, civilians killed to civilians wounded by police, and civilians killed to killings generally, can be used comparatively to suggest that deadly force is used more cautiously in some cities than in others; we might call these "disproportionate violence ratios." If the number of killings by police is a large percentage of all homicides, that suggests that the police may be using a disproportionate amount of deadly violence in relation to the actual hazards of their work and of life in the city; if the number of civilians killed is enormously larger than the number of police killed, that suggests that the police may not be using their weapons exclusively in response to threats from gunmen, as is so often claimed in official accounts of police shootings. Lastly, if the police kill many more than they wound, that suggests the use of deliberate violence against some of the victims; in the usual pattern of shootings, in war as well as in police work, the number killed is only a fraction of those wounded. The figures I use are often rough, and the results are only suggestive; nevertheless, the differences among the cities are so striking that I think the figures are sufficient to show a genuine contrast. The contrast does not become dramatic until the fifth chapter and afterward; the numbers of police killings in São Paulo and Jamaica have been relatively so large until recent years, and the ratios have shown such a disproportionate use of force, that they seem to call out for a comparison with other cities and for an explanation of the violence.[18]

THEORETICAL FRAMEWORK: INTERNAL VIOLENCE AND THE GOVERNMENT

The relative prevalence of the use of violence in ordinary police cases has to be understood as a reflection of a slow process of change in the use of violence between citizens and in the use of violence by government against its citizens.[19]

The European Model

In Norbert Elias's account of the growth of "civilizing" influences, the peoples of Western Europe gradually became more refined, less tolerant of outright brutality before their eyes, and thus less willing to use violence against or accept violence from their countrymen, at a time when the state was centralizing and seeking to deprive citizens of their prerogatives to use violence. France was Elias's paradigm case, where under the Old Regime, local notables were drawn to the seat of government, trading their privileges to govern, fight, and punish at the local level for a place at the king's court. As the state acquired a monopoly of the legitimate use of force, the use of violence at the domestic level became more and more unmentionable. In this model, however, the violent impulses do not disappear; as the guns are turned outward, war between states becomes more violent and destructive and colonialism increases.[20]

From the point of view of social control and punishment, the domestic changes are particularly notable. As early as the late middle ages, government authorities took from the people the prerogative to exact vengeance themselves, replacing it with the violent punishments of the criminal law. Like other changes in the use of internal violence, changes in punishment depended on changes in the power of the state and in the consciousness of its citizens. During the Enlightenment, there was a rising revulsion against cruel and brutal punishments, particularly in public. At the end of the era of the Old Regime, Benjamin Franklin argued that hangings and whippings ought not be public, because they excited in onlookers pity and either hard-heartedness or a contempt for law, and in the victim, if he survived, an increasing tolerance for violence. Franklin's views show a growing sense of common humanity with the victims at the same time as a desire to sanitize the violence by putting it out of sight; they reflect the rationalization of government as well as the privatization of personal life.[21]

The available evidence suggests that during the nineteenth century, and up until perhaps the First World War, there was a general decline in urban violence in Western Europe, not only by the state but among private persons as well.[22] This civil pacification accompanied increased state control of the legitimate instruments of violence as well as the processes of urbanization and the relative rationalization of government. It was in this period that modern urban police forces were developed and came to symbolize much of the pacification. The armed forces were hardly used anymore to control the domestic population.

Some of the spirit of the change is captured in Weber's ideal model of modern society, bureaucratized and rationalized. People are managed by government rather than merely coerced; at the same time, the management becomes legitimate. The change is accompanied by the growth of modern law and the expectation of regularity and rights under the law. Present-day writers emphasize what Weber perhaps discounted—an increased demand for participation and citizenship. The satisfaction of the demand depends upon the recognition of civil rights and at least the appearance of dialogue with the government. The simmering class war between capital and labor begins to fade into a government-sponsored negotiation between organized labor and business. In penology, deterrence and the "correction" of offenders replaces punishment as the chief justification of criminal penalties.[23]

The expectations attendant upon citizenship and the possession of civil rights, however, are at the same time in conflict with other elements of the dynamic of change. The relative pacification of personal and state violence has been accompanied by increased powers of surveillance. As Anthony Giddens has pointed out, modern participation was accompanied by a vast increase in communications, through urbanization and literacy itself; the people consume and make opinion, and the government is eager to persuade them of the wisdom of its policies. But the other face of communications is the power of surveillance. Michel Foucault has sketched for us a sort of zero-sum economy of social control, in which, as the external control by terror decreases, the direct control by government management of people increases. And in response, both in the effort to avoid the surveillance, as well as the reality of conflict and violence that persists primarily as a thing to be shunned, greater value is placed on privacy, with the effect of weakening the public life implied by citizenship.[24]

The Model in the Americas

In the Americas, the formation of the state and modern government, viewed from the perspective of the European historical model, has taken a rather different course. Governmental institutions often have had less complete control of the instruments of legitimate force, and violent private vengeance has persisted in many places.

The United States

Americans have never quite ceded a monopoly of legitimate force to the government. Through the frontier and its symbolism, the problem of the establishment of government and its imposition of order has continued. Vigilantism was accepted as informal social control, without much hope of official intervention, until almost yesterday. In 1918, the NAACP recorded 3,224 lynchings in the previous thirty years, mostly of black people, and that figure included only the lynchings that were relatively easy to document.[25] To this day there is a great deal of vigilantism in the United States, against thieves, drug dealers, and sometimes against people who are just thought to be deviant; the difference in contemporary life is that the government tries to assert its hegemony over the situation by arresting and trying the perpetrators.

No doubt the citizenry is not completely "pacified," in the sense of accepting the lawful order of the government, in any society. Yet Americans, urban as well as rural, seem to resist tenaciously the pacification that comes from the power of the state. Their police departments have been relatively "democratic" and traditionally closely allied with the political powers that run the cities. As Wilbur Miller pointed out, in comparing the more "undemocratic" but more neutral police in London with those in New York in the nineteenth century, the latter were vastly more violent, even brutal. The reasons were not only that the New York police worked in a more socially diverse and more unpredictably violent society, but that the society accepted summary violence as a way of controlling people. The use of overt violence had not been swept out of sight in the process of state-formation. The police were doing things that the citizens would otherwise do themselves; they were "delegated vigilantes."[26]

The United States has shared some political characteristics with other countries in the New World. When the democracy was new, and again when the cities were being flooded with migrants, including blacks fleeing the aftermath of slavery in the South, clientelism in politics was widespread. The urban political machines delivered services and patronage, and corruption was rife in all municipal functions. The sense of participation as a citizen, with rights in relation to the government, was slow to develop, at least among the newcomers in the cities.

When the sense of citizenship began to grow in U.S. cities, particularly after the turn of the century, the idea of rights in a liberal legal system seized the imagination of Americans, strongly defining their sense of their relation to the government in a way that does not prevail elsewhere in the New World. It is important to see that the growth in rights-consciousness has been part of the process of pacification: citizens came to expect the government itself to be pacific, limited by law. Citizens have defined themselves, and minority groups have organized politically and fought against discrimination and even for their identity, through the language of rights, with all its limitations. Oppressed groups, like blacks, Hispanics, and homosexuals, have found a place in the polity through claims about rights. As a result of this struggle, police violence against a member of a minority group is very likely to be perceived as an act of discrimination, an attack on group identity, so much so that it raises a risk of civil disturbance. Thus the ancient conflict for the police, between keeping order and enforcing the law in a narrower sense, is dragged into the light again by the demand that the police act in a neutral and lawful manner. It is a demand never satisfied, because reproducing order is an implicit part of the job, but it does produce pressure for greater accountability and more caution in the use of violence.

Latin America and the Caribbean

When the guns of European states were pointed away from their own populations, they pointed in the direction of the New World as well as Asia and Africa. Some of the violence that was withdrawn in the interests of civility in Europe was exported as slavery and colonialism. While brutal and public punishment was fading in Europe, it was still being used against slaves and, by extension, against other dispossessed people. Thus in Rio de Janeiro in the nineteenth century, rough police practices developed in controlling slaves were then applied to the underclass after the abolition of slavery at the end of the century.[27] The system of public violence in the interest of terror has not been repudiated to the same degree as it has been in Europe.

When direct colonialism receded from Latin America and the Caribbean, the landed classes and other local economic elites inherited many of the class and status attitudes of the Europeans; in Jamaica, direct colonial control did not end until the 1960s. Even in Latin America, however, where nations obtained their independence much earlier, such class relations have tended to persist because the region has not escaped the effects of colonialism; in many respects, Latin America is still dependent on the nations of Europe or on the United States. Inequitable land-ownership relations and the consequent poverty of the landless masses have led to urban centers too swollen to be functional for their societies and to despair and fear about the urban underclass.

Under these conditions, a sense of citizenship and participation in many cases has not developed in a way that contributes strongly to the voluntary acceptance of peaceable civil governance. Where there are democracies, as in Jamaica and from time to time in Brazil and Argentina, the relation between leaders and voters has often been clientelistic. The sense of equality before the law and the expectation of being treated in a fair and predictable way by the legal system has tended to be weak. Thus the ideological supports for urban "law and order" have been shaky, and the reasons to cede a monopoly of legitimate force to the government have been correspondingly weak.

At the same time, the military has not withdrawn from civilian governance in many parts of Latin America outside Mexico; the military has continued to act on the belief that it has a mission not so much to support civil government but to save the nation when civil government seems to be floundering. Thus the distinction that took place in Europe, in which the military no longer acted against the civilian population, except in the most extreme cases, and domestic police patrolled the cities, was never drawn quite as sharply in many Latin American countries.

During the Cold War, encouraged and directed by the United States, the tradition of the national mission for the military took a violently repressive form in Argentina and Brazil, as well as elsewhere. The military developed an ideology of "national security," directing their energies against what they saw as subversive and other morally destructive elements within their own countries. The authoritarian tradition on which the military drew for its interventions is radically at odds with the rights- and citizenship-based forms of governance that have developed elsewhere since the end of the Old Regime; some of the arguments for military rule, particularly in Argentina, literally reach back to the anti-liberal justifications for the Old Regime.[28]

The military governments that took power in the sixties and seventies saw their enemy within not only in political subversion and dissent but in common crime as well. While the suppression of political dissent largely disappeared with the passing of the dictators, the violence in ordinary law enforcement continued. To some extent it had always prevailed in the treatment of the poor; when the dictatorships receded, law enforcement reverted to business as usual. The anti-liberal strand in the military tradition has made it more difficult to form the sense of common citizenship that would condemn discrimination against the poor, while at the same time it has made it easier to accept the imposition of violent authoritarian governments.

Pacification in the Six Cities

U.S. cities differ enormously from one another in their acceptance of police violence. Los Angeles (chapter I), which is
spread out and weakly organized politically, with little effective
contact among citizens, also has had police, both at the city and
county level, who draw upon a military model. In Los Angeles
the use of deadly force as well as lesser violence is high for the
United States, and accountability is low. In New York City
(chapter II), on the other hand, the police are bureaucratized,
the city is relatively centralized, and there is strong control over
the use of deadly force. In U.S. cities, the use of nondeadly force
for purposes of social control has continued, accompanied in
many cases by corruption, and a central issue in the first three
chapters is how to shape systems of accountability to control
police abuses. In the fourth chapter, to clarify the comparison
with Latin America and the Caribbean, I sketch the history of
problems of police violence and of political control of the
police in U.S. cities, including corruption, the use of torture to
obtain evidence, and the abuse of deadly force. Although the
political and management problems with police have sometimes been strikingly like those in Latin America and Jamaica,
the growing public confidence in the government and the
system of law has enabled the system gradually to minimize the
abuse of confessions and substantially reduce the number of
shootings, while other violence had continued.

São Paulo (chapter V) has in recent years had the highest
level of deadly force among the six urban areas in the study, as
well as continuing use of torture for corrupt purposes as well as
to obtain information. Correspondingly, government, even at
the local level, and public confidence in the political and legal
system have been weak. The sense of citizenship and obligation
between citizens has suffered, and vigilantism is very common;
while government efforts to reduce it are increasing, the problem of vigilantism is still not under control. Until recently, with
high levels of crime and poverty, there has not been any substantial objection to police violence either by the population
or by the elites, although this has finally begun to change.

Controls (or the lack of them) over police violence in São Paulo will be compared with the rather different situation that prevailed until recently in Rio de Janeiro.

Buenos Aires (chapter VI) has a smaller problem with crime and poverty than São Paulo, but it has long suffered from the use of torture in many cases, as well as from some spectacular police homicides. The government has emphasized the sense of public insecurity, encouraged by police violence, as a way to try to control the people and consolidate the power of the state. Both in Argentina and Brazil, the dictatorships that passed away a decade or more ago have encouraged a "military" approach to crime, with weakened public confidence in the effectiveness of the legal system.

Jamaica (chapter VII), unlike Argentina and Brazil, has an unbroken tradition of democracy during its independence and earlier period of self-government under British rule. But clientelism is strong in politics there, and the sense of common citizenship is weak. Vigilantism is widespread, and the constabulary have used deadly force with great frequency, in a pattern very similar to that of São Paulo. In the last few years, the government has become increasingly concerned and has tried to take control of the official violence.

Mexico City (chapter VIII), like Buenos Aires in Argentina, is the seat of the national government, which is strong and centralized, and until recently has had the allegiance or at least acquiescence of the populace. Since the revolution more than seventy years ago, the Mexican government has worked very hard to keep control of the use of force, and there is no widespread problem of vigilantism. While corruption is endemic in the city's police, as it has been in other parts of the government, and torture has been widely used to obtain evidence, there has not been a notable abuse of deadly force in the Federal District. Thus the centralization of the government and its avoidance of a military model for the police have kept deadly violence in check although they have not controlled torture.

In emphasizing the process of pacification as an explanatory model, I am by implication marginalizing other possible explanations for the relative prevalence of violence in ordinary police work. Increased police violence might be thought, for example, to be a reaction to rising criminal violence in the cities. The empirical evidence, however, is against that explanation; police violence has dropped over time in many cities, even in the face of rising crime. The terms of the same explanation might be shifted, to attribute police violence to a reaction to public fear of criminal violence. Fear does in fact have some driving force; it has been used regularly to try to excuse police violence in the United States as well as Brazil, Jamaica, and Argentina. But it is not an "explanation" for police violence, because in some cities, like New York, where the fear is strong, the incidence of police violence is nevertheless relatively low, while in Buenos Aires, the insecurity is used as a tool to strengthen control by the government. Fear of crime, in short, is too easily manipulated by officials as a way of perpetuating past patterns of abuse.

Some, like former Police Chief Daryl Gates in Los Angeles and the military police in São Paulo, have sought to explain police violence even more simply as an effort directly to intimidate would-be criminals and thus produce more peaceful streets. But that explanation begs the question why direct repression is chosen rather than lawful means. The choice is especially puzzling because it is not clear that the effort works or that less violent means would not work just as well.

Disproportionate police violence has also been viewed, notably in Jamaica, as a desperate official reaction to crime when resources are lacking for a more sophisticated response. But that explanation fails to account for the vast differences in the police use of violence among the cities in Latin America and the Caribbean, not to speak of the United States.

The violence might be viewed as a reflection of the elite's fear of the poor, in places where disparities in wealth and income are extreme. This explanation has some validity, as we shall see in succeeding chapters, but again it fails to account for the differences in the use of violence in the cities. This explanatory factor is easiest to understand if it is brought around to join with the process of pacification. Where economic disparities are high and the government does not have some strong allegiance from its citizens, together with a tradition of pacification, extreme police violence is to be feared.[29]

The comparison of cities in the United States with those elsewhere in the Americas introduces an element of ambiguity into the process of explanation, because the United States bears some responsibility for political conditions in the other countries, for example for the support and encouragement of the national security strategy of the military in Argentina and Brazil, which shaped the dictatorships there in the sixties and seventies. Some Latin Americans I interviewed claim a direct responsibility: they accuse the United States of actually having trained their police to torture and kill during the seventies and before. So far as I can tell, the evidence does not support that conclusion; it shows instead that the United States acquiesced in and failed to take any action against abuses until 1975, when the Foreign Assistance Act put a stop to most foreign aid for police forces. Since that time, the United States has generally been supportive of human rights, although we have also sometimes been hypocritical about it, as in the case in 1990 when U.S. drug officials appeared to be annoyed that Mexico was increasing the rights of suspects.[30] Thus, although the experience of the dictatorships has certainly contributed to police abuses in succeeding years, it would seem that police practices have generally been developed locally and may legitimately be compared from city to city.

The study of the six urban areas will remind us that the pacification model is very rough, and its workings have never been simple. While on the one hand the "civilizing" process has never been completed, on the other hand it has begun to break down. In the last generation, whatever sense of civil pacification there was in the cities has begun to dissipate, with claims that crime is out of control. The legitimacy of civil rights and the sense of a common bond that contributed to citizenship are under pressure. Penology is confused, having lost the sense that criminal justice can control crime through relatively rational processes like deterrence and rehabilitation, while being unable to replace them with another consistent policy. David Garland comments, "After more than two centuries of rationalization, even our 'experts' have begun to recognize the limits of social engineering and the dark side of social order."[31] In the United States, where the control of the most serious forms of official violence is relatively strong, a fantasy of repressive violence in a *Blade Runner* world is always pushing at our consciousness, breaking out in acts of private or official vigilantism. Nevertheless, the dynamic of the original pacification, legalization, and rationalization is still being worked out, while the reaction is setting in; thus the death penalty has been largely abolished in Western Europe and Latin America, while its use is rising in the United States, and the fear of criminal disorder is increasing everywhere. Under these circumstances, the control of official violence becomes critical; when people are more fearful of crime and more despairing of correcting offenders, the temptation to punish summarily, even by eliminating the suspect, is correspondingly strong.

CONTROL OF POLICE VIOLENCE

One of the points of this book is that the potential for police violence and the rhetoric that would justify it are endemic. The control of violence, then, is not automatic; it is a matter of policy effected through many institutions, including the management of the police itself as well as separate institutions of accountability. Among them are the prosecutors and the courts acting against police abuses as crimes. The prosecution of police turns out to be a very blunt instrument for control, although it is useful in places like Buenos Aires, where other institutions have failed. Furthermore, the courts can control the use of torture through the rejection of coerced confessions in criminal cases; this has been quite effective in the United States as well as Latin America. The legislature can help to control police violence by increasing the penalties for it and by requiring the courts to exclude coerced confessions from evidence. In each of the localities, I have also tried to examine the work of the courts in awarding damages for injuries due to police violence.

Internal administrative disciplinary procedures as well as external systems such as civilian complaint review boards are useful, but their effectiveness is limited by the very fact that they review acts after they have happened, on a case-by-case basis. More effective are oversight bodies, similar to the commissions that are organized in the wake of police scandals, to examine the overall workings of the police departments. The problems of oversight suggest that nothing can replace the vigilant oversight of the police as a whole, who must be constrained by regulations on the use of force.

Throughout the book I consider national institutions for control of human rights violations; characteristically, these are strongest in Mexico (chapter VIII) and the United States (chapter III). In the end, in countries where domestic institutions of accountability are weak, it is the international standards of human rights that create a space for reform in police violence, through political pressure by international organizations, nongovernmental organizations, and foreign governments.

IN SUM: SCOPE AND PURPOSE

It is part of the drama of human rights that dissenters, who are often intellectuals—people not very different from those who protest human rights abuses—are tortured and shot just on account of their ideas. This study, however, is not primarily about that drama; it is about the use of violence in day-to-day policing. I make a rough distinction between official violence that is calculated and directed at political enemies, and the seemingly more routine police violence in dealing with crowds and crimes; it is this distinction that makes it possible to compare police work in the United States with Latin America and the Caribbean. We make the distinction in this country; we are concerned about "police brutality," usually thought of as directed against an underclass, but we expect very little overt violence against dissenters. Conversely, it is not difficult to imagine a situation where there is deadly violence against political enemies but much less against poor people in the streets;

some former authoritarian socialist governments fit this pattern.[32] Police brutality often gives us the impression that the police are "out of control," that they are not obeying the bureaucratic-legal norms of the state; political repression, on the other hand, we view as a calculated act by a centralized authority. Ultimately, as I shall show in the last chapter, the distinction will not hold up. But the "police problem" that seems repeatedly to confront us at the present time, and for purposes of this comparative study, is the problem of mistreatment of poor people and ordinary citizens, rather than the problem of partisan political harassment. We treat these two as though they were functionally separate, and I shall follow our practice, concentrating on the routine police work.

For each of the six places, the book makes an empirical study of the use by the police of torture and deadly force, as well as, in some cases, other forms of violence. In all the chapters, I have relied on my own research, conducted in São Paulo and Rio de Janeiro in 1987 and 1992, and in São Paulo alone in 1991, always aided by the Center for the Study of Violence, at the University of São Paulo. The research in Buenos Aires, with the cooperation of the Center for Social and Legal Studies, was conducted on the ground in 1991 and by mail in succeeding years; in Jamaica, the research, aided by the Jamaica Council for Human Rights, was conducted in 1986 and 1993. All of this research has contributed to field reports prepared for Human Rights Watch/America, upon which I have relied, as I have on other human rights reports, government data, and newspaper reports.[33]

In 1993, I conducted field research in Mexico City aided by Human Rights Watch/America. I have relied on the field work I did in Los Angeles in 1993, and on my intermittent work in New York over the last twenty-five years, conducted more systematically since 1992; the work in those two cities is described more fully in the short prelude that follows.

Through the comparison of the six urban areas seen as part of their national cultures, the book then picks out the circumstances in which violence is used, relates those circumstances to the characteristics of the society in which they occur, and finally talks about how the violence might be controlled. The factors I draw upon in accounting for official violence in each case are chiefly these:

1. The nature of the government, whether it has made a serious effort to monopolize the use of force and to exclude the military from domestic peace-keeping, as well as to prevent the police from turning into a quasi-military force.

2. The sense of citizen participation as well as reliance on the legal order, which are commonly affected by class conflict and economic inequality.

3. The prevalence of private dispute-settlement by violence.

4. The growth of regularity and oversight in government relations with citizens, both in the direction of government regulation of citizens and in the the direction of the accountability of government to its citizens. In this connection, I have also studied the prevalence of corruption in the police as well as in government generally.

In each chapter, I have described the successes and failures of institutions of accountability, including the courts, the executive, and the police themselves. In the third chapter, I survey and critique institutions of accountability in the United States as a whole.

In every case, the governments make at least a colorable claim to adhere to international standards for the control of police violence; the governments always claim that almost all shootings are justifiable and deny that torture is used systematically. The international standards are thus norms that have been accepted by the legal opinion of the governments. The political problem is to find institutions, and social support for the institutions, that can bring the police closer to adhering to the norms.

This book, then, is an empirical study of police violence, in a theoretical frame of politics and sociology, with the aim of approaching fulfillment of the international standards.

Los Angeles and New York in the Americas

The governments of New York City and Los Angeles, which lie on opposite coasts of the country, have taken almost opposite approaches to policing. The Los Angeles police, both in the city and the county, have had a reputation as the quintessential anticrime force, with a semimilitary attitude both to the job and the public. There have been no major corruption scandals for decades, and morale has been good among the police, at least until the Rodney King scandal. In contrast, the New York City Police Department (NYPD), which is more than three times the size of the Los Angeles Police Department (LAPD), has been concerned with controlling the discretion of its officers and maintaining good relations with the public and political forces. In the 1990s, the NYPD embraced a philosophy of community policing, through which more police would be put on foot patrol, and, with stronger links to the local communities, the department hoped to reduce crime as well as convey a sense of greater safety. The relation between superior officers and the rank-and-file in the NYPD is often wary, at best, and there are periodic corruption scandals, both large and small.

The reasons for the divergence in the styles of policing in the two urban areas lie in the differences in municipal government and the history of the cities and their police, as the two chapters that follow will show in more detail. The result of the divergence, for purposes of this study, has been that, while each of the cities has had endemic problems with the abuse of non-deadly force—police brutality—as have many other American cities, Los Angeles made no serious effort to control such violence before 1991, while New York yielded much earlier to the pressure to set up at least some systems of accountability. New York long ago took the lead in the nation in trying to make officers accountable for and reduce the use of deadly force through stringent internal regulations, while the police in Los Angeles have continued to shoot more people than any other police department in the largest U.S. cities. Some of the keys to the problems, then, lie in the management of the departments and in the systems of accountability for acts of violence; accordingly I have discussed those systems as they are found in New York, Los Angeles, and, in chapter III, the United States as a whole, in an effort to glimpse what a workable system might be.

I have not selected the police in New York and Los Angeles for this book because either of them is an example of the best or the worst, on some scale that we might invent. News stories appearing as this is written suggest that the police in New Orleans are probably more corrupt and violent than they are in either New York or Los Angeles.[34] Such scandals, however, obscure the fact that we have neither information nor standards for deciding what it would mean for a police department to be the best or the worst.

One reason for selecting these two cities, apart from the fact that they are perhaps the most talked-about urban complexes in the United States, is that there has been so much interest in their police. It would be a sin to ignore the superb work that has been done in Los Angeles since the spring of 1991 by commissions investigating violence by the police in the city and in the county surrounding it. The Christopher Commission investigated the city's police in the wake of the Rodney King beating, triggering an equally thorough account of the county sheriff's department by the Kolts Commission. These reports, tracing the traditions of violence, showing the failure of accountability, and recommending series of reforms, afford an unparalleled comparison of two contiguous departments during the same period of time. There have been periodic progress reports in subsequent years from the Kolts staff and from the LAPD itself which have shown, I think, that the reforms, although of the greatest importance, have not been entirely successful.[35]

I have been watching the problems of the New York City police at intervals since my 1969 study *Police Power: Police Abuses in New York City*.[36] By sheer chance, an investigation was provoked by a corruption scandal in 1991 just as I was really digging into my work on the city. The resulting Mollen Commission report of 1994 revealed a connection between corruption and the incidence of violence which I surely could not have uncovered with my own feeble resources.[37] For both Los Angeles and New York, I have of course relied on my own field work as well as other studies.

It must be admitted that the NYPD is difficult to study. Bureaucratized as it is, it turns a bland face to the public as well as to scholars. Everything has to be done through channels; hardly anyone in the department will talk to an outsider without approval from above, and once the approval is obtained, hardly anything of substance is revealed.

The fate of the Mollen Commission report and its recommendations is typical. After the report was released in July 1994, it became difficult to obtain a copy; once the commission had finished its work, there was no place, or at least none that anyone knew about, from which the report was distributed. Out-of-towners who wanted to get a look at it sometimes called to ask me to send a Xerox of my copy. Then the mayor refused to implement the principal proposal of the commission, to establish an outside monitor to investigate corruption. Thus encouraged, the new police commissioner, William Bratton, dismissed the department's own corruption trouble-shooter, who had been introduced in the first place in an unsuccessful effort to quiet the worst publicity arising from the Mollen Commission investigation. He was replaced by a department insider, about whom Bratton said, "[His] experience in narcotics investigations and his strength as a communicator in public forums will make him highly effective in his new post."[38] Business as usual, in short.

So far as I can tell, the exasperating secretiveness of the NYPD nevertheless does not conceal any colossal pattern of violence; it is, rather, an excess of bureaucratic caution directed at any potential source of bad publicity, especially any connected with corruption. It is a caution rooted in a history of conflict with the generally liberal constituency of New Yorkers, who continue to be suspicious of the NYPD, looking for bad faith behind every incident of violent conflict.

Citizens in every city take incidents of violence one at a time; one reason for writing this book is that people rarely are conscious of how violent their police are in relation to the police in other cities. Thus New Yorkers do not realize how much more gingerly their police act in comparison to the police in Los Angeles; to a New Yorker reading the chapter that follows this, the violence in Los Angeles may seem quite out of control. And yet police violence in Los Angeles, however alarming, is relatively rare in comparison with some other cities in the Americas. The comparison between New York and Los Angeles, taken alone, would suggest only a narrow band of the spectrum encompassed by this study about the comparative use of force. The use of deadly force is relatively infrequent in those two cities, and torture has virtually disappeared.

If we were to make no more than a bald comparison among the six places in this study, using cases and statistics out of context, the prevalence of torture as well as deadly force would seem incomprehensible, not to say incomparable to the United States. It will require a historical perspective on police violence in the United States, such as I will undertake in chapter IV, to reveal the skeleton of police problems that the United States has in common, under the skin, with the cities of Latin America and Jamaica.

CHAPTER I

Los Angeles: City and County

They give me a stick, they give me a gun, they pay me 50Gs to
have some fun.
—LOS ANGELES POLICE OFFICER[39]

INTRODUCTION: POLICE AND POLITICS

The national reputation for violence, and even cruelty, that has
been visited on the Los Angeles police since the Rodney King
incident in 1991 has elements of tragedy. Until that moment,
Los Angeles had a department that was much admired;
although it had its critics, many of whom knew of episodes like
Rodney King's and worse, the LAPD was widely considered
one of the most "professional" forces in the United States. It
was brought low as a consequence of some of the very characteristics for which it was admired.

In 1990, the authors of *Beyond 911,* a leading work on police
reform, gave this glowing endorsement: "It [the LAPD] operates
with a high degree of autonomy, discipline and self-confidence.
For four decades it has avoided major corruption scandals. It
polices a vast terrain and varied population with half the officers per capita of some big city departments. It boasts sophisticated specialties rivaling the expertise of much larger organizations.... It is the apotheosis of reform policing."[40]

The LAPD's reputation for honesty and professionalism was
an extraordinary accomplishment, because before World War
II, the department was well known for graft and political influence. Police took bribes, in some cases actually worked in the
rackets, and were protected by politicians. The police reformer
August Vollmer, who was chief in Los Angeles for one year in
the twenties, wrote:

> Any chief of police who attempted to do his duty and eliminate
> those iniquitous dens [of gambling and prostitution] would soon

have suffered a shortening of his career. The business of vice there-
fore continued to flourish, the protests of the people were wantonly
flouted, the morale of the law-enforcing officers was inevitably
threatened, and the result of the whole matter was to strengthen
the hands of the politicians who daily corrupt the government of
our cities.[41]

William Parker, who was chief for sixteen years beginning in
1950, succeeded in separating the department from "politics,"
in the sense of interference in departmental affairs, and in virtually eliminating corruption. It was a stunning performance. To
bring it about, Parker infused a strong semimilitary spirit and
esprit de corps. The Los Angeles police were well paid and
proud of their "professionalism," but it was close to the professionalism of an army. Parker spoke of the "thin blue line,"
embattled against an invasion of crime, and even hosted a television program with that title.

The chief's office had civil service status—the chief could not
be removed without cause—and in fact had had it for decades,
although no one before Parker had been determined enough to
make full use of the status. The discipline of officers was also
run completely by the department, limited by strong protections for officers through the civil service laws. The chief,
whose power was buttressed by secure tenure and internal discipline, was insulated politically to an extent that was rare
among U.S. cities. There was and still is a civilian police commission, which was intended to oversee police management
independent of narrow political concerns, but it had long since
been captured by the police and did not function as an effective
control; indeed, since the chief had tenure and control over his
own personnel, it is hard to see how the Police Commission
could have controlled him.[42]

The chief's and the department's powers, although they were
the engine of reform in a city and a department that had been
honeycombed with corruption and even more serious crimes,
contained the seeds of contemporary problems. The chief's
tenure was rooted in the progressive reform idea that the police
had to be separate from politics, but in fact Parker imposed his

own politics on the department. It was repressive, anti-Left, and suspicious of minority groups. He fostered an ideal of the "hardnosed, proactive" policeman, less interested in relations with the community than in the paramilitary fight against crime. The security of tenure, so far from insulating the chief from politics, made him an independent political actor.

The theme in Los Angeles police work that Parker advanced had long been present. The LAPD had always had a reputation for the sort of violence—against demonstrators, labor agitators, and the merely unemployed or poor—that disaffected Angelenos used to call "cossackism," although the flavor was much more peculiarly American than European. Parker and those who followed him, up through Chief Daryl Gates, thought it was so important for a policeman to be aggressive that excess was scarcely a failing. From the fifties to the nineties, it was proverbial that a policeman would be dismissed for an action that "embarrassed the department," such as taking a bribe, but would not be severely disciplined for the excessive use of force, even for shooting a civilian. In the sixties, Parker disciplined a policeman who was critical of the department on issues of civil rights and suspended him for six months, at a time when he avoided disciplining other police for violence; ironically, that policeman's departmental hearing occurred two weeks before the Watts rebellion.[43] In the eighties and nineties, Daryl Gates repeatedly showed that he thought police violence against people connected with crime was justified. In the Larez case, in 1986, in which the police beat a suspect and tore apart his house searching for a gun they never found, Gates said Larez was "lucky" not to have suffered worse. Gates topped that in 1990 when he advocated before Congress the shooting of casual drug users.[44]

Although these rash statements, which would be suicidal in many big-city departments, may be thought of as a result of the bravado that comes with tenured status, in fact the Parker-Gates style of policing has mostly suited the politics of the city and county over the last fifty years. The Los Angeles Sheriff's Department, which serves under contract as police in many municipalities in the county that are not technically part of the city, has problems with police violence that are similar to, and sometimes worse than, those of the LAPD. Because of Los Angeles's urban sprawl, fitting roughly into the county but well beyond the confines of the city itself, it is necessary to look at the whole region, including the police problems of the sheriff (often designated the LASD) as well as the city police. It is characteristic of Los Angeles that it is vague as a political concept, referring as needed to the city or the region.

There is great economic and social disparity, as well as diversity, in the region. White non-Hispanics (white Anglos) make up 40 percent of the population of the county, while another 40 percent are Hispanic and about 12 percent are black. Although per capita income is high, economic inequality is sharp; as many as 30 percent of blacks and latinos are below the poverty line. Crime has been on the rise, driven by poverty and the dislocations of migration.

For decades, until relatively recently, the city was run by a downtown elite, opposed to labor organization and impatient with the poor and minorities; the elite always encouraged the LAPD Red Squad and actions against vagrants. During their hegemony, there was a strong streak of western vigilantism in Los Angeles life which was absorbed into police conduct. As Joseph G. Woods put it, "Apparently a willingness to evade, subvert, or override the law whenever necessary imbued most judges, policemen, civic leaders and ordinary citizens. Given this atmosphere, the willful insolence of the police was understandable." Nevertheless the Los Angeles boosters liked to call it "the White Spot of America," in reference to its supposed freedom from crime as well as its racial purity; on either count, the name was something worse than an exaggeration.

The boosters tried to make it come true through constant development of new communities; moving to get away from undesirables and erecting barriers to keep them out became a way of life in Los Angeles. The dispersion of the residents through the county made for weak governmental coordination and control over citizens, as well as for poor communications among the communities. There is hardly an issue about which the residents of the county would have common ground to meet together, nor a natural forum for them to do so. As Paul Hoffman says, "South Central Los Angeles, the flashpoint of the civil disorder in April and May 1992, might as well be on another planet for most residents of Los Angeles County." Even within the city itself, the process of fragmentation and isolation has taken hold; the city council has allowed street closings and the creation of closed neighborhoods, many of them with private guards.[45]

The rule of the older downtown elite has passed from the city; Tom Bradley, its first black mayor, was elected by a liberal coalition in 1973. With power dispersed between the city council and the mayor, however, the city has a structure that does not make for strong governance. The scattering of neighborhoods and communities has continued; if Los Angeles, because of its ethnic diversity, is the "Capital of the Third World," as David Rieff called it, it must be so mostly in the eyes of the thousands of newcomers to the region. White Anglos often do not know how or even clearly where the newcomers live. Control of the police by other branches of the the municipal government is particularly weak; thus the police, more than other agencies, have retained an older repressive style.

The police no longer repress labor but rather the poor and the underclass, which is of course enormous both in the city and the county. Much of the police harassment discriminates simply by race or ethnic background. For example, on the pretext of traffic violations, both the LAPD and sheriff's deputies stop black people driving expensive cars, apparently on the theory that such people are likely to be criminals; sometimes the victims are forced to take the "prone-out" position, face down on the ground. The stops occasionally net celebrities; basketball player Jamaal Wilkes and movie star Wesley Snipes, among others, were stopped and humiliated by the LAPD in 1991. Jeremiah Randle, a high school teacher driving a BMW, was stopped by sheriff's deputies in 1991; when he asked the reason, a deputy said, "Look, nigger, I don't have to tell you

39

shit." When Randle complained and asked for the deputy's name, the deputies arrested him and kicked him repeatedly in the right knee, then charged him with obstructing an officer.[46]

The biggest operation to detain and search minority people was Operation Hammer, which began in the spring of 1988 after a woman was killed in crossfire in Westwood, a shopping village that is the gateway to the University of California. In April 1988 alone, more than fourteen hundred minority youths were arrested, many of them only to be released later for lack of any charges. For two years, black and Hispanic youths who ventured into middle-class neighborhoods were very likely to be stopped, forced to "kiss concrete," and searched.[47]

All this was justified by the claim that the police were in a war, described in a fantastic combat rhetoric that seemed to borrow not a little from the films that are made close by. When Operation Hammer began, a police official said, "This is Vietnam here." In 1990, when Chief Gates advocated shooting casual drug users, the Los Angeles Times reported him to have explained, "'We're in a war,'...and even casual drug use 'is treason.'" District Attorney Ira Reiner said he agreed "in concept...although not with his 'colorful choice of language.'" Thus Los Angeles officials live in a world of violence they have created to put them on a war footing; this same Ira Reiner claimed in a 1992 report that there were 150,000 gang members in Los Angeles County, and he later said that half the young black males in Los Angeles show up in gang "data bases," some of them presumably derived from the Operation Hammer arrests. A captain in the sheriff's department told a lawyer that there were sixty gangs just within the few square blocks of the Lynwood substation.[48]

One effect of the "war" actions against minority people is to reinforce the divisions between communities and to keep minorities in the districts where most of them live. Consistent with Los Angeles politics, this has not been unpopular with many middle-class voters nor with the majority of the city council over the years. They liked the Parker-Gates style of policing: repressive, exclusionary, technocratic, and squeaky clean. Although there was more than a generation of agitation against the police street tactics, by the ACLU of Southern California among many other organizations, there was little substantial change before 1991.

THE POLICE, THE SHERIFF'S DEPARTMENT, AND THE USE OF FORCE

The County has about nine million people in more than eighty cities and towns. In 1991, the Los Angeles Sheriff's Department worked as police in forty-one of those communities and unincorporated areas that did not have their own departments, serving two and a half million people in a sprawling region. The LAPD serves three and a half million people in a more confined area. Each of the forces had about eight thousand officers; the LAPD is notably small, serving a larger population than comparable big-city departments. The sheriff is elected countywide, while at that time, of course, the chief in the city of Los Angeles was appointed with civil service status. The city's Police Commission continued to function, but had little control over the LAPD.[49]

Excessive Force Without Firearms

Both departments operated on the principle, as an LAPD witness at the Christopher Commission put it, "that excessive force is treated leniently because it does not violate the department's internal moral code." The officer went on to say that "'some thumping' is permissible as a matter of course." As in the days of Parker, other offenses were thought to pose a greater disciplinary problem. The Kolts report on the sheriff's department notes that "it is ironic that while discipline in excessive-force cases is rare, and notice of excessive-force incidents seldom is included in the personnel records of deputies, more than 40 deputies had comments in their files regarding suspensions or reprimands arising out of traffic accidents, or just notice of vehicle-related activity."[50] In southern California, careless driving is a serious matter.

Under these circumstances, incidents of serious brutality are numerous. In April 1988, members of the LAPD pursued Luis Murrales for a traffic violation; Murrales did not stop until he struck a police car, and then he ran and tried to hide. When they caught him, the officers beat him with batons and kicked him in the face and body until he finally lost his sight in one eye; the city paid damages of $177,000. The Christopher Commission reported: "Describing the incident, the commanding officer acknowledged that a lynch mob mentality appeared to have existed once Murrales fled the scene on foot. However, after an LAPD investigation, no allegations were sustained against the officers involved. Four officers who used force on Murrales had similar prior incidents."[51]

Dana Hansen's career in the LAPD is indicative. After the Rodney King incident, Hansen was successfully prosecuted by the federal government (the local district attorney having declined to prosecute) for violating the civil rights of Jesus Martinez Vidales, aged seventeen, whose skull he had fractured. After searching for Martinez Vidales, on a charge of driving a stolen car, Hansen, in the presence of witnesses, struck the youth repeatedly in the head with his baton, trying to pull him from his hiding place under a truck. Hansen had a second federal case against him, again for brutality, that was dropped after he went to prison in the Martinez Vidales case. In addition, the city had paid substantial damages for his beating of a woman in 1986, and he had been cleared in a shooting of a teenager in 1983. Nevertheless, Chief Gates said he was inclined to give Hansen a leave of absence to serve his federal sentence.[52]

The situation was much the same with the sheriff's deputies. It seems that both in the LAPD and the sheriff's department, recruits were trained on the street to use violence. When recruits began their work on patrol, they were mentored by a field training officer (FTO), who taught them how to work in the field. In both departments, the FTOs were selected for their aggressiveness and their arrest records; hardly any attention was paid to complaints they had received for excessive force, even in the unusual case when the complaint was sustained. Thus violent members became FTOs.[53]

Brutality was used against those who defied or even criticized the police, especially when they belonged to ethnic minorities. As the Kolts report said, "This is the worst aspect of police culture, where the worst crime of all is 'contempt of cop.' The deputy cannot let pass the slightest challenge or failure immediately to comply. It is here that excessive force starts and needs to be stopped." In April 1989, Demetrio Carillo, a Hispanic, reproved some deputies, who were issuing a traffic ticket, for driving up on the sidewalk across from his home. He was grabbed and beaten, while a woman deputy called him a "goddamn Mexican"; finally he was charged with obstructing a police officer. Many of the cases arose after car chases, which are of course acts of defiance, as in the famous Rodney King case and the Murrales case, where the victim lost an eye.

In their typed conversations with one another on their computer equipment, the LAPD used expressions calculated to degrade and sometimes dehumanize those with whom they had to deal. After the Rodney King beating, there occurred a now-famous exchange: "You just had a big time use of force...tased and beat the suspect...Big Time." And from the station: "Oh well...I'm sure the lizard didn't deserve it...HAHAHA I'll let them know, OK?" Many of the transmissions contained violent racial slurs, of which one of the mildest was "looks like monkey-slapping time."[54]

Although torture in the classic sense of "the methodical infliction of pain to get information" was rare, there was deliberate infliction of pain to punish and degrade. The LAPD and the sheriff's department routinely used special weapons and techniques in ways that police in other cities find astounding. Dogs were used extensively, were trained to bite suspects rather than simply to find or even just intimidate them, and were used in a disproportionately large number of cases involving black and Hispanic suspects; after viewing a video about the LAPD's use of dogs, Hubert Williams, formerly chief of the Newark police and now head of the Police Foundation, commented, "This is incredible.... I've never heard of this before." The LAPD used the taser—a sort of gun, which fires barbed darts attached to a wire that delivers an electric charge into the body of the suspect—as routinely as a club, although in other departments in the country the weapon is unusual. The taser was used on Rodney King as it has been on many others, and it is clear from the transmission after the King beating that it was used as a form of summary punishment.[55]

For many years, the LAPD had used, as a means of subduing suspects, chokeholds that cause the person to pass out. According to James Fyfe, most police consider chokeholds a dangerous form of deadly force, but the LAPD used them as a routine way of forcing compliance; an LAPD policeman told me that they used to subdue a suspect with a chokehold if he did no more than refuse to give fingerprints. The department stopped the routine use of the chokeholds in the eighties, after one victim who survived brought a federal action and proved that sixteen people, fourteen of them black, had been killed in five years. An ironical twist is that after the Rodney King incident, police in Los Angeles claimed that a reason for the violence of the beating was that the police were not permitted to use chokeholds for compliance; I was told this more than once, and it appeared to be a widespread belief among officers. The argument runs that if the officers had been able to choke Rodney King, they would not have had to use their batons (and, incidentally, the affair would not have looked on videotape like mayhem).[56]

The argument assumes, of course, that the officers had to use their batons; the officers claim that they had to force King to lie prone, and they had to do it with the clubs. I still find these arguments eerie. Since the officers could not use the chokehold, they were not going to put their hands on Rodney King, for their own safety, they claimed. Yet it is puzzling why King had to be forced to lie face down at all; if he was to be arrested, it is not clear to anyone outside Los Angeles that he had to be taken from the "prone-out" position that the LAPD uses to control people after mere traffic violations or just for investigation. Taken together, the arguments say that the purpose of the techniques is "control," and control that distances the police from the people, that keeps the police clean and safe but makes people into objects. The approach to the work is technical, in the sense that it ignores the fact that the objects of the techniques are citizens. The use of the chokehold is more desirable than the baton because it is simpler and less messy; the danger of the technique is beside the point (although it is fair to say that Los Angeles police often claim that chokeholds are not dangerous).

Yet it is clear that the police know that a technique of control is also a means of degradation. They do not use the chokehold on middle-class white people, nor make them lie down on their faces on the pavement. It is interesting that in the first computer-radio exchange about Rodney King, the station referred to him as a "lizard," a reptile that is always prone. A police officer told the Christopher Commission that the use of the prone-out technique in minority communities was "pretty routine," that the police had been taught "that aggression and force are the only things these people respond to."

All the police actions and words, together with the attitudes that infuse them, are justified in the name of a war on crime, particularly against gangs. But all the violence and rhetoric, including the analogy to war itself, with its conception of part of the population as an "enemy" to be conquered, come down to the enforcement of the barriers between places where different classes and races live and the consequent control of the lives of the predominantly poor people with whom the police have to deal. The Kolts report described the genesis of one sheriff's department shooting, in August 1991, as "a lethal version of 'I'm going to show you who's boss around here.'" Sometimes the police make the purpose explicit. In one of the most notorious cases during Operation Hammer, when LAPD units, including its Gang Task Force, literally destroyed four apartments on Dalton Avenue in 1989, on the mistaken theory that they were crack dens, some police spray painted on the wall "Gang Task Force Rules."

In the case brought against the sheriff's department for harassment in the town of Lynwood, a woman whose house had been twice ransacked without a warrant testified, "I cannot take any more of this. If I could afford to move to another city I would." That would seem to be the point.[57]

Deadly Force

The Los Angeles city police shoot more people, in proportion to the size of the force, than any other major U.S. police department. That alone, of course, is no cause for criticism; they also make proportionately more felony arrests than police in other departments. Consistent with contemporary U.S. law, the LAPD's written regulations restrict the use of deadly force to situations where the suspect poses a threat of death or serious injury. The figures on shootings, moreover, in relation to officers shot and general homicide statistics, do not by themselves point clearly toward any covert policy encouraging the deliberate abuse of firearms:[58]

OFFICER-INVOLVED SHOOTINGS AND GENERAL HOMICIDES	1991	1992
Los Angeles City Police		
Civilians killed by police	23	25
Civilians wounded	38	52
Police killed	n/a	1
Police wounded	n/a	5
County Sheriff's Department		
Civilians killed by deputies	23	18
Civilians wounded	40	31
Deputies killed	0	2
Deputies wounded	10	6
Homicides in General		
County	2401	2589
City	1047	1095

These figures are consistent with the past; the LAPD has shot about the same number of people for the past decade. Nevertheless, there are a number of shootings that appear to be unjustified and some that must be called deliberate abuses.

The shootings by sheriff's deputies are best known and best

documented. The investigation that resulted in the Kolts report was prompted by four killings in August and September 1991: the victims were shot in the back, witnesses claimed that the shootings were unnecessary, and there were no disciplinary proceedings. In a set of muckraking articles, the Los Angeles *Daily News* analyzed 202 on-duty shootings by deputies between 1985 and 1990, finding 56 of them to be questionable, in the sense that the person shot was conceded to be unarmed or that there was serious criticism by uninvolved witnesses concerning the circumstances of the shooting. One notorious case, for which the county wound up paying a million dollars in damages, was the killing in 1988 of Hyong Po Lee, shot seventeen times when the deputies finally cornered him after a car chase. The deputies claimed that Lee had tried to run them over with his car, but a Long Beach city police officer who was a witness said that the car was parked. It seemed that the shooting perhaps started because one deputy apprehensively jumped away from the car, and the others panicked. The Long Beach police witness testified that he said to his partner at the scene, "We just observed the sheriffs execute somebody."

More disturbing are the shootings by deputy Paul Archambault. In March 1987, deputies responded to a call that a Pascual Solis had struck his wife and might be under the influence of the drug PCP. Archambault found Solis in the backyard of a neighbor, Ernest Machuca, where he shot at him six times, reloaded, and shot four more times, killing him. Archambault claimed that Solis wrested away his baton and menaced him with it, but Machuca saw Archambault fire a number of times while the man was crouched behind a car and Archambault still had the baton on his belt. Machuca heard another deputy ask if Solis was still moving; Archambault said, "He's moving, he's moving," and fired again. The medical evidence later showed that Solis was probably crouching when he was shot, and was not under the influence of PCP; the county paid substantial damages for the death.

In May 1990, Archambault and his partner were searching for a man known as "Twin," in connection with a shooting.

The deputy apparently mistook one Elzie Coleman for Twin, chased him, and fired twenty-three rounds at him; he hit Coleman six times but did not kill him. Archambault claimed that Coleman pointed a gun at him, but Coleman and other witnesses say that Coleman was running away with empty hands and that they saw the deputies plant a gun. Coleman was later acquitted of the charge of possession of a gun.

Archambault was neither disciplined by the sheriff nor prosecuted for these shootings, which is, as we shall see in more detail, typical in such cases. He was made a field training officer instead; his performance evaluation said that he "handles emergencies very well. He is able to maintain clear thought and reason while in stressful situations."[59]

That evaluation is so opaque and strange that it must make us ask ourselves what the deputy's thinking could have been in those stressful situations, why in fact he fired so profligately. Comparing the Coleman and Solis incidents with Hyong Po Lee and other similar cases, I can only conclude that the overheated "war" footing on which the police have placed themselves, abetted by other public officials and the media, has made them apprehensive about situations, perceiving danger where it does not exist. When the victims are black or Hispanic, the misperception only increases. If an officer is trigger-happy under those conditions, it is partly because neither the sheriff's office nor any other actor in the criminal justice system restrains him.

The abuse of deadly force was sometimes more systematic in the LAPD. In accordance with police reform philosophy, the LAPD has various specialized units; the difficulty is that they sometimes become a law unto themselves. One of the units has the uncommunicative name Special Investigations Section (SIS); its job, in fact, is to keep surveillance over suspected violent criminals, robbers and burglars, and catch them. In the years between 1965 and 1992, SIS shot fifty-five people, killing twenty-eight of them. Its detectives claimed that those shot were armed and dangerous, but in all that time, only one SIS detective was shot—accidentally by a police shotgun.

At the end of the eighties, finally, reporters exposed the methods of the SIS. As David Freed of the *Los Angeles Times* put it, "Officers routinely stood by until the suspects they were watching had committed violent crimes. Many suspects were shot when they returned to their getaway cars." To put it bluntly, it appears they were ambushed.

In 1989, SIS had a group of Hispanics under surveillance for a string of robberies of McDonald's restaurants. In early 1990, detectives trailed the group of four to a McDonald's. The manager called 911 to report that some Mexicans were trying to stick up the place; the police dispatcher sent a patrol unit, but the SIS detectives called it off. They waited for the long-suffering manager to be tied up and robbed, then they boxed in the robbers' car with their own and shot them. They killed three and almost killed the fourth. The police claimed that the robbers reached for their guns, but in fact the "weapons" they had with them were empty pellet guns used to intimidate the victim of the robbery.

Incensed by this assassination, as he called it, the aggressive police-brutality lawyer Stephen Yagman brought a civil action for damages for the survivor and the families of the dead. The jury understandably had little sympathy for the robbers, but so outraged were they by the police methods, that they awarded $44,000 in purely punitive damages against Chief Gates and the officers personally. The city council, ever obedient to police needs, voted to have the city pay the damages anyhow. Gates's comment on the case made the assassination purpose quite clear: "If we had taken them outside [the restaurant before they entered it], they would have been out on bail today, and probably robbing someone else. Now there won't be any more of these robberies at McDonald's. Perhaps we accomplished something."[60]

Accountability and Impunity
Before Rodney King

Until the changes in 1991, the handling of civilian complaints both in the LAPD and the sheriff's department was free-wheeling. There was no external review of complaints, nor any specialized investigative staff, nor even a separate office in which complaints were to be filed. In response to an inquiry in 1990 by Los Angeles *Daily News* reporters, Sheriff Sherman Block said, "I have the ultimate review board—I was just elected with 68 percent of the vote." A complaint form was simply filled out at any police station or sheriff's station. Officers frequently failed to fill them out, failed to file them, or, worse, intimidated complainants from filing a complaint, sometimes by threatening to arrest them. There was, furthermore, no consistent procedure for processing the complaints if they were made; officers at the station level could usually terminate investigations if they chose. Under these conditions, 2 percent of the allegations of excessive force were sustained by the LAPD, and 6 percent of the complaints against the sheriff's deputies were sustained.

Particularly discouraging was the performance of the departments concerning shootings. At the sheriff's department, deputies were virtually never disciplined for shootings; they were not to be disciplined unless the district attorney thought the conduct criminal, and the district attorney never indicted. The LAPD did only slightly better; shootings were found to be against regulations in thirty-nine cases, but the discipline imposed was minimal. The most severe penalty was nineteen days' suspension, and in a majority of cases, there was no suspension at all. One officer, according to Amnesty International, was involved in five shootings that were found to be against regulations; in 1989, he killed an unarmed Hispanic youth after a car chase, a case for which the city paid almost a million dollars in damages. Nevertheless, he was not dismissed and appears to have resigned or retired.[61]

More surprising is the fact that the district attorney never prosecuted any of the officers for the shootings. On paper, the procedures for criminal investigation of shootings looked good; since the late seventies, both departments operated under a system called Operation Rollout, in which an assistant district attorney is invited to observe the investigation of any shooting in which an officer has been involved. The system, however, was not very effective; the lawyers did not get to talk to the witnesses until after the police had interviewed them.

More important, the police and the district attorney did not seem to differ very much in their judgment about the shootings. In effect, the test used by the prosecutor's office was simply whether the shooting was done in the line of duty and in good faith—that is, for a purpose related to police work and not, for example, to settle a personal score. Under that test the killings by the SIS would not be indictable in Los Angeles—and, sure enough, there were no indictments. It appeared that police and other elements of the law-enforcement system in the county shared a cultural norm about what police conduct ought to be punishable, and neither procedures for investigation nor even the law of homicide could move them.[62]

Both the Christopher Commission and the Kolts report found that there were many officers against whom a disproportionately large number of civilian complaints had been filed. The "problem officers" were relatively easy to pick out; in fact, one LAPD official testified that the department knew who they were. But neither of the departments had ever tracked them or tried to improve their performance, because officials did not read that performance as poor. Even when complaints were sustained, they commonly made little difference in an officer's career. Written evaluations by superiors were usually pro forma and were not intended seriously as praise or criticism; that is perhaps the reason for the startling evaluation of deputy Archambault. More important, officers who had received many complaints were routinely promoted; the police who participated in the famous Dalton Avenue raid, in which apartments were destroyed and the city paid some four million dollars in damages, were promoted, some to sergeant and lieutenant, some to field training officer. The radioed wisecrack that is the epigraph to this chapter was perhaps not as much of a joke as it seems at first.[63]

Despite the ineffectiveness of the system of complaints, the police had an arsenal of devices to insure their impunity. First was, and undoubtedly still is, the universal device of the code of silence; officers virtually never testify against one another, and if they do, they run a risk of ostracism. The departments, moreover, viewed officers' lying as a venial sin; the departments did not discipline for lying, as if it were expected. In the case of the Dalton Avenue raid, for example, some police had been charged with criminal vandalism; at their trial, the judge commented, "I cannot think of a case...where I have seen more false testimony." The police were acquitted, and nothing was done about the perjury. In the sheriff's department, deputies were trained by field training officers to falsify reports to incriminate people arrested.

Police also covered themselves by arresting people they had roughed up and charging them with a crime. The Kolts report found that the use of cover charges by deputies was systematic. Jeremiah Randle, who objected to being called "nigger," and Demetrio Carrillo, who was beaten after he told deputies not to park on the sidewalk, were charged with obstructing an officer, a typical cover charge. There have also been claims that weapons were planted to make shootings appear justified.[64]

The failures of internal discipline and even of prosecution, however discouraging, may not seem too surprising; such problems are old in American policing. What seemed amazing in the Christopher Commission report, when it first appeared, was the failure of the civil tort claims system to have any effect on police policy; the Kolts report only confirmed the conclusion.

Police brutality litigation has become a cottage industry for lawyers in Los Angeles County. There is a police misconduct lawyers referral service, called Police Watch, the likes of which I have not seen anywhere else. It has a hundred cooperating lawyers, who pay a small percentage of their fees to keep the one-person complaint office going; in 1990, the office received over a thousand complaints against the LAPD and the sheriff's department. And Police Watch lawyers do not by any means handle all the police brutality litigation in the county.

In 1993, I was told by an attorney for the city of Los Angeles that the city pays between seventeen and twenty million dollars a year in damages for "police malpractice"—some of it, of course, for simple mistakes and not for excessive force. The Christopher Commission found that the city paid more than

$20 million just for the excessive-force cases that the Commission was able to trace between January 1986 and 1990. The Kolts report found that in the three and a half years between January 1989 and May 1992 the county paid more than $15 million for excessive-force cases.[65]

Although these payments are large, even relative to payments in other cities such as New York, the main point about the cases is not the amount paid but the nature of the abuses. They were incidents of "clear and often egregious misconduct resulting in serious injury or death," as the Christopher Commission said, in which the public took an interest and huge damages were paid, like the Murrales case of the man who lost an eye in a beating after a car chase, or the Dalton Avenue raid. The Kolts report said what should have been obvious, that "the verdicts in this litigation represent findings by an independent trier of fact that the force used was excessive," and even most of those that were settled "represent clear examples of excessive force." The departments did nothing systematic about the cases; they did not track the litigations nor take them into account in discipline or promotion; the results were usually not even entered into the personnel files of the officers involved. More important, the departments did not learn anything about repeated problems; the Kolts report picked out seven repeated patterns of abuse to which the sheriff's department had paid no attention. In cases of shootings, for example, investigations sometimes found that, while deputies had acted within the law, they had panicked in a situation or misperceived it. In some of those cases, the jam that the officer was in or thought he was in could have been avoided, for example, by calling for assistance. The Kolts report said, "Our staff reviewed many cases in which officers unnecessarily walked into or created situations which ultimately required the use of deadly force."

The reports took the position that the departments ought to try to rectify the problems the civil litigation system revealed; as the Kolts report put it, "the kinds of incidents that are repugnant to juries should also be repugnant to the department." Sheriff Block did not agree; he said he did not monitor civil suits because he had little faith in the results, and Chief Gates took a similar view. The departments did not want to learn anything from the damage settlements and verdicts, because they did not accept the judgment of the civil law. The city and the county certainly could have done something about this; they could have insisted that the departments change their tactics to reduce the damages. It is clear, however, that in the last analysis they did not substantially disagree with the sheriff or the chief. In two cases, including the SIS assassination of the McDonald's bandits, in which exasperated juries assessed punitive damages personally against the police officers and their chief, the city council, apparently exasperated, in turn, at the jury and sorry for good old Gates, voted to pay the punitive damages.[66]

Why did the departments fail to track the cases and try to control the damages? Why did the city and county accept the situation for so many years, when they could have saved money by insisting that the departments pay attention to the judgments in discipline and policy? Behind these failures lies the familiar and powerful hidden belief that violent police tactics decrease the amount of crime by terrorizing and deterring criminals. It follows that, if the department is small in relation to the population, as is the LAPD, the department will have to be more violent to keep control over crime. The alternative would be to hire more police, which would be, as Fyfe and Skolnick point out, a great deal more expensive than paying the injured. Thus the damages seemed a gruesome sort of "cost of doing business." The city literally and figuratively got more bang for its buck.

Gates made the hidden belief all but explicit, something he was always good at. He argued that Los Angeles was the "safest of the big cities" because of his policies, pointing to the high arrest rate of the LAPD. If that were so, it would not really be a justification for the violence nor any comfort to innocent people who were beaten and shot, but it would certainly be a powerful argument in these United States that are at once vengeful against criminals and in perpetual revolt against higher government expenses. Fortunately, it is a myth. The figures show that serious crimes were not low in Los Angeles and that it was not the "safest of the big cities"; let us not forget that Los Angeles law-enforcement people also like to argue, perversely, that they are at war against a rising wave of crime. What evidence there is, particularly James Fyfe's work on the restriction of shootings in New York, indicates that a reduction in police violence is not accompanied by a reduction in the arrest rate or by a rise in crime. What all this suggests is that the governments could cut their expenses by changing police policies, without changing the size of the departments and without increasing crime.[67]

After Rodney King

Overnight, it seemed, on March 3, 1991, the most "professional" of U.S. police departments was out of step; Joseph McNamara, the former chief of the San Jose police, said that "Mr. Gates' military style of policing is at odds with the rest of the country, and it's time police leaders publicly repudiated it."[68] Was the reversal so sudden because the Los Angeles boosters had been successful for so long in presenting the city as a progressive El Dorado? Or was it because popular belief has always suspected a dark undercurrent of violence in sunny California? No doubt we easterners, at least, cannot entertain El Dorado without the undercurrent. In either case, or both, the country was ready to watch the videotape that might sweep away the military model of policing in the United States.

The beating of Rodney King was a curiously appropriate case to precipitate an avalanche of investigation and reform. The victim was typical: a poor, black man with a criminal record. It was by no means the worst case of abuse in the city or the county; so far from being a case in a thousand, it was like a thousand others. Karol Heppe, who runs Police Watch, told me, "People who run from the police here take their lives in their hands; they are liable to be shot, beaten, or bitten by a dog." There was no room to claim that King's case was an aberration. The videotape the networks displayed to the world reminded us that there is no such thing as a garden variety case of police brutality; they are all brutal.

The investigations by the Christopher Commission and Special Counsel Kolts turned out to be powerful instruments of accountability in themselves. They identified problems, prescribed solutions, and under the political pressures of the day the two departments had little choice but to say that they would follow the recommendations. The departments started to track civil litigation and have a liaison with the county or city lawyers to try to improve practices. They began to track complaints about the use of force and to identify the problem police, seeking to retrain and counsel them. They started to use complaint histories in promotion decisions. They began to train police in getting situations under control using less violence, and the sheriff's department began to investigate shootings more consistently. The LAPD was trying to get police to exhibit less racism; they were even trying to fight the code of silence.

One of the most important things the Christopher and Kolts bodies have done is to try to keep the effects of the public interest alive by producing or receiving reports every six months on the progress the departments are making. Thus they have been acting in effect as outside auditors or ombudsmen.[69]

There are political changes that may point toward less reliance on force in Los Angeles's law enforcement. Daryl Gates was replaced by Willie Williams, a respected black chief from Philadelphia. The sheriff's department finally punished five officers for improper use of deadly force in 1992, and the district attorney obtained a conviction of an LAPD officer for beating a Salvadoran accused of jaywalking.

There have also been some changes in the structure of the departments. The county established an ombudsman to run the complaint process in the sheriff's office and to try to facilitate results; in cases where a person is still dissatisfied with the result, he or she is able to draw on a member of a panel of judges to review the case and make a recommendation to the sheriff. By an amendment to the city charter in Los Angeles, the perpetual tenure of the chief has been ended and he can now be removed by the political process. A civilian now sits on the

Board of Rights, the trial board for the most serious disciplinary cases in the LAPD, and the Police Commission has charge of taking complaints from the public. Apart from this, there is little civilian participation in the disciplinary process.[70]

There are just as many signs, however, that the process of change is going to be much more difficult. At the time of the Rodney King incident, there was some sense that the main problem was that the Los Angeles police were just "old-fashioned," held back by Daryl Gates. Unfortunately, it seems that a large part of the population had just the police they wanted. Chief Williams has faced tremendous resistance, as a black person and an outsider in the LAPD. Racism has not died in the LAPD, and more important, it has not died in Los Angeles. The separation and fear between people, which underlay the tactics of the police, are still there.

CHAPTER II

New York City and Its Police

The one truly iron and inflexible rule we can adduce from the cases is that any person who defies the police risks the imposition of legal sanctions, commencing with a summons, on up to the use of firearms. The sanction that is imposed depends on at least three factors: the character of the officer, the place where the encounter occurs, and the character of the person with whom the encounter is had. The police may arrest *anyone* who challenges them (as they define the challenge), but they are more likely to further abuse anyone who is poor, or who belongs to an outcast group.

*   *   *

In the police canon of ethics, the lie is justified in the same way as the arrest: as a vindication of police authority, by proving that defiance of the police is a crime in fact if not in law. A member of a pariah group, or anyone who defies the police, being guilty at heart and sometimes potentially guilty in fact, deserves to be punished out of hand.... By lying, the police enforce these folkways of their own, while preserving the shell of due process of law.

—*Police Power,* 1969

THE CITY

New York City has changed enormously in the more than twenty-five years since I wrote those words. John Lindsay, who was the mayor in 1969, had been swept into office during one of the periodic waves of reform. Traditionally, however, the city was governed by the Democratic Party in the five counties that make up the city. Leading commentators in the fifties remarked upon how the apparent "one-party" system had in fact become pluralistic and responsive; Tammany, as the hegemonic party organization was called, was driven from office by reformers from time to time, but it tried to absorb the reform impulses and return to office, as it was to do after the Lindsay administration. The demands of citizens as well as organized groups went to the central city government more than to local or county officials. The city government was indeed "metropolitan," with regulatory systems established in the interest of ordering the city that were complex and bureaucratized; "Go fight city hall" was a New York proverb for a quixotic endeavor. Coping with, rather than fighting city hall offered opportunities for political influence as well as outright graft.

The "cosmopolitan constituency" that backed Lindsay's liberal administration, with the cooperation of minority voters, supported social and cultural expenditures, and by the middle seventies, the city confronted a fiscal crisis at the same time as an increasing conservatism about those very social programs. Mayor Ed Koch attacked the crisis by encouraging the financial and real estate interests in the city, through an administration less socially activist and at the same time more decentralized than in the past.

Minorities have since become a majority of the city's population, although a slight majority of those who vote are still non-Hispanic whites; a great many of the minority population are immigrants. Industrial jobs have been abandoning the city for more than a generation, although some of them have gone underground, to jobs in sweat shops and other factories in the informal economy. Jobs in finance, insurance, real estate, and communications have not replaced them in the economy, especially since the stock market break in 1987. Economic inequality has increased sharply, even more than it has in the nation as a whole. In 1987, there were more than a million people below the poverty line in New York City, some thousands of them homeless. Crime has increased over the period, although in the nineties it is said to have stabilized and begun to drop.[71]

New York can thus be seen as a postindustrial city with a large immigrant population and severe economic problems that are not dissimilar to those of Los Angeles. Nevertheless, as every Angeleno and New Yorker knows, it is very different from Los Angeles, because it is still relatively centralized politically and culturally. The government has intervened constantly in the lives of citizens, although less so since the seventies, and the New York constituency, with its liberal-Democratic past, has expected it to do so. Public opinion, at least on some issues, has been at odds with opinion elsewhere in the country; in the mid-eighties, opinion in New York City still favored government assistance and support programs and was radically in favor of reduced defense spending.[72]

There are strong signs of increased social conflict. One of them is a rise in vigilantism; the shooting by Bernhard Goetz of four black teenagers on the subway is a symbol of white fear of and backlash against crime by blacks. In 1991, it was reported that some private security firms had started to use violence to intimidate criminals, especially drug dealers. The city and especially its police have tried to discourage any such moves toward self-help. Goetz was vigorously although not very successfully prosecuted, and some of the security guards were charged with assault; the police have always been inhospitable to self-appointed security groups, such as the Guardian Angels.

Nevertheless, the resolve of the city authorities against private violence is perhaps becoming a little less firm. Especially indicative for me is a series of episodes in the Crown Heights neighborhood in Brooklyn that appear to be stages in a vendetta between blacks and Hasidic Jews. In August 1991, there was a riot after a car belonging to a Hasidic rabbi struck a black child. In the ensuing melee, a rabbinical student was stabbed and later died; an investigative commission found that the police had failed to contain the disturbance, and the Hasidim claimed that the city's neglect was deliberate. On two occasions in 1992, a black man was beaten by a group of Hasidim and both times the attackers offered as their principal explanation that the victims had been caught trying to commit crimes. The question how that could be an excuse for beating them up was largely lost in the argument as Mayor David Dinkins came under attack as having favored blacks against Jews.[73]

THE POLICE

The city's police department (NYPD) is the largest in the country; there are two much smaller departments, the housing and transit police, that the NYPD is in the process of trying to absorb. According to its own figures, the NYPD had more than twenty-eight thousand police personnel in 1993, of whom almost twenty thousand were at the police officer (patrol) level; studies in the last decade have repeatedly remarked that, apparently as a result of the fiscal crisis in the seventies, the department has too few people at the rank of sergeant and above. The department has changed in the twenty-five years since 1969, encompassing two major corruption scandals, investigated by the Knapp Commission in 1972 and the Mollen Commission in 1993–94. The reforms of Commissioner Patrick V. Murphy following the Knapp Commission report covered issues affecting the use of force as well as corruption. He established command responsibility, so that if officers in a precinct had a disproportionate number of complaints, the commander had the job of doing something about it. He also established an "early intervention" program to try to identify and counsel officers who were prone to violence.

The NYPD is highly regulated and bureaucratized. There is relatively little of the atmosphere of violence that pervaded the LAPD until 1991. Exotic tools like the taser are used, but not very often, apparently less often, for better or worse, than the firearm. Dogs are not used to harass and bite suspects. Vehicle pursuits are discouraged. In fact, in most cases the NYPD will try to avoid tactics that look like a show of force and might offend some liberal members of the New York public. An inspector told me how, during the Democratic party convention in 1992, officers concealed the riot gear they had brought with them, by putting it under the orange cones used to deflect traffic. There is no rhetoric of violence and combat. It is interesting, in fact, that one area of tactics in which the NYPD consistently seems to be weak is crowd control in disturbances— and that is one area in which police work most resembles military deployment.[74]

Some of the attributes of a military bureaucracy remain. Everything has to be done through channels, and officers are supposed to go by the book. This does not work well, because, unlike soldiers, police have enormous discretion and are almost always on their own when on patrol. Supervisors are often ignorant about what is actually happening on patrol; they are also accustomed to being criticized without warning by opinionated New Yorkers. One result is that the department is quite secretive and tries to control the information that reaches the public; the department probably gets hit harder by scandal because of its secretiveness and its cozy public relations. Another is that the rank and file are cynical about the regulations and the opinions of superiors and resentful of public criticism; from their point of view, they are surrounded by legalisms and misinformation. They close ranks against their bosses and the public, making the code of silence almost ironclad.

The Police and New Yorkers

The relation between the NYPD and the citizens is wary at best. Like people in other cities, New Yorkers seem to view police work as a "tainted occupation"; they are not very well-satisfied with the police, but they do not seem to expect a great deal more of them. A *New York Times* poll in 1994, after the revelations of the latest corruption scandal, found that 48 percent of the sample thought the police were doing a "good" or "excellent" job, while 93 percent thought that corruption was either "widespread" or at best "limited."[75] A great many New Yorkers, furthermore, although they expect the government to step in and help the citizen, are at the same time suspicious of authority and jealous of their rights; minority people often find police to be racist.

Perennial demands for more control, either over police violence or corruption, have led to increased bureaucratization. The rank and file have become more resentful of the population, and the bunker mentality, the sense of "us versus them," combined with the great secretiveness of the department, has soured relations; the police, it appears, find New Yorkers hypocritical, demanding protection but not being willing to let the police do their job as they see fit. For me, the police problem in New York City which epitomizes conflict with the public has not been shootings, which are comparatively controlled, nor beatings, which are more common, but the arrest of witnesses and people who complain about police work at the scene of police actions. I would not think for a moment of commenting audibly about bad police work if I saw it; and the worse I thought it was, the less inclined I would be to say anything to the police doing the work. But New Yorkers, those legalistic beings, not infrequently comment hotly to the police at the scene of arrests or summonses. The police are often exasperated and sometimes arrest the person, usually on the charge of interfering with an officer. The person is "run through the system," by being locked up, verbally abused, and left to wait hours for arraignment. In one of the worst of these cases, in 1989, such a bystander had been arrested and was languishing in the lockup; when he and other prisoners complained about not being able to use the telephone, the police beat up—no, not the bystander, as you might have expected, but instead a hapless black derelict, in the presence of the others, to intimidate them all into keeping quiet. Through this degradation the police wanted to teach the "liberals to keep your mouths shut," as one policeman put it in that case.[76] But of course, it does not work with the sort of people who criticize police—they just become hotter police reformers than they were before they were arrested.

The New York police have an affinity for actions intended to show their power and independence that only make people more determined to limit that power and independence. In September 1992, the union, the Patrolmen's Benevolent Association, sponsored a rally at City Hall to protest policies to control police, including a proposed civilian review board for complaints and the Mollen Commission investigation of corruption. The crowd of off-duty police broke through the scarcely manned police barriers to swarm up the City Hall steps and to block traffic to the Brooklyn Bridge. A policeman on duty in uniform at the police barriers waved them on, shouting what the department later called "racial slurs." They cursed then-Mayor Dinkins, who is black, and held up signs with racist caricatures; they called a city councilwoman and a television cameraman "niggers." They were nevertheless not really a mob out of control; there was no personal violence and only a small amount of property damage. Their anger was political. Rudolph Giuliani, who was campaigning against Dinkins for mayor, was egging them on.

In a report three weeks later, the police commissioner noted unhappily that the demonstration "raised serious questions about the department's willingness and ability to police itself." He ordered discipline for forty-two police who were identified from videotapes. They had committed one of the worst offenses; they had created, as the commissioner said, "an embarrassment to a department widely respected for its professionalism." Shortly afterward, the department had to grin and bear it when wholly external investigation of civilian complaints was instituted.[77]

The order that is represented and reproduced by the NYPD is characteristic of the city. It is bureaucratized but not really rationalized. The department as an institution is trying to maintain the relations of uneasy tolerance among racial and other groups; it is trying to keep the peace, while it is very apprehensive about whether that can be done. The government, including the police, very much fears vigilantism and (usually) tries to control it by arrest and prosecution.

Thus the policies tend to be spotty and inconsistent. There is no technological or other show of violence; as a former police official stated the department's philosophy: "We want no hard-noses out in the street.... We are not an attacking force. We are not an avenging force." Yet those words were uttered to contrast the aims of the department with the uncontrolled police violence in repressing a crowd in Tompkins Square Park in 1988, an event that will be described in more detail here shortly.[78] In the end, the police, or some of them, know that they are being asked to control people, and sometimes to do it by harassment or force.

Some aspects of the order are reflected in the relations between the NYPD and its members. Although the organization is highly regulated and the regulations are constantly being changed to try to minimize violence, the supervisors as well as the rank and file know that repression goes on in ways that they cannot account for or control. So the rank and file experience the bosses as both unpredictable and hypocritical. At the City Hall protest in September 1992, some of the police demonstrators shouted at administrators who appeared in plainclothes, "Empty suits!"

DEADLY FORCE

The change from twenty-five years ago in the use of deadly weapons has been enormous. In the late sixties, the old common-law rule that permitted a policeman to shoot if necessary to prevent the escape of any person accused of a felony (the "fleeing felon" rule) was being abandoned, while new strictures were being imposed on shootings. The words of Howard Leary, who was Mayor Lindsay's police commissioner in 1967, captured the changing moral atmosphere:

> [p]ermitting the police to shoot suspected criminals, who are not a danger to life and limb, would, I believe, not only increase the risk of riots in sensitive communities, but also subtly increase the tolerance of—indeed glorification of—violence which is a significant problem in our society. (Similarly one must consider the effect of killing someone upon the police officer involved. Our department has had to retire men or reassign them to non-patrol functions because of emotional problems caused by having been the killer in a situation that was technically a justifiable homicide under the traditional rule.)[79]

In 1972, following a year when his police had killed at least eighty-seven people, Commissioner Patrick Murphy reined them in by establishing guidelines on deadly force that forbade the use of firearms except as an instrument of last resort against people who posed a threat of serious physical injury. He also established the Firearms Discharge Review Board to investigate, at the precinct level and then by review of the findings at the highest level, every incident when a shot is fired; the Firearms Board has been functioning for over twenty years and does from time to time find that a shooting has violated the guidelines. Officers are trained in simulations to react to dangerous situations; they learn to take cover and call for backup. A shooting may be justifiable as a matter of law, they learn, but it might be avoided if the officer called for help. There are dozens of occasions when police are fired on and do not return fire, usually because of risk to other people; they are taught that the preservation of life is a central value.[80]

Recent figures on shootings and general homicides suggest that the controls are strong:

OFFICER-INVOLVED SHOOTINGS AND GENERAL HOMICIDES IN NEW YORK CITY				
	1990	1991	1992	1993
Civilians killed by police	41	27	24	25
Civilians wounded (shot) by police	60	84	66	61
Police killed	0	2	1	1
Police wounded (shot)	17	31	12	26
(stabbed)	n/a	11	7	12
Murder and nonnegligent homicides	2,245	2,154	1,995	1,951

The number of people killed by the police has, moreover, generally been dropping since the high in 1971.

Instances of shooting civilians for purposes of summary punishment are extremely rare; the 1994 Mollen Commission report on corruption records an instance of a rogue officer who shot a drug courier to get his money.[81] Serious mistakes are made, however; I have analyzed two cases here that were not among the notorious ones that received intense public scrutiny.

Bobsy Miller Shooting[82]

Bobsy Miller is a native of Jamaica with a considerable criminal record involving drugs and weapons. At about eight o'clock one August evening in 1991, he was shot once by a policeman on the top floor of a tenement at 15 Hawthorne Street, near the corner of Flatbush Avenue, in Brooklyn. The officers involved were interviewed by superiors the same night, as the first stage in a firearms discharge review. The officers claimed that Miller had shot a person on Flatbush Avenue and had run into 15 Hawthorne Street with a gun in his hand, pursued by two patrolmen and ignoring shouts to stop. On the top landing, he turned toward one of the policemen, still with the gun in his hand, and the policeman shot him. The two patrolmen who pursued him received departmental recognitions for their actions.

Miller survived and was charged with possession of a gun and menacing the police; when he was tried for those charges some months later, he was acquitted by the jury. His defense was successful, almost certainly, because a woman named Donna Zephyr who lived at 15 Hawthorne Street and was apparently not involved, said she saw the shooting. She claimed she was curious when she heard running up the stairs and heard a policeman shout "Stop, motherfucker, or I'm going to shoot you," and that she went out of her apartment and silently followed the police up the stairs. When Miller turned toward the police, she said he had his hands up with nothing in them. After the policeman shot him, she said "My God, you've killed him," and another officer pulled her away from the scene. But the police had never interviewed her as a witness.

Miller claimed that he had heard the shooting on Flatbush and had started to run, as did others. His story was that the police mistook him for the perpetrator, chased him into 15 Hawthorne Street and shot him; they then planted the gun and framed him to cover their mistake. He sued the city and the policemen in a civil rights action that was tried in federal court in 1993. The jury found damages for Miller of $50,000, which implies that they thought the police were at fault, although it would be a small award if they took Miller's story at face value; nevertheless, under the circumstances, in my judgment, it was a substantial recovery.

What were the circumstances? It appears that Ms. Zephyr did see the events she described, but that neither Miller nor the police told the whole truth. The key to interpreting the case seems to lie in a puzzling aspect of the police account of the shooting.

There was a door to the roof of 15 Hawthorne Street, with

steps running up to it from the top-floor landing. *After* Miller was shot, the police said, they saw him dash up those steps, jump up on the bannister of the stairway, and then fall down onto the floor of the landing, where he was arrested. Upon looking up into a skylight above the door, the police found a pistol where Miller had desperately jammed it; a third policeman who arrived on the scene corroborated the story that the pistol was in the skylight.

This is very odd. Supposing that Miller had the physical agility and the presence of mind to jump on the bannister and put the gun in the skylight after being shot, why would he do so with armed witnesses staring right at him? And why would the police merely let him go on, with a gun in his hand, without shooting him again? On the other hand, as the city's lawyer pointed out in her summation in the civil case, if the police had planted the gun, why wouldn't they have just put it on the floor? Why reach up and stick it in a skylight?

All good questions. The only story that explains most of the facts is that Miller had a gun with which he ran up to the top floor, ahead of the police, hoping to make it out the door to the roof. Unfortunately, the door was locked; he jumped up and put the gun in the skylight to get rid of it. When the police arrived seconds later, he turned around with his hands up, hoping to surrender and be able, in effect, to say, "What seems to be the trouble, officer?" But he relied too much on their presence of mind; the policeman shot him as he turned, before Miller could pull the trigger of the gun the patrolman believed he had. After having shot him, the police were no doubt very relieved to find the pistol in the skylight.

The initial mistake by the police was understandable. The patrolman could probably have told the truth, saying that he thought that Miller still had the gun in his hand, without being found in violation of the law or the regulations, but he would have had to do endless explaining to his superiors. As it is, it seems surprising that the superiors did not inquire more into the odd story about the skylight; but of course, they never found Ms. Zephyr to make them realize how odd it was. In the end, I think we have to fault the firearms discharge review process for not having gone to the scene and inquired more deeply into the facts. We have to fault the patrolmen even more for having charged Miller with having menaced them with a gun. That was a lie, and as I sit here I think that a large part of what the jury awarded was probably compensation for that charge and Miller's defense against it.

Jacques Camille Shooting

The Camille shooting is very different from the Miller case. There is almost no dispute about what happened, but the event is so simple that it is difficult to interpret.

On a spring morning in 1992, Jacques Camille, a Haitian immigrant who had been working as a cab driver for only four days, became involved in a crime after he picked up two passengers, black men, in midtown Manhattan and took them downtown. At one point, below Greenwich Village, they asked him to double-park so one of them could get a sandwich; presently the man came rushing back, and the two told Camille to drive on uptown. At their direction, he made a right turn onto Fourteenth Street. As Camille stopped at a corner, one passenger got out on each side; one was arrested by police following the taxi, but the other faded into the crowd. Camille drove on a short distance to get out of the way of the traffic and stopped.

The man who had got out of the taxi while it was double-parked had in fact gone into a delicatessen and pulled a robbery, and the number of the taxi had been broadcast to the police. Police converged on the cab on Fourteenth Street, a major thoroughfare, at rush hour. They were apprehensive because the report was that the robbery had been committed by two black men; one had been arrested, and the only remaining black male was the driver. It appeared to them that the driver pulled away from the scene after he had stopped, and stopped again when he encountered police coming toward him; thus Camille was a suspect.

A lieutenant in a car driven by patrolman Sean Gelfand responded to the scene; he ordered Camille to put his hands on the dashboard, then opened the door and pulled him out. Camille complied with an order to put his hands on the roof of the cab, and the lieutenant began to frisk him while Gelfand stood with his pistol drawn. Camille was completely surrounded by police, and the situation was under control; one officer even got into the passenger seat of the taxi. At one point, Camille, with his hands still on the cab, turned slightly to the right, and Sean Gelfand shot him in his midsection. Camille survived, although he lost a kidney and has a damaged liver.

Gelfand later testified that he saw Camille take his hands off the car roof, turn quickly, and drop his hands to his waist, but no other witness saw such a thing. Gelfand was indicted for felonious assault and was tried before a judge without a jury. Although the police witnesses did their best to make Gelfand's action look reasonable, saying that Camille was "fidgeting" or even resisting arrest, all the civilian witnesses were clear that Camille merely turned a little from the cab. Gelfand was finally convicted by the judge of misdemeanor assault only, which leaves unanswered the question of why he shot Camille. The only possible explanation, I think, is that Gelfand, tense and wary, interpreted what he saw as the act of a robber trying to escape, and thus saw something different from what the others saw.

Camille settled his civil claim for $1.5 million from the city, with $5,000 from the officer personally.[83]

These cases, like others that are better known, suggest some conclusions about the use of deadly force by the NYPD. The department does try to restrict the use of guns to situations in which there is reason to believe there is a real danger to life. The plausibility of that belief in the worst cases of abuse, like that of Sean Gelfand, is stretched to the limit of credibility. In 1986, plainclothes police tried to stop a black and a white man together in a car, unarmed, on a deserted street in the poor neighborhood of Coney Island by blocking the car with two unmarked cars. Supposing their assailants to be criminals, not police, the driver rammed the unmarked cars trying to get away, and the police fired on the car; fortunately they missed, although they wound up beating the two mercilessly. The police later claimed they thought the men fit the description of two robbers and that they were armed, an explanation so feeble that the court ultimately awarded some $6 million in damages.[84]

A disproportionately large number of those shot are Hispanic or black, like Jacques Camille and Bobsy Miller. These are the NYPD's figures for fatalities by race for 1989–90:

	WHITE	BLACK	HISPANIC	ASIAN	TOTAL
1989	10	10	9	1	30
1990	3	15	23	0	41

Since all or almost all of the shootings are justified under the guidelines and the criminal law, I cannot conclude from the statistics alone that there is racial discrimination in the choice to shoot. Nevertheless, when a situation is ambiguous, many police may perceive a black or Hispanic person as more likely to be dangerous; in any case, the disproportion in the numbers creates a lot of resentment and makes every shooting of a minority person into a socially explosive act.

The civil and criminal justice systems in New York City react to the abuse of firearms. The district attorneys seek indictments in cases that appear to be criminal homicides or assaults, and they have been doing so since the seventies. The prosecutions are usually even less successful than the Sean Gelfand case, but, like the assistant DA in that case, the lawyers often try very hard to get the convictions.[85] And damages are paid in many cases where the police are at fault.

The climate for deadly force is different in the counties of New York City than it has been in Los Angeles County. The Firearms Discharge Review Board has been favorably compared with the review system for shootings in Los Angeles.[86] Yet on paper, the investigative systems in Los Angeles do not look bad; the district attorney is notified and can "roll out" to the scene of a shooting or to the relevant station house. In New York City, the district attorney is notified but hardly ever goes out to investigate unless the police actually ask for an assistant DA to be present. There is a consistent system of review in New

York that makes it difficult to cover a mistake, but as the Bobsy Miller case shows, it is, like other systems, no better than the people who do the investigating. The Los Angeles system should have made it difficult to cover a mistake, except that for many years, the definition of "mistake" was very expansive; there was no effective policy anywhere in the criminal justice system which would make police cautious in the use of firearms. Members of the NYPD, on the contrary, seem to recognize that all the participants in the New York City system are backing such a policy.

The problem with the use of deadly force in New York is not that the policies are defective, or that the system does not take the policies seriously, or that the shootings resemble executions; on the contrary, even the abusive shootings appear to be errors, although sometimes grotesque errors, of judgment. The problem in these cases—even the simplest ones, like the Camille shooting, that occur in front of many unimpeachable witnesses—is that the police are not straight about them; they don't tell the truth about what they themselves have done nor about what their fellow police have done.

FORCE WITHOUT FIREARMS

The physical coercion of suspects to elicit a confession is a rare complaint in New York. A New York City police official explained to me in 1993, "Everyone knows that if you get caught beating a prisoner, you go to jail." It would certainly seem they know it now. After a group of police officers in Queens were caught in 1985 torturing black suspects with an electric "stun gun" to force them to confess to minor drug sales and to the location of other drugs and money, they were sentenced to prison terms for assault, and the victims collected a million dollars in damages from the city.[87] The problem abuses in New York now occur mostly in the street, far from the problems of coerced confessions.

The thread that ties together deadly force and abuses of non-deadly force, in which people get roughed up or beaten, is the perception on the part of the police of a threat; in the case of deadly force, it is a threat of death, while in the case of lesser force, it is often a threat to authority, such as defiance or criticism. And in all the cases, the police shape the facts to justify what they have done; they still systematically impose charges such as resisting arrest on those they abuse. The words at the beginning of the chapter could be written today about abuses of nondeadly force, although there are probably not as many incidents as there were years ago. A classic occurred near Tompkins Square Park, in Manhattan, in 1988; while it is a case of the failure to control a crowd, it is also a police action against defiant outcasts.

Tompkins Square, a park of only three square blocks on the Lower East Side, has been a gathering place for the poor and dispossessed, resulting in collective conflicts with the police, for more than a hundred years. In 1874, in what the leading history of the New York police calls "the decisive confrontation between police and labor," a meeting of "workers interested in public works to provide for the unemployed" was charged by mounted police and beaten. In the 1960s, as part of what is still called the East Village, the park became a haven for hippies. On Memorial Day 1967, during a show of art and music in Tompkins Square, the police tried to get a group to stop singing and get off the grass; those who refused to go were arrested and some were beaten.[88]

In the 1980s, the park was a borderland between gentrification and the older East Village world of cheap housing and an increasing number of squatters. The chief of department put it stylishly in a report to the police commissioner: "The park serves a racially, ethnically, economically and politically diverse East Village community and has generated a need for police attention since the 1960's. As a result of its diversity, the community has long been known for its tolerance of a wide variety of lifestyles."[89]

During the stifling hot summer of 1988, a number of people, some dressed in punk style, hung out there at night, partying and in some cases taking drugs. Homeless people were camped there. People who lived near the park complained, and in a compromise typical of New York, especially the Lower East Side, the police began to clear the park of all revelers by 1 A.M., while permitting the homeless to sleep there. The people who hung out in the park resisted the closing as part of a loose political agenda, opposed to increasing gentrification and consequent middle-class respectability. That process, which was making Manhattan more a city for the monied, was in fact a chief source of prosperity during the Koch administration for the municipality itself as well as the real estate interests; the people protesting in the park apparently thought that they were among the very few actively trying to keep New York from becoming a city of the rich. At later demonstrations, participants attacked the doors of a recently renovated condominium and hung up a banner that read "Gentrification Stops Here."[90]

The police and the neighbors were understandably peeved that some protested the relatively mild curfew; there was a clash with police on July 31. On Saturday night, August 6, there was another rally after midnight, whereupon some protesters left the park and unexpectedly massed in the middle of an avenue, stopping traffic. According to the police, people threw bottles and fireworks at the police; the police, including mounted officers, tried to push the crowd out of the avenue, to free up traffic. At about the same time, the local commander sent out a call for "all available personnel" to respond. As the chief of department wrote, "Over the next several hours radio cars with officers from all over the city responded." A police helicopter hovered overhead, making the people present even more excited; one naive student called it "a hell of a light show."

Henry Stern, the perennial commissioner of parks, who is old in the ways of the city, later remarked: "Why did it happen here?... Because it's unique as a political park. A few months ago, President Reagan was impeached by the people here. Periodically various Americans are put on trial for war crimes. If you read the posters in the park, you'd think that revolution was imminent." Indeed, some of the demonstrators did not seem to have any idea what they were up against with the police. One young man said he threw bottles "to distract" some mounted police, and was chased and hit.[91]

All hell broke loose as hundreds of police converged on the area, beating people and (rarely) arresting them. As in the Rodney King incident in Los Angeles three years later, videotapes of the events controlled the official response. At first Mayor Koch and Police Commissioner Benjamin Ward defended the police actions, but after they saw the videotapes displayed on television, they were dismayed; by August 23, the chief of department's memo frankly referred to the "appalling behavior of some members of the department."

The police action swept up everyone in its path, and in some cases stepped out of its path. The story was reported over and over again of the woman manager of a local restaurant who protested when a policeman, demanding to know who had thrown a bottle, hit one of her waitresses; the police kicked the manager in the stomach, knocked her down, and dragged her out by the hair. She was among the few arrested; some neighborhood residents were beaten repeatedly without being arrested as they tried to make their way through the streets. People who simply stepped out of drinking places on a Saturday night were beaten with clubs. In its report on the action, the department's Civilian Complaint Review Board concluded:

> There appeared to be little or no attempt to identify and arrest those demonstrators who had thrown objects at the officers (only nine arrests were effected). Many individuals, including several merely passing through the neighborhood on their way home or to other destinations were subjected to verbal abuse and physical assault by one or more officers. Force used by officers included potentially fatal overhand blows with nightsticks to the head and bodies of individuals who were offering no resistance and were not arrested for any crime.[92]

Why did this happen? The official explanation was that there was a failure of command, that the senior officer in charge was in fact absent, and that when the police were summoned from all over the city, no one took charge and coordinated them. Commissioner Ward said that new training and guidelines for

crowd control needed to be drawn up.[93] But these "explanations" hardly explain anything; they just clothe the problem in
bureaucratic garb. The question is, What prompted the police
to behave the way they did? Put in bureaucratic terms, Why is
so much control by superior officers needed in mass police
actions?

It is true that there was a failure of direction because the
unidentified police who arrived had no more than a general
notion that they ought to "clear the streets." But much more
important was the police reaction to the situation; most, if not
all, of the police present had little connection with the community to which they responded. They found outright defiance of
police orders, as well as a sense of danger produced by the call
to all personnel and the helicopter droning overhead and light-
ing up the scene. What they knew was that police had actually
been attacked, and by a ragtag group identified with squatters,
drug users, and "punks"; they thought they had carte blanche
to clear the streets of people who were the worst enemies of the
city's policies. Much of the violence, furthermore, was deliberate; the police knew that they were using excessive force, and
that if they were caught they might be in trouble. They took
advantage of the cloak of anonymity provided by the "all available personnel" call; a lot of them actually took off name tags
and covered the numbers on their badges with the black band
that is supposed to be used for mourning a dead fellow officer.
Relatively few arrests were made because there was relatively
little need for the usual cover. The situation presented a recipe
for repression, and the police vented their fury against the
people on the streets as if they were all outcasts, calling black
people "niggers" and several people "faggots." And some of
the respectable approved of what they had done; the East Side
Chamber of Commerce sent a letter to the police commissioner
praising the "necessary and measured response."[94]

Excessive force does not occur only in situations like Tompkins Square, against people the police see as outcasts attacking
authority; it is also used sometimes to punish suspects summarily. The Mollen Commission, appointed in 1992 by Mayor

Dinkins to investigate police corruption after some New York police had been arrested on Long Island for selling drugs, found a pattern of police violence linked to corruption. The commission report of 1994 describes some of the crimes of corruption in these words:

> Corrupt officers usually raided drug locations for profit, but sometimes also to show who was in control of the crime-ridden streets of their precincts; sometimes to feel the power and thrill of their badges and uniforms; sometimes because they believed that vigilante justice was the only way to teach a lesson or punish those who might otherwise go unpunished.

Later the report talks of brutality:

> Officers also told us that it was not uncommon to see unnecessary force used to administer an officer's own brand of street justice: a nightstick in the ribs, a fist to the head, to demonstrate who was in charge of the crime-ridden streets they patrolled and to impose sanctions on those who "deserved it" as officers, not juries, determined. As was true of other forms of wrongdoing, some cops believe they are doing what is morally correct—though "technically unlawful"—when they beat someone who they believe is guilty and who they believe the criminal justice system will never punish.

It is significant that the police who talked to the commission thought of their corrupt as well as their brutal acts as aspects of vigilante justice. Corruption is power; those from whom the police took bribes or drugs, or to whom they sold "protection," were unable to complain because they had put themselves entirely in the grasp of the corrupt police. The police showed their power over the criminals, as well as others, by beating the victims. Thus both corruption and brutality demonstrated control, the domination of the situation by the police. One officer, famously called "the Mechanic" because he so often "tuned people up," testified that he and his friends beat people up "to show who was in charge. We were in charge, the police."[95]

These important findings affirm something about the connection between corruption and illegal violence that seems generalizable to all the cities in this book. Writing twenty-five years ago, I did not see the connection; nevertheless, subsequent chapters will show that it is clear in the history of police in U.S. cities as well as in Latin America and Jamaica. Both corruption and brutality can be used for social control, as part of the police endeavor, found everywhere, to enforce order directly, without intervention by other parts of the criminal justice system or the government generally. The police who were caught by the commission were creating a renegade system of justice in which it was their function to control crime by taking its profits and administering punishment.

The commission assures us that the cases its investigators found are rare. Most likely the commission is right, at least with respect to serious crimes connected to corruption; summary punishment of suspects, however, appears to be more common. In any event, the assurance is less comforting because the very police methods of accountability for the crimes of corruption, and connected acts of brutality, have tended to conceal how widespread the problems are.

ACCOUNTABILITY AND IMPUNITY

The Mollen Commission's investigation of the reasons for the NYPD's inability to catch and prosecute corrupt officers tells us a great deal about the problems of accountability generally, as applied to any abuse of police authority. Following the scandal investigated by the Knapp Commission twenty years earlier, the NYPD had instituted a centralized Internal Affairs Division (IAD) to investigate corruption, combined with field internal affairs units at the local level, to permit senior officers to control corruption in their own commands. The commanders, in turn, were supposed to be accountable; if they did not root out corruption among their people, they were to be replaced.

It is not clear whether this system ever worked well; certainly it failed in the long run because no one, not even the Internal Affairs Division, was interested in withstanding the scandal presented by revelations of widespread corruption. Superior officers did not want to root out corruption, both because it might threaten their jobs and because they wanted to maintain a good image for the department. The Mollen Commission pointed out a curious phenomenon that appeared in similar commission reports in Los Angeles as well; the written evaluations of violent and corrupt officers are absolutely bland, filled with routine phrases such as "meets standards." One reason such evaluations get written is that patrol people have a lot of discretion and their supervisors often do not know what they are doing, especially in New York, where there is a shortage of managers. More important, field supervisors actually have limited power over rank-and-file police, who are civil servants, difficult to get rid of and more difficult to replace; supervisors see it as more in their interests to retain the good will of the rank and file, to get their cooperation when the command needs it.[96] Most important of all is that everyone in the police has come up through the ranks, and superiors share the values and experiences of those under them; this is especially strong at the level of sergeant, but it extends up the line.

The effect of shared experience is visible in a multitude of ways. Lying by officers to cover themselves or to fill in gaps in proof is expected. The Mollen Commission found that there was virtually no effort to punish police for lying when they got caught, that supervisors taught them how to prepare convincing false testimony, and that they were even taught in the academy that it is a basic survival tactic to "cover your ass." Superiors do not seriously disapprove of brutality by those under them, at least if it is restricted to those who are thought to be criminals; the policeman who was called "the Mechanic" says he got the nickname from his sergeant. As the commission put it, many supervisors tolerate brutality because they "share the perception that nothing is really wrong with a bit of unnecessary force and because they believe that this is the only way to fight crime today." And this solidifies both the code of silence and the link to corruption; the commission says, "brutality strengthened the bonds of loyalty and silence among officers and thus fostered corruption tolerance."[97]

Even in connection with corruption, then, there was a general sense that everyone had a little something to hide; the NYPD as a whole consequently had a lot to hide. Senior officers at the Internal Affairs Division put especially sensitive cases, involving people they wanted to protect, into a "tickler file," where they could keep track of them. The anticorruption office was thus itself a little crooked, and its policy was to make all the corruption investigations look like low-level, individual matters, so that they would not balloon into generalized scandals. The IAD tried to do this with the group of police that was ultimately arrested for selling drugs on Long Island, with the result that the case did balloon into a scandal and the corruption was revealed. More dismaying, they followed the same course in a case in the Ninth Precinct on the Lower East Side in 1991. During an investigation in which anticorruption officers had a plan to catch at least a dozen police taking drugs and discussing their crimes at a party on Staten Island, a commander ordered the arrest of just one policeman, effectively warning all the others that an investigation was afoot. The thinking of the IAD in this case was a monument to small-mindedness; one inspector testified that the publicity from an arrest on Staten Island, where he himself lived, would have been "outrageous." They wanted you to believe that there is crime in the streets of the ghettoes, it seems, but not in the backyards of semisuburban Staten Island. The end result was that the corruption in the Ninth Precinct has not been exposed, and for all we know, those officers are as of this writing still out in the field.[98]

These findings suggest that the review of civilian complaints of brutality, if it is conducted by an internal police body, is likely to fail. Since police violence is generally viewed less seriously by the police than corruption, we would expect the police to treat most of the excesses leniently and in any case to try to protect the department from scandal. And those are the basic reasons that proponents of civilian review of police abuses have always used to advance their cause.

When more than 120 civilian complaints were filed about the Tompkins Square incident, the case became a test for the Civilian Complaint Review Board (CCRB), which had been revamped in 1986 to make half of its members civilians appointed by the mayor; half of the investigators were still police personnel. It was the most difficult sort of case, because so many of the officers were unidentified. The code of silence was total; not one officer came forward to give evidence. The videotapes were the main source of identification, but without some guidance from the police, they were no doubt difficult to use except in the most obvious cases. Several officers were disciplined just for having concealed their identity with their mourning bands. In the end, the CCRB succeeded in having administrative charges presented in seventeen cases, and officers were disciplined in thirteen of them.

Proponents of civilian review were bitterly disappointed by these results. I have to say, however, that it looked to me as though the CCRB tried very hard against difficult odds and did surprisingly well. My problem was not so much with the CCRB as with the entire complex system, as I shall explain in more detail in the next chapter, which made it virtually impossible to tell what the final outcome had been. The CCRB did not have exclusive jurisdiction of the complaints; the district attorney could prosecute for criminal acts and the NYPD could investigate through other branches. Moreover, the CCRB had no control over what the commissioner did with the cases in which the complaint board had recommended charges; in fact, in 1993 the CCRB was unable to tell me what had been the result of its seventeen Tompkins Square cases, and I had to inquire laboriously of the department in writing. In addition, in some cases charges had been brought independently by the department itself, and criminal charges were preferred in some cases by the district attorney. The latter seem to have been dismissed, for reasons that I cannot determine, while the former no doubt resulted in some sort of discipline. In short, a principal difficulty with the system of review for civilian complaints was that, in a literal sense, it did not afford much "accountability" at all; one could not with reasonable effort get an account of the result of the process.

In 1993, the city completely scrapped the internal system of review, making the complaint review board, as well as its staff, independent of the police. The question is whether such a body can really do better than the CCRB has done in the past or whether accountability should be organized in some other way. I shall try to unravel this issue, which has been a political battleground for thirty years, in the next chapter.

CHAPTER III

New York and the United States: Accountability and Control

New York City presents the problem of police violence at close to its most basic level. The NYPD is not a notably abusive department in the big cities of the United States. Although some unforeseen scandal may destroy that impression, which the NYPD has cultivated, there is evidence to support it. A lawyer who specializes in damage actions for police brutality in Los Angeles told me he would starve if he had to practice in New York. Why, then, are there acts of excessive force and brutality in New York? A small number might be explained simply by the size of the force; out of any group of almost thirty thousand people, some are going to be criminals and even more are going to make serious errors. But how explain the prodigious abuses like the Tompkins Square beatings? How explain the attitude of supervisors, as the Mollen Commission found, that excessive force is so much a part of the job that they can overlook it?

The answer must arise in part out of the fact that an irreducible aspect of the job is order-keeping and control, typically done through coercion. Always in tension with the protection of life, which is taught as a value in police training by the NYPD, are the peculiarities of police work captured in Bittner's conception of the police role as "a mechanism for the distribution of nonnegotiably coercive force employed in accordance with the dictates of an intuitive grasp of situational exigencies." It has been the lack of negotiability and the intuitive grasp of situations (or the lack of it) that have given rise to disagreements about the proper scope of police use of force, even in cases where there is no reckless abuse of power.

A discussion between Wayne Kerstetter and Wesley Pomeroy, both former police executives, shows how difficult the choices can be. Kerstetter quotes a civilian complaint investigator from Chicago saying, "If you are going to be an authority figure in

Cabrini Green or the Robert Taylor homes [crime-ridden public housing projects] then the people there have got to be afraid of you." Pomeroy answers that proposition by saying, "A fair assumption is that there are authority figures in those projects such as parents, priests, and teachers who *are* effective even though they are not feared." He takes the uncompromising position that "police officers have absolutely no identity or power as police officers outside the law." It seems to me that neither of these views is quite adequate. It will not do to say that police have no identity outside the law, because as a matter of practice, they always have had an order-keeping function that is not encompassed by law. On the other hand, in this country, we consider authority through fear to be scarcely authority at all.

A view similar to Kerstetter's is very widespread; so many police seem to think that it is their job to dominate a situation in which they find themselves, often by an overt threat of force, that we ought to pause and think about whether they are right. I think we have to recognize that the view is persuasive just because in some unknown number of cases it *is* right. There unquestionably are people who cannot be persuaded or directed to an action even when it is obviously in their interest; they have to be forced. And it is to that sort of person that authority through fear is directed; the trick is to be able to pick those people out from those who will respond to arguments or commands. William Muir has tried to show that the very best police are those who can learn how to handle even potentially violent situations without using force; no doubt he is right, but we cannot expect all police to be that skillful.[99] And therein lies one source of police abuse; police use force when, upon reflection, they did not need to. Some of them are going to continue to do so, especially because they use "rule through fear" as a general strategy, when it should be applicable to only a few. The police have been cut off for so long from the community they police that some of them no longer see occasions when they could avoid coercion, and finally do not even want to see them because they have distanced themselves so much from those on whom, as well as for whom, they work. Thus in the end, even setting aside deliberate acts of violence, there will be legitimate civilian complaints, because if police have power to use coercion according to a judgment of what is reasonable under the circumstances, they are bound to make mistakes, some of them very serious. Through the bland bureaucratic facade of the police, the frequent corruption, and the code of silence, the serious abuses are going to be hard to pick out. The generalized question, then, is how to make the system accountable for those mistakes, and how to minimize them.

The institutions of accountability used in this country are many and overlapping; their relation to the minimization of abuse is complex and often unclear, as I shall show in more detail in this chapter. Intergovernmental accountability, in which the federal government oversees local compliance with constitutional standards, is an option that has been used rarely. The courts, either at the state or federal level, may prosecute the police through the criminal process or award damages to compensate for abuses, and can also set minimum standards for acceptable police conduct. At the local level, special investigative bodies and ombudsmen periodically audit the work of the police, while the police may monitor their own work through management review. The one set of institutions that has received constant public scrutiny is the system of discipline for individual police—the review of administrative actions after they have been performed, to determine whether they complied with the law and administrative regulations. Although it does tend to deter abuses, such review is cumbersome and unlikely to be effective unless the supervisors accept the laws and regulations and can tailor incentives to ensure compliance. Nevertheless, because the smoldering public debate about control of police violence almost always is reignited over the question of justification for a particular incident—often a shooting—the politics of the minimization of abuses has concentrated on discipline after the fact; and it has centered on proposals for review outside the police—civilian review.

ADMINISTRATIVE DISCIPLINE

Until recently, neither New York City nor Los Angeles had a system of external review for police complaints. Nevertheless, the two systems were as different as the NYPD and the LAPD themselves. Although Los Angeles had formalized procedures for the trial of officers when complaints were sustained, the procedures for taking in a complaint and deciding whether it should be sustained were in the hands of the Internal Affairs Division and local commanders. In practice, the Christopher Commission found, civilians were actively discouraged from filing complaints; when Rodney King's brother went to the local station in March 1991 to complain about the now-famous beating, the sergeant in effect refused the complaint by failing to fill out the form. Since that time the intake system has been partly transferred and formalized, but the rest of the system has not been replaced. The Police Commission and the investigative commission have tried to keep monitoring the changes in the LAPD.

In New York City, the procedures for civilian complaints have been centralized since the sixties in the Civilian Complaint Review Board (CCRB), which has its own offices and its own intake procedures and investigators. Complaints could be filed with the CCRB, at local community boards, and at police stations. Complaints about police harassment of those who complain at the station did occur, but they did not seem to be so systematic as in Los Angeles. After 1986, half the members of the board were civilians appointed by the mayor, and many of the investigators were civilians. In 1993, in the Dinkins administration, the city took the final step, separating the board completely from the department, having all members and all investigators independent of the police. New York joined twelve other major cities in the United States that had entirely external review procedures; a majority of big cities have at least a hybrid system, in which, for example, the police investigate but civilians sit on the board that recommends discipline. The powers of the New York board, like those in the other cities, are very limited nevertheless; the board only recommends charges to the commissioner, who must reach his own conclusions. And in any case, the NYPD can still investigate any case it chooses on its own and without the participation of the civilian board.[100]

Civilian review of complaints is an exceptional bureaucratic procedure. Standard management practices would suggest that superiors be responsible for the work of their subordinates and then be answerable to those above them, in this case, the political system. When the sheriff of Los Angeles County commented that he had the ultimate review board because he had been elected by the voters, he was not just making a snappy remark to a reporter; he was reiterating an old point about administration. As a former police chief in Los Angeles put it, "When the right to discipline is vested with management, management has the essential tool with which to attain the desired behavior from employees." In his comparative international analysis of policing in 1985, David Bayley concisely stated the case for the effectiveness of internal review:[101]

> In principle, internal processes are to be preferred, for at least three reasons. First, internal regulation can be better informed than external. A determined police can hide almost anything it wants from outside inspection, certainly sufficiently so as to make outside supervision haphazard. Second, internal regulation can be more thorough and extensive. It can focus on the whole gamut of police activities, not simply on the more dramatic and visible aberrations. Third, internal regulation can be more varied, subtle and discriminating than external. It can use informal as well as formal mechanisms that are omnipresent in the professional lives of police personnel.

Sometimes such internal command responsibility has been taken seriously and has worked well. In New York, after the incidents of torture with a stun gun in Queens in 1985, Commissioner Ward warned all commanders that "they could forget about promotions if their subordinates generated too many brutality complaints. Then he fired the entire chain of command leading from police headquarters to the offending precinct."[102]

It is, then, very easy to see why police, especially senior police officers, for so long resisted civilian review of complaints. Essential to the concept of a "profession" is that professionals impose their own standards and discipline; the cherished ideology of policing as a profession is thus irreparably damaged by external review. And police are afraid of an administrative lynching in cases where public feeling runs high. Given the belief that right conduct in a policing situation requires an intuitive sense of the situation and that there is no way to do the job that cannot be criticized from a different point of view, police are extremely concerned about having outsiders judge their work.

Yet, as Kerstetter has pointed out, those very characteristics of police work have created a dilemma for police discipline; outsiders mistrust internal police review just because its standards seem subjective. Some version of civilian review of police complaints is becoming accepted, by the public and even by police adminstrators.[103] The questions we must ask are: Why do people want it so much? and why are police beginning to accept it?

Some of the arguments for external review could be applied to any bureaucracy. It is not enough that managers are "accountable" to the public, as the sheriff of Los Angeles County said he is, if the managers have complete control over the facts of every determination of misconduct. It may be wiser to have an outside body determine the facts concerning an allegation of misconduct, because many administrators sweep the facts under the rug to avoid the implication of failure of oversight that results from a finding of guilt against a subordinate. In a democratic polity, this argument is especially vivid in the case of police, just because they are the body appointed to use force against citizens. They make fine-grained choices in situations in which there is a tension between order and violence, situations in which the power of the state in relation to society is most dramatic.

Public demands for civilian review are especially vociferous for the police because of a widespread perception that many supervisors in the police do not really believe that the excessive or unnecessary use of force—within some ill-defined bounds—

is wrong. The recent commission reports from Los Angeles and New York support that perception. Minority groups have pushed especially hard for civilian review because they do not see effective control over racist actions by police. All the sources for the demand for civilian review betray a public mistrust of police administration, which is in turn a reflection of the estrangement of the police from the urban populations among whom they work, a problem that has persisted in U.S. cities for generations.

Proponents of civilian review have faulted internal procedures for lax and incomplete investigations, for a low rate of substantiation of complaints, and for failure to inform the public of the reasons for the results of complaints. There is something to the charge of lack of enthusiasm in investigations. Complainants and witnesses in the Tompkins Square beatings said in many cases that investigators were uninterested in the process of finding the facts, that they failed to follow up on information that people gave them, and that they failed to see the complex connections among the various pieces of the puzzle. While these are subjective impressions, they are easy to believe. Given the nature of police work, any police person investigating an ordinary complaint is likely to be aware of other examples that are as bad or worse, or perhaps herself to have been guilty of some minor infraction of the regulations. The existence of corruption in some departments makes the problem all the more difficult. Someone in the department is likely to "know" something that is at least slightly embarrassing to anyone investigating a complaint or making a decision about it. Furthermore, police are organizationally and personally offended by serious abuses; they hate to find that a terrible crime involving their fellow officers has occurred. This dynamic is very clear in the failures to investigate corruption in New York, and I have been told by experienced people that a similar problem existed, much less systematically, among police who worked for the Civilian Complaint Review Board.

On the other hand, civilian investigators and even members of police boards often are or become police buffs. It was a *civil-*

ian investigator from Chicago whom Kerstetter quoted as saying that an officer has to prevail through fear in tough housing projects; Kerstetter noted that investigators for Chicago's Office of Professional Standards, who are all civilians, "give great deference to police officers and are extremely cynical about complainants."[104] Furthermore, because they know that police actions are often matters of judgment in which police have wide discretion, investigators of any background are likely to give the police the greatest latitude allowed by the law.

The vigor and effectiveness of investigations is related to the rate of substantiation of complaints. All review boards, no matter how they are constituted, sustain a rather small proportion of complaints—20 percent or less. The reasons are several. The number of complaints received is not necessarily related to the prevalence of police abuses; it may well be related instead to the political attitudes of citizens, or to public confidence in the review process, or to the way complaints are handled. At the time of the Rodney King incident in 1991, for example, New York processed twice as many complaints in relation to its population as Los Angeles. Some of the complaints thus received will be without merit, and presumably a great many more will be impossible to authenticate. In the vast majority of cases, there will be no witnesses except the complainant and the police; even where there is more than one police witness present, the code of silence means that the case will be one of the complainant's word against the police. In 1989, when some members of the CCRB in New York were civilians appointed by the mayor, the board reported that it had never had a case in which a police witness testified against another; investigators routinely gave little weight to police officers' stories when they corroborated the account of another police officer.[105] Thus, whether a case can be substantiated bears no relation to its seriousness but rather to what evidence is available to prove it. So whether complaints are sustained or not is almost haphazard in relation to the number and seriousness of actual abuses.

Even when there are independent witnesses, there are factors that make it hard to substantiate a complaint, as the investigation of the Tompkins Square beatings demonstrated. In that case, even though there were videotapes and many witnesses, it was often impossible to identify the officers; the CCRB found charges sustained against named officers in seventeen cases, but it found misconduct in twenty-nine cases in which the officers could not be identified. Though critics argued that the investigators could have identified more officers if they had worked harder at correlating the statements of witnesses and analyzing the tapes more closely, it is not clear that they could have done a great deal better. It is interesting, for example, to compare the Tompkins Square investigation with the entirely internal investigation of the police demonstration at New York's City Hall in September 1992. The investigators succeeded in charging more than forty officers in less than two weeks. Surely the pressure was at a maximum and resources were available in that case to nail those who had so publicly embarrassed the NYPD. But literally thousands of police had been present at the rally, many times more than at the Tompkins Square incident, and according to the report submitted by the commissioner, the department could identify only eighty-seven of them; that is just slightly better than the record in the Tompkins Square case.

The words of David Bayley quoted above in support of internal review are surely correct when investigations are carried out in good faith: internal review is likely to be more thorough and better informed than the work of outside investigators. If the lack of witnesses and the code of silence are the chief roadblocks to substantiation, then surely an entirely civilian investigative body is at a disadvantage, for the blanket of silence would probably be more complete, if such a thing can be imagined. And a civilian board would not usually have more investigators and other resources than a board under the control of the police; it might well have fewer.[106]

Review boards, moreover, whether internal or external, find complaints unsubstantiated even in many cases in which officers are identified and there are independent witnesses. Officers are often justified in the use of force in circumstances where civilians would not be; for example, at Tompkins Square in August 1988, police would have been justified in acting against people who were stopping traffic, forcing those who would not go willingly off the pavement or arresting them. Thus the board might find an action justified while a witness would not. Furthermore, if the facts about the justification are in doubt, the board is usually going to decide in the officer's favor because the complainant's side has the burden of proof.

Although formally the burden of proof is no more than the usual standard in civil cases of a "preponderance of the evidence," in practice disciplinary bodies use a higher standard.[107] An example is the rule of thumb that the complainant does not prevail unless she has some way of corroborating the complaint, usually through the testimony of another witness. No such rule is used in ordinary civil matters; although a case is obviously stronger if it is corroborated, trials in which the jury has to decide whether the plaintiff or the defendant is telling the truth are conducted every day, and juries sometimes decide against the defendant on the word of the plaintiff alone. But in police disciplinary matters for civilian complaints, the police respondents win virtually all the time, unless they fail to give a legally sufficient explanation of their actions or the complainant is able to corroborate her side of the case. Thus damages may be and often are awarded in civil actions against the police although, in the parallel review board investigation, the complainant's case had been found "unsubstantiated."

When I asked a staff member of the New York review board, before it became completely external, why the board did not stop using the functionally high standard of proof and decide the cases according to the probabilities as they saw them, the response was that the commissioner would likely reject the findings unless very strong evidence was presented against the police. And that brings us full circle: because review boards, whether civilian or internal, cannot discipline anyone, cannot do more than present investigative findings, the chief official of the police does finally retain the power to determine who shall be disciplined. There is no serious movement in the United

States to change this power, which is generally written into the civil service laws; it is very unlikely that the legislators could be persuaded to change those laws to give review boards the ultimate power to determine the fate of public officials.

That is surely one key reason that police officials have decided in many cities to give in and accept civilian review or some hybrid of civilian and police review: it is not going to lead to very different results. It undoubtedly will lend some legitimacy to the review process and thereby to the police departments, where it is badly needed. For example, in the Tompkins Square case, the claims that police investigators were not interested and not thorough might well have been made about civilian investigators as well, but they would have carried a different weight. There would have been no implication that the case had been "fixed" by the police, that the investigation was a mere facade.

In some cases, furthermore, civilian review boards will improve the process for civilian complaints simply by establishing a set of intake and fact-finding procedures that are publicly known and routinely followed; at least they are not going to intimidate complainants and throw away complaints, as the LAPD sometimes did before the Rodney King case. They always serve to control police department secrecy. In very embarrassing cases of gross abuse, presumably they will not be tempted to sweep the facts under the rug (assuming they can get the facts at all). It is apparent that some commentators have come around to accepting civilian review because their experience with internal review, however much they may have favored it in theory, has been discouraging; superior officers did not take advantage of their management powers to minimize violence. David Bayley, who preferred internal review procedures in 1985, commented tartly in support of external review in 1991 that "discipline is unlikely to be undermined, as is often argued, because it is largely ineffectual now."[108]

Unfortunately, it is just those departments in which the intake and investigative processes are most in need of overhaul which will probably be the last to get it. New York, which already had a clear-cut and formal procedure, has gone to external review, while Los Angeles, which had a formless procedure, has not gone to external review and still seems to have a formless procedure.

For me, the principal political problem in all review systems as instruments for minimizing abuse grows out of the self-evident fact that they put so much emphasis on the disciplinary process. If they do not produce a lot of substantiated cases, then they foster an illusion that the department has no problem with police abuses. In New York, police commanders were able to persuade themselves that the hundreds of complaints of unjustified force made to the CCRB, for example, did not represent a systematic problem because most of them were not sustained. In *Beyond 911*, a book that pleads the case (based on the authors' studies in several police departments) for community policing, the authors add this explanatory note to their chapter on accountability: "*Genuine complaints* are those that were made out of sincere disappointment with an officer's behavior. Many complaints, perhaps as many as two thirds, are motivated by something else—for example, a desire to exercise malice, obtain revenge, thwart or obstruct a prosecution, acquire some political gain, or get unmerited police attention."[109] No authority is cited for this; it is offered as an idea which is likely to obtain ready assent. But I suspect that it reflects conversations with police officials who think that complaints, in the main, are so much baseless trash. A moment's reflection will suggest, I hope (I, too, offer ideas that I think will obtain ready assent), that this is very unlikely; it is likely that most people who go to the trouble to make a complaint are sincere. And some unknown portion of those complaints are true but unprovable. The police officials have been mystified by the magic of due process, blinded by their own inflated standards of proof into believing that the mass of cases does not reflect real problems. They think they are doing some sort of favor for a misguided community in having a complaints process at all, not that they are instead tapping into an invaluable source of community feedback and information. Their views limit the effectiveness of review either as a deterrent to abuses or an instrument of policy.

Such views have contributed to the failure to use the civilian complaint process as a way of explaining to the public the reasons behind the decisions in cases, whether sustained or not, and thus of making the process more legitimate. In New York, for example, the department has not made any real effort to inform complainants of the ultimate outcome of their cases. If a case is serious, the police may ignore the review board, investigate the case internally, and send it for trial on the resulting disciplinary charges; in short, if it is "serious," then it tends to be handled as an internal management matter and not as one to be publicly aired. Much of the possible effect in educating the public both about the disciplinary process and the department is lost.[110] In the Tompkins Square case, as I pointed out in the last chapter, the investigation was spread among the CCRB, entirely internal NYPD investigations, and the resulting administrative trial processes. The work that was done on the matter as a whole was simply lost on the public.

The unstated view that the mass of complaints does not represent anything important also results in failure to make use of the complaints for management or for making policy. In Los Angeles, the Christopher and Kolts investigations of the LAPD and the sheriff's department made the discovery that a relatively small number of officers accounted for a disproportionately large number of complaints; this finding, which is probably generalizable to other departments, was never made before because the departments did not track complaints in any systematic way. New York had an "early intervention system" established in the seventies, but it had apparently not been keyed to civilian complaints; according to the NYPD, the department has now begun to monitor officers who receive more than four force complaints in two years. It is essential that the NYPD and other departments make use of the past records of officers.

Civilian complaints also fall into patterns of conduct, such as particular types of questionable searches, for example, or a concentration of complaints of force in a single neighborhood. These could be used, whether substantiated or not, to improve training for the conduct complained of, or to inquire whether there is some reason for a concentration of activity in a neighborhood. In the seventies, for example, the New York Civil Liberties Union brought a case against the NYPD practices of arresting bystanders at police actions, either because they complain about the police work they see or just to eliminate witnesses. Together with a group of volunteers, I scrutinized the files of the CCRB, looking for the pattern; I found many examples of bystander arrests, together with other patterns of cases so much alike that they could almost have been carbon copies. Nothing was ever done by the department to try to find such patterns, and the review board was never encouraged to make policy recommendations to the department.[111]

In 1991, David Bayley succinctly put the arguments for civilian review from the management point of view just as persuasively as he had put those for internal review in 1985: "Civilian review deflects unfounded criticism, isolates the persistently erring officer, strengthens the hands of police middle-managers and attests to the good faith of the police. Civilian review is an important tool for managing the risks of dispersed police actions."[112]

Nevertheless, I do not think the process of review of civilian complaints is an easy answer for affecting police department policy and thus minimizing the abuse of force. The departments do not want to take policy guidance from review boards; if the NYPD was so reluctant to take suggestions from its internally controlled board, it is surely much less likely to take them from an external board. The remedy must lie in a police department monitor, with internal and external components, that can make use of all the available information for policy review. I will take up this proposal in more detail at the end of this chapter.

CRIMINAL PROSECUTION

Criminal prosecution is the most cumbersome tool for the accountability of officials. As an instrument for policy, it presents the difficulties with disciplinary proceedings writ large:

the charges are made after the fact; it is a matter of hazard which cases can be proved and which cannot; and because the burden of proof is extremely high, the likelihood of success is small. Prosecutions are brought in the few cases where the evidence happens to be available, and the results thus create a patchy deterrent; they may have no effect on police policy at all if police executives do not agree with the decision to prosecute. Furthermore, the standards of the criminal law usually cannot delineate what is good police work that will minimize the unnecessary use of force—that must be shaped by police regulations, training, and practice. Police standards for the use of firearms, for example, are commonly more restrictive than the criminal law of justification, because a shooting may be "wrong" in the sense that there was a better way to handle the situation, without being "wrong" in the sense of a flagrantly offensive act that ought to be punished as a crime. The state prosecutions in California for the Rodney King beating present a rather complex example of the problems. The police who beat King were first prosecuted in state court for felony assault and were acquitted; one of their defenses was that they believed King was a threat to them and that they responded as they claimed they had been taught to respond. Thus, within limits, poor police practices throughout a department can aid the defense of a criminal case by suggesting that there is no criminal intent on the part of a police defendant.

It is very important, nevertheless, to prosecute acts that are clearly criminal, whether deliberate or reckless. The prosecution of the cases of torture with a stun gun in New York's Queens County in 1985, for example, were essential to make a statement that the calculated infliction of pain must be punished. And as a result, there seems to be a general recognition that the infliction of torture is in fact a crime. Such cases do have a broad deterrent effect, making officers aware that the lawful use of force is always at the border of actions that may be criminal. NYPD Chief of Department John Timoney, for example, talked to police at station houses in 1994 about his former partner, the only NYPD officer convicted of homicide on duty in the last twenty years, warning that "cooler heads have got to prevail"; implying both that police have to avoid brutal force themselves and that they have to intercede with other police.[113]

Prosecution probably would be most useful where the internal disciplinary systems for violence are weakest, such as Los Angeles; in such a case, the criminal law might set at least a minimum standard in some cases. It is just in such places, however, where prosecution is least likely in this country, because if the police tolerate violent misconduct, the rest of the criminal justice system may do so as well. When the officers in the Rodney King beating were indicted for assault, they undoubtedly believed, with some justification, that they had been singled out for political reasons, because prosecutions for police violence hardly existed in Los Angeles County before that case.

Twenty-five years ago, prosecutions of police for violence were rare everywhere in the country, including New York; it was generally believed that local district attorneys needed the cooperation of the police so much that they could not afford to antagonize them by prosecuting errant officers.[114] In the intervening years, Los Angeles County and the counties in New York City have diverged in their approaches to such prosecutions. In New York, criminal charges began to be brought in the seventies, due in part to an increasing sensitivity to civil rights, as reflected in the willingness of grand juries to indict in cases that they would earlier have dismissed. At the same time, and for the same reasons, there was a growing sense on the part of the district attorneys that there was a political cost to ignoring the cases. There is of course a political cost to pressing the cases as well: on the one hand, the police will claim that their people are being sacrificed on the altar of politics, and on the other hand, if the officers charged are acquitted, as they frequently are, there is a risk that the community will be more agitated by the case than if there had never been any indictment. If the remedies in the Rodney King case, for example, had been restricted to the administrative dismissal of the police and the payment of substantial damages to the victim, the Los Angeles riot of 1992 might never have occurred. Unfortunately, it is very doubtful that the system in Los Angeles could have delivered adequate administrative discipline at that time.

Prosecution is a powerful and socially explosive tool that should be used only in the clearest cases, where the failure to prosecute would bring the justice system, including the police, into disrepute for granting impunity to officials. Criminal law is thus not a system of "discipline" for police misconduct; it defines the outer limits of what is permissible in society, applicable to the police, with some exceptions, the same as to other people.

CIVIL DAMAGES

The amount of civil litigation over police abuses in the United States has been growing over the last twenty years. There is no question that major lawsuits that change underlying constitutional law do force states and cities to alter their practices. In 1985, for example, the U.S. Supreme Court held that the old rule permitting the police to shoot a person fleeing a felony arrest was unconstitutional in cases where the person was not armed or dangerous; that decision obliged states that still adhered to the old rule to apply the new constitutional standard. And the Supreme Court has also held that a department's "deliberate indifference" to constitutional standards of behavior can give rise to municipal liability under federal law. Some commentators have observed that increased exposure to liability has made police executives more cautious and careful in policies and training.[115] This may be true in smaller departments, where the effect of a single judgment could be devastating, or where insurance rates might go up. But in Los Angeles and New York, the effects of civil tort damages, taking all the cases together, have been surprising small.

The damages the city governments of New York and Los Angeles have paid would seem to have been large enough to make them sit up and take notice. According to the Christopher Commission, the City of Los Angeles paid out more than $20 million for police excessive-force suits in the five years 1986–90, averaging more tha $1,300 per officer in 1990. The

City of New York, according to figures supplied by the city's financial officer, the comptroller, paid out more than $50 million for "police misconduct" for the six years 1987–92, averaging about $400 per officer for a much larger department. It is likely that the actual trials of such cases, in which officers testify and may be found liable, make some difference in the way individual officers think about their work and react to situations. But trials are relatively rare; most civil cases are settled. The officers almost never pay the damages themselves, even when they are technically held personally liable. And the total damages are very small in relation to the police budgets, more than $1 billion dollars a year in New York and more than $400 million in Los Angeles; the damages, moreover, are not even paid out of police budgets but out of general city funds, of which they are but the tiniest fraction. The cities are self-insured; they have no outside insurance company telling them their rates will rise unless they change their practices.[116]

The damages paid had little effect on police policies before the Rodney King incident. In Los Angeles, the Christopher Commission studied more than eighty lawsuits in which substantial damages had been paid, finding that the facts established often seemed to show serious abuses and that the LAPD had failed to take the suits into account in evaluating officers or in setting departmental policy; the Kolts Commission reached similar conclusions about the sheriff's department. In 1992, a study by New York City's comptroller found that the NYPD had not been monitoring the results of suits for police misconduct and had not taken the patterns those cases revealed into account in discipline, in training, or in other policies.[117]

The city's lawyers in New York explained to me the failure of the damage actions to affect police policy by saying that the results of tort claims were idiosyncratic; except in a very few cases, there were no patterns about which the lawyers thought they ought to warn the police. On the one hand, they claimed, when cases go to trial, juries are erratic; at times they award damages unexpectedly. On the other hand, when the city settles the case before trial, the settlement proves nothing; the city and the police officer do not admit that they did anything wrong. I heard this same set of reasons given by officials in Los Angeles to explain why they had ignored the significance of the civil claims made in that city. It is easy to see how a city's damage lawyers fall into this habit of thinking. Their job is to defend the city and usually the individual officers from claims; for them to press severe criticism of an individual officer will often create a conflict of loyalties.[118]

Nevertheless, the claim that the damage actions for police abuses, those that are tried as well as those that are settled, offer no substantial basis for guidance to the police department deprives the civil damages system of any deterrent or normative effect it might have; the money paid becomes just another cost of doing business. City officials do not have to take that approach; they can give the tort system a normative edge if they choose to do so. Even though juries, like lawyers, may sometimes make mistakes, their judgments are binding. And although a "settlement" may prove nothing as a technical matter, city officials can make their own judgments about whether the underlying facts of a given case demonstrate that an officer's actions were violent. In 1992, the New York City comptroller described a case that had been recently settled for $900,000:

> The plaintiff alleged that he was accosted by two officers, struck about the face, head and scrotum, and incarcerated for 26 hours without medical attention despite his complaints of pain. The record shows that plaintiff had no prior criminal record and all charges against him arising out of the incident were dismissed. Both police officers had multiple prior civilian complaints of alleged brutality filed with the Department, although in most cases the complaints had been withdrawn or the complainants had failed to appear. One officer was the subject of a subsequent unrelated civil action, also charging assault, and both officers were the subject of subsequent unrelated civilian complaints alleging excessive force.[119]

If the police did nothing about the officers involved in such a case, that was in itself a judgment of policy about the accountability of police and the willingness of the department to control violence; if the city did not insist that the department take disciplinary action, then the government as a whole shared in that judgment of policy. And the judgment is, in effect, that the social costs of police violence are not great enough to require the city to act against them.

James Meyerson, a New York lawyer who has handled many damage actions against the police, brought a case that threw a revealing light on the interlocking failures of the systems for discipline and for civil damages. In 1987, during a peaceful demonstration about housing, a black man who called himself Posr Amojo Posr, was beaten with clubs and arrested by officers of the NYPD. The criminal charges against Posr were dismissed, and he made a civilian complaint against the officers; despite the fact that Posr had several witnesses who supported his story that he had not attacked the officers, his complaint was found unsubstantiated. Posr sued and ultimately won an award totalling $10,000 in compensation and $20,000 in punitive damages against two policemen; the city paid the $30,000 on behalf of the officers, as it usually does. Following this, frustrated by the failure either of the disciplinary or the civil damages system to make any difference to the officers, Meyerson and Posr decided to treat the punitive award as if it were an "appeal" of the administrative finding that the complaint was unsubstantiated; Meyerson wrote the police commissioner requesting him to bring charges against the police officers based on the unambiguous decision of the jury that they had acted illegally. The commissioner did not answer the letter, and Meyerson brought another case to compel the commissioner to discipline the officers.

No doubt the case was a very long shot; the city's lawyers attacked it as "frivolous" and got it dismissed. The city could have taken a broader approach, however, and used the case as an occasion to start to change the relation between the police and the civil damages system. The city could have insisted that the NYPD take the results of civil actions into account in evaluating officers, especially in cases where punitive damages have been awarded.[120]

So far as I can tell from the scattered evidence, the nexus between police accountability and civil damage claims is generally very weak almost everywhere in the country. When the Police Foundation in Washington did a survey of the legal consequences of police use of force in 1991, only about one-third of the departments responding gave any information about civil actions. The report comments: "The limited number of agencies supplying data was largely attributable to the fact, as explained on a number of questionnaires and in follow-up interviews, that many departments did not keep information concerning civil suits. Instead, such data were maintained by the city attorney or some other outside entity."[121]

This situation may be beginning to change. In the 1990s, juries are more willing to make large awards, and the totals paid by the cities have been rising.[122] The corporation counsel of New York City has refused to represent a few officers and the comptroller and has insisted that they sometimes pay damages; Sean Gelfand paid a small part of the damages in the shooting of Jacques Camille. In connection with the comptroller's report in 1992 that the NYPD was not monitoring police abuses through civil damages claims, the department began to collect reports on the civil cases and said that it was taking them into account in evaluation and promotion. The LAPD made similar changes after the Christopher Commission report.

Nevertheless, the cities, which usually have detailed knowledge about the cases at the time they dispose of them by trial or settlement, ought to make much more active use of them; they have missed an opportunity to use a legitimate tool of accountability for the police. One way to make police departments take more notice of civil actions would be to require that the damages be paid out of police budgets rather than general city funds. But it is not enough to ask the police to take civil actions into account through their bureaucracy; the city ought to follow through to make sure that the police department acts against officers who lie about an abuse, as well as those who perpetrate it, in cases where the city is convinced there has been abuse. It would reduce the costs to the cities, increase the oversight of police, and probably improve relations between city government and citizens.

FEDERAL OVERSIGHT
OF UNCONSTITUTIONAL POLICE ACTIONS[123]

In the last forty years, the U.S. tradition of policing as the quintessentially "local" governmental function has been in growing tension with a growing federal role in the activities grouped under the umbrella of "law enforcement." We now think of crime as a national problem with local roots; thus a predicate for charging a person with the federal crime of "racketeering" is his involvement in a series of underlying felonies, many of which would ordinarily be prosecuted as local crimes. At the same time, we have become increasingly conscious of federal constitutional rights that limit and control the order-keeping and investigative powers of local government. The Supreme Court has imposed national standards on the investigative work of police by excluding even from local trials evidence that is the fruit of a constitutionally invalid search or involuntary confession. During the same time, the Court made it possible to bring a federal damage action for the infringement of constitutional rights by the police. As recently as 1989, the Court finally recognized definitively that police use of excessive force in an arrest is an unreasonable seizure of the person under the Constitution's Fourth Amendment.[124]

The tension between federal power and local control of policing has been traditionally eased, if not resolved, by a federal reluctance to take any action that would affect the internal governance of police departments. The federal government thus minimized the risk of any outright conflict of principle with local police; the custom was undoubtedly reinforced by the frequent cooperation in investigations between federal, state, and local law-enforcement agencies, which discouraged federal officials from looking into local misconduct any more than they absolutely had to. John Dunne, then assistant attorney general in charge of civil rights in the federal Justice Department, expressed the policy perfectly when he testified before Congress during the flap about police brutality following the Rodney King beating in 1991: "We are not the frontline troops in combatting instances of police abuse. That role properly lies with the internal affairs bureaus of law enforcement agencies and with state and local prosecutors. The federal government program is more like a back-stop to these other resources."[125] The federal government made this point of view seem right and inevitable by failing to keep essential data about local police violations of rights and by maintaining restrictions on the power of federal institutions to act against those violations. Until 1994, the restrictions extended to every aspect of the federal government, to the powers of the attorney general in civil and criminal cases, to the self-imposed limitations on the powers of the courts, and to the executive in carrying out federal programs.

Criminal Jurisdiction

Statutes first passed during Reconstruction give the federal government the power to prosecute officials acting "under color of law" for depriving individuals of their constitutional rights; it is these laws that were successfully used against Los Angeles police for the Rodney King beating after they had been acquitted of the assault in the California courts.

These statutes are even more difficult than local criminal laws to use against the police. To get a conviction, the prosecution must prove "specific intent" on the part of the local official to violate a federal right, as distinct, for example, from an intent simply to assault the victim. There is a long-standing policy in the U.S. Justice Department against pressing such a prosecution as long as the local district attorney is vigorously pursuing the case under local criminal laws; the federal prosecutors rarely act as they did in the Rodney King case, pursuing the federal case after the state case has been completed. People who are experienced in the investigation of civil rights complaints have claimed that FBI agents often take little interest in investigating such cases; while that may be true sometimes, the problem runs deeper than that. The usual difficulties in prosecuting police in any system, combined with the high standard of intent and the deference to local prosecutors, mean that federal criminal law contributes little to the accountability of local police for acts of violence.[126]

Civil Jurisdiction

More surprising than the limited effectiveness of the criminal remedy have been the curbs on civil injunction actions in the federal courts. In the 1970s, for example, the federal attorney general as well as private citizens brought separate injunction actions alleging a "widespread practice of violating the rights of persons" and a departmental policy of encouraging the abuses and discouraging civilian complaints, against the Philadelphia police, who were then notorious for their brutality under Frank Rizzo, first as police chief and later as mayor. The courts held that the federal attorney general had no power to bring such a case, a power that would not be conferred on the attorney general until Congress passed the federal Crime Bill of 1994.

The decision in the parallel private case, *Rizzo v. Goode,* had even more far-reaching and lasting effects. After a long trial, in which the plaintiffs proved a number of incidents of abuse, the trial court ordered the city to draft "a comprehensive program for dealing adequately with civilian complaints." This decision was approved on appeal, but when it reached the Supreme Court, it was reversed on grounds that were to affect all cases brought against police executives to put a stop to abuses by the rank and file. The Court held that there was no "pattern" of violations of rights, because the problems were so routine; they were, as the trial court had said, "typical of [those] afflicting police departments in major urban areas." The failure to act against such abuses, the court reasoned, did not establish responsibility for them; furthermore, the Court recognized no enforceable duty on the part of superiors to take any action. More important, the Court held that the trial court should not have directed the reform of the complaint system, because, in light of the "delicate issues of federal-state relationships underlying this case," the court had exceeded its powers when it "injected itself by injunctive decree into the internal disciplinary affairs of this state agency."[127]

Although the legal doctrine in *Rizzo* is not always clear, its political import for federal-state relations is unmistakable: it expressed a federal reluctance that approached a horror of interfering in local police matters. The thread of that reluctance runs through many other decisions, using a number of legal doctrines to limit federal jurisdiction. In *Los Angeles v. Lyons*, the Supreme Court held that Lyons, who had once been arrested and subjected to a potentially fatal chokehold by Los Angeles police, had no standing to obtain an injunction against the LAPD's use of the practice, in part because the city's policy authorized the chokehold only in cases when the subject resisted. Lyons could not make a credible claim that he was likely to be arrested, resist that arrest, and be subjected to the chokehold again; the decision did not need to point out to us that no living person, much less the family of anyone unfortunate enough to have been strangled to death, would ever have standing to get an injunction.[128]

I do not want to paint too bleak a picture; injunctive actions in the federal courts are still useful to groups of private citizens in some cases. They do mobilize public interest in the issues; opinion ran high in Los Angeles against the use of chokeholds during the *Lyons* case, and the LAPD eventually limited their use to situations in which the use of deadly force was justified. Injunctive actions focus the attention of the city and the department on a problem in a way damage actions hardly ever can, and they may lead to administrative changes. In the seventies in New York, for example, after I had for several years been collecting cases for the New York Civil Liberties Union of arrests of bystanders and people who complain about police work, that office brought an action alleging a pattern of abusive arrests based on some thirty-five examples. The police department and the city's lawyers worked out a consent decree under which they agreed that the mere presence of a third party at the scene of an arrest, even if the person is complaining, recording badge numbers, or taking pictures, is not grounds for arrest. The decree was publicized in the police stations, and it slowed down the abuse for some years. In the eighties, the abuse began to come back, and the order had to be renewed and reinforced by the police and the Civil Liberties Union.

Injunctive actions may also be effective if the plaintiffs can prove that the abuses are deliberate and are likely to be used against them repeatedly. In Los Angeles County, the NAACP Legal Defense and Educational Fund brought a case against sheriff's deputies for systematic brutality, including shootings within the area covered by the Lynwood police station. Because the abuses were concentrated within the area of that station, where they were likely to recur to the same people, and the plaintiffs made a showing that the acts were "condoned and tacitly authorized" by policymakers, the courts have allowed the case to go forward.[129]

It is clear, however, that the unsuccessful case against the Philadelphia police, together with *Lyons* and similar cases, drastically limit the use of federal injunctions by private citizens against the police. In *Lyons,* the Court pointed out that even though the plaintiff had no standing to get an injunction, he did have some remedy through a claim for damages. It seems clear that the effect of decisions like *Rizzo* and *Lyons,* if not their overt strategy, is to push claimants toward damages actions and away from systematic relief against cities and police departments. This response seems particularly inadequate in light of the widespread failure of police departments to take account of the results of damage claims.

Changing Federal Policy

After the Rodney King beating, the U.S. attorney general announced that he had asked the National Institute of Justice, the research arm of the Justice Department, "to determine the correlation, if any, between the incidence of police brutality and the presence or absence of police department training programs and internal procedures to deter police brutality." Although the National Institute did make some modest grants for preliminary work on the problems of police violence, in truth the Justice Department was not equipped to carry out the project, and the habits and policies of national data collection had made it next to impossible for anyone to carry it out. The

Bureau of Justice Statistics (BJS) has been collecting superb data on many aspects of the justice system, both federal and local, for decades. It prepares reports on how many crimes are reported, on the cost of and public response to crime, and on sentencing and corrections, but virtually nothing on human rights, civil rights, or police misconduct. After the Rodney King incident, the annual BJS *Sourcebook on Criminal Justice Statistics* picked up some data on public opinion about the police, but that was the extent of it. The BJS had no statistics on police misconduct and very little information about any police conduct, too little to enable anyone to begin to compare the departments. The lack of data has disabled the national government from coming to grips with local police abuse or devising programs about it, even though many if not most police abuses are violations of federal constitutional rights.

The lack of data has made it extremely difficult for scholars inside or outside the government to think about police problems on a comparative basis from city to city. To choose just one example, the BJS reports very careful statistics on the number of law enforcement officers killed and assaulted; it does not release and apparently does not keep any data on the number of persons shot or killed by police. Of course, such figures taken by themselves prove almost nothing. But taken in conjunction with the number of police in a given department, the number of arrests made, and the reported crime rate, those figures may suggest which departments use deadly force more freely, and may suggest ways of trying to control the use of deadly force through better regulations. In comparing Memphis, Tennessee, with New York City in the seventies, for example, James Fyfe was able to show, by contrasting the number of police, the number of felony arrests for violent crimes, and the number of shootings, that the rate of shootings by police, in comparable situations of danger, was three times as high in Memphis as in New York.[130] If we had statistics on police shootings, it should be possible using the other BJS statistics, to carry out a similar comparison for all the major cities in the nation.

The Rodney King scandal, combined with the increasing

political emphasis on crime as a national problem, brought some (possibly temporary) change in the studied federal ignorance about local police. In the Crime Bill of 1994, the U.S. attorney general for the first time got the power to bring injunctive actions against "patterns and practices" by police which violate the Constitution or federal laws. The attorney general would be required to collect data "about the use of excessive force by law enforcement officers" and to publish an annual summary. Furthermore, under the first title of the act, federal funds were allocated to pay community police officers in a "cops on the beat" program; the attorney general could establish guidelines for carrying out the program, and every project funded was supposed to be monitored and evaluated for its compliance with such guidelines.[131]

Provisions such as these could be used to set standards to minimize violence in local police work. The government could set standards for the use of lethal and nonlethal weapons, for adequate systems of command, and for systems of review of police misconduct. The government could go further and condition the receipt of grants on compliance with basic principles of due process and human rights. Grants should be refused to abusive police departments, and the evaluation process should be tailored to assure that departments that have engaged in a pattern of abuse while expending federal funds are eliminated from the program; the attorney general's new data-collection function could be used to single out the departments that should not receive federal support. As this is being written, however, only a few months after the crime bill was passed, Congress is in the process of revamping the provisions of the bill that provide for any federal control over the way the money is used; the federal government may be reverting to its traditional relation to local police.

Without something like the provisions of the 1994 bill, it is doubtful that the United States can comply with its obligations under international law. Codes and principles adopted by the United Nations envision that standards should be set by the national government and that the government should ensure that officials comply with them. The U.N. Basic Principles on the Use of Force and Firearms call for the adoption of rules and regulations governing the use of force, including the use of firearms, and the establishment of "effective review and reporting procedures" for shooting incidents by the police. The U.N. Convention against Torture and Other Cruel, Inhuman or Degrading Treatment or Punishment, which has only just made its way through the U.S. Senate, requires each state party to "keep under systematic review interrogation rules, instructions, methods and practices as well as arrangements for the custody and treatment of persons subjected to any form of arrest, detention or imprisonment in any territory under its jurisdiction, with a view to preventing any cases of torture." It also requires every party "to prevent in any territory under its jurisdiction other acts of cruel, inhuman or degrading treatment or punishment which do not amount to torture," by training and educating law-enforcement personnel, by investigating complaints, and by ensuring that complaints are promptly and impartially examined by the authorities. At the time of this writing, the United States cannot in fact comply with the treaty or meet the demands of the Basic Principles, but it could do so through the powers to gather data and bring injunctive actions and the implementation of the guidelines for federal funding of local law enforcement. If the federal government did that, for the first time we would know what problems exist across the country and could then determine what might be done to control them.[132]

LOCAL AND NATIONAL REFORM

Despite all the arguing in Washington, there is little reason to believe that federal policy toward police practices is going to change radically. Most likely, we are, at least for the foreseeable future, stuck with trying to improve the police on a municipal basis, and we ought to try to see how to make the most of it.

I began to take this effort most seriously in 1992, after talking to an old police reformer in São Paulo (who will appear again in chapter V); for him, municipal control of the police was a transformation devoutly to be wished for, because he thought that control by the state government had separated the police from the people and turned over the administration to a less progressive and more repressive government. So, also, in the United States, we ought to remember that standards set by the federal government might well be so minimal or retrograde as to be little better than nothing and that the standards set by a local administration may be better.

At first glance, the conclusions about the local devices for accountability that I have discussed above are not very encouraging. Disciplinary procedures, whether external or internal, have not been very effective, nor have the criminal or civil liability systems. The problem with these, as I see it, is that they work on a case-by-case basis, and what is needed instead is an institution to bring the implications of the cases home to the departments. Some recent developments suggest useful approaches. In Los Angeles and New York, investigative commissions have collected documents and other evidence from the departments and have reviewed abuses systematically; thus they are able to make equally systematic recommendations. These auditors should be institutionalized, as an auditor has been in San Jose, California, for example, instead of being established every time there is a crisis and later abandoned. In addition, there must be an official inside the departments, an inspector general, who will listen to the outside auditors and also oversee the workings of the department from within to try to assure that the instruments of command really are minimizing violence. We need a permanent, tripartite system of accountability including a fact-finding body for complaints, an auditor with power to obtain documents from the department, and an internal inspector general who can make sure that the findings of the other bodies are turned into working policy by the department. This tripartite system should function to control corruption as well as other police abuses. I recognize that such a strong system of accountability will not be put in place unless police management as well as external political forces want to obtain control over violence, but I see no viable alternative on a local basis—none of the devices, taken alone, has come close to being effective.

Powerful institutions of accountability, such as the tripartite system, are needed because the police are the chief institution for the employment of force in urban government. Because police departments are integrated vertically, there is virtually no lateral entry; if there were, those at the top might have different values from those further down, and internal accountability might be more effective. As it is, the customs of solidarity within the ranks tend to dissolve accountability. Another possibility for reform would be to introduce lateral entry; but that change seems even more improbable, and more uncertain in its effects, than the tripartite system I have just proposed.

The New York City police, as well as the federal government, have taken a rather different tack, through community policing, which is supposed to put "a cop on the beat," as the federal Crime Bill of 1994 put it, and to make that cop a problem solver for the community. As the New York police describe the proposed changes, "The community policing philosophy reaffirms that crime *prevention*, not merely responding to calls for service, is the basic mission of the police. Crime prevention is accomplished by having a visible police presence in neighborhoods and undertaking activities to solve crime producing problems, arrest law violators, maintain order and resolve disputes before they result in violence. In community policing it is understood that police and citizens are partners in the maintenance of safe and peaceful neighborhoods."[133]

That philosophy seems to imply the possibility of a radically new sort of accountability, through which the police might actually answer to the community in the partnership. The police departments are trying to solve the perennial problem of their estrangement from the public, a problem that has pulled in its train a bunker mentality on the part of the police and a mistrust on the part of the public. Under community policing, commands are supposed to be decentralized and directly responsive to the community.

It is tolerably clear, however, that the radical possibility is not to be realized; the police do not propose to cede any real decision-making power to the community. As critical commentators have put it, "the community police perspective offers instead a vision of shared values, a 'coproductive' relationship, most often characterized as a 'partnership' in which communities offer input, advice, and guidance to police while working hand-in-hand to carry out strategies to fulfill their mutual objectives."[134]

Community policing nevertheless expresses an important drive toward reform on the part of the police: the effort to increase police legitimacy by reducing conflict with the community. As its critics have pointed out, however, community policing may encourage local police to slight the rights of some people in favor of others who call themselves the relevant "community" and may thus lead to a kind of balkanization of police work and discrimination in the enforcement of rights.[135] It cannot eliminate police abuses and will not obviate the need for powerful systems of internal and external accountability.

Chapter IV

Past and Present: The United States, Latin America, and the Caribbean

The panoply of institutions of accountability obscures the recurring problems of violence in contemporary U.S. police departments. In a historical perspective, however, from the founding of the departments in the nineteenth century to the present, the connection among political influence, venality, and violence appears perennial, and it is clear how much effort has been required to reduce the abuse of suspects, either in the station house or in the street. Viewing that history in light of the problems in the other cities of the Americas, we will see that familiar issues are raised, in language that is much the same. The familiar language, however, is used to explain and excuse much more systematic violence in contemporary São Paulo, Jamaica, or Buenos Aires.

POLITICS, CORRUPTION, AND REFORM

Politics and corruption have been a thread running through the history of U.S. police departments, just as they have in the Third World. In the United States, reformers have been fighting the vices of the police for generations, alleviating some problems while creating or encouraging others.

Cities in the United States were, and sometimes still are, run by political machines, a version of clientelist politics by which, in return for votes, politicians deliver a variety of jobs and services. These have included jobs in the police department, as well as policing itself, and other social services, such as legal assistance or subsistence payments, and "protection" for activities that the dominant society often sees, or pretends to see, as vice. Many residents of the cities have been poor newcomers, learning to be integrated into a modern, urban society; as clients of the machine, they have also been subject to its rule, including that of the police. When "Clubber" Williams, a police inspector famous in New York in the nineteenth century, acted on his philosophy that "there is more law in a night stick than in all the statute books," poor New Yorkers were not in a good position to disagree or to formulate a different philosophy. If at first many of them did not have a strong sense of participation as citizens, having little choice but to support the machine, they did learn how politics worked, while receiving some of the things they needed to survive.

Machine-style politics encouraged some enduring values in policing in the United States. Almost all police are organized as services to cities and towns. The U.S. Justice Department has estimated that there are more than fifteen thousand "enforcement agencies," of which four-fifths are local forces, many of them very small. Although in the nineteenth century state officials sought unsuccessfully to wrest the management of the police forces from the city machines, we now have a strong cultural commitment to local (city and county) police. The idea of a national police force has been systematically denounced in the United States as unworkable and a potential instrument of tyranny, most memorably by J. Edgar Hoover, who promoted the Federal Bureau of Investigation as a specialized detective agency that would not interfere with generalized local policing; even state police forces were feared as potentially violative of citizens' rights as well as of local prerogatives. Although the federal courts have set broad national standards for a few law-enforcement practices and there has been some successful work by federal agencies cooperating with local police in the prosecution of national crimes, until recently there has been little federal intervention in local law enforcement beyond the collection of data about the number and characteristics of crimes and criminals and the like. Local politicians and police officials, aided by federal reluctance, have prevented any effective national control or even policy coordination for local police.[136]

The local forces combined the functions of patrol and order keeping, called "preventive policing" in the United States just as it is in Latin America, with those of detecting and catching— sometimes slipping over into punishing—those suspected of crimes. It was once common in the English-speaking world, as it is in Brazil and Mexico, for the investigative part of the criminal justice process to be viewed as a function of the judiciary, rather than of the local police. Nevertheless, in part because of the ineffectiveness and venality of detectives outside the police, and the failure of the judiciary to control them, as well as for political reasons, crime detection came to be attached to patrol and prevention as a police job. The separation of the functions, which is not unusual outside the United States, now seems to us in this country to be awkward and artificial.[137] The detectives were absorbed by the vertically integrated police organization, so that they, like superior officers, are drawn from the ranks of patrol people who come in at the bottom. This has made for a hybrid hierarchy, protomilitary and at the same time democratic, in which almost no one is separately trained and laterally employed to be over others, but all theoretically have an opportunity to rise, either to a command or detective position.

Politics, in the most direct sense, has been part of the police as the police have been part of politics. In the United States, jobs in the departments in the early days were assigned and taken away as a matter of patronage, so that police were expected to oversee the polls at elections, to make sure that the machine was successful. One of the first great investigations of police corruption and brutality, the Lexow Commission in New York in 1895, found that "almost every conceivable crime against the elective franchise was either committed or permitted by the the police, invariably in the interest of the dominant Democratic organization." Similar complaints were made in Chicago and other cities.[138]

Corruption has been endemic in the police. Machine politicians in the United States depended on graft to pay salaries and patronage and to conduct campaigns to keep the machine in office; in the thirties, a Los Angeles politician summed it up in the aphorism "The purpose of any political organization is to get the money from the gamblers." Under such circumstances, the police were expected—more, encouraged, practically obliged—to take graft to deliver to the politicians. To be sure, the police have also been offered opportunities apart from organized political graft. As Egon Bittner said, "It is difficult to imagine a profession in which there is more opportunity and a greater temptation for corruption than policing. This is most obvious in criminal law enforcement, where an officer only has to look the other way to earn a bribe." Nevertheless, most police corruption has been part of the larger pattern in the government as a whole, whether of election fraud or graft taken from vice rackets; the situation that prevails in New York City, where police corruption is said to be developed independently of other graft, seems to be the exception.[139]

Some policemen have committed crimes more seriously in conflict with their order-keeping and law-enforcement purposes, participating in the rackets directly as organizers or committing so-called hard crimes such as burglary. It is a problem that never completely fades in any police system. As recently as 1994, the largest single category of formal disciplinary cases in the New York City Police—19 percent—was for criminal acts; and in New Orleans, federal agents investigating corruption in the police department overheard a local policeman casually arranging the murder of a witness to an act of police brutality.[140] More commonly in earlier days, politicians had gangs of toughs or gunmen as enforcers, to keep the machine in office and protect against the depredations of rival racketeers and politicians. Officials protected such toughs against prosecution, offering bail and corrupting other parts of the criminal justice system to keep them out of jail. Magistrates were bribed or kept in line by the patronage of the machine. The office of district attorney is usually elective in the United States, a situation that judges and prosecutors trained in the continental tradition, including those in Latin America, continue to view with astonishment as an open invitation to corruption. And indeed, district attorneys frequently were products of the machine, who protected the toughs who were the protectors of the machine, and sometimes took bribes to dispose of cases in ways favorable to defendants. It was not until the 1930s, with Thomas Dewey in New York and Earl Warren in California, that the notion of a "career professional" district attorney took hold.[141]

Progressive reformers at the end of the nineteenth and the first part of this century sought to shape the organization and functions of the police so as to eliminate political manipulation, corruption, and involvement in crime. They favored a group of reforms, including the formation of squads for specialized functions and lateral entry to specialized positions. They tried to narrow the scope of the police job to a "crime-fighting" model, so that it could be regularized and "professionalized." They believed that the status of the police would be raised, appointments and management would be separated from politics, and an objective internal review of the quality of the work would be made by managers. To ease the problems of organization and integrity in the police, many reformers were drawn to a military analogy, which had its historical roots in the development of the police out of bodies such as the militia, in the United States as well as in Latin America. Police had duties, furthermore, that bore a resemblance to those of the military, including the right and sometimes the obligation to use violence. The analogy was superficially attractive because the military was a classic form of public bureaucracy, considered generally honest, with clear lines of authority and well-defined aims, and independent of and sometimes "above" politics.[142]

The drive for reform was successful in many ways. The profligate interference with the police by politicians was reduced; the reformers, with the support of much of the rank and file, obtained civil service status, including competitive merit appointments, for police employees, as well as internal management control of status and discipline. Specialized squads have been formed and have proliferated. The central purpose of the job, at least, if not its day-to-day practice, was narrowed to the "anticrime" function; thus the detective, far from his origins as a separate operator, became the ideal policeman. Campaigns against corruption, including the formation of special internal investigation squads to find crooked officers, are constantly conducted, sometimes, as in Los Angeles, with lasting success.

These were part of a strong "good government" drive that led to the general reform, if not complete abandonment of machine politics, at least in its raw spoils-system form in the big cities. The economy had resources available for reform, for a less clientelistic distribution of pay and other benefits controlled by the political system. It is striking, for example, and notably different from Latin America and the Caribbean, that almost all historians concur that big-city police in the United States were not badly paid. Even in the early days, they were paid as well or better than most working-class people, and after the reforms took hold, they were paid even better. Thus it was possible to discipline them through their desire to keep a good job, and any drive to venality created by sheer need was at least reduced.[143]

The reforms have not been a complete success. On some issues, the reformers made almost no headway; lateral entry particularly, intended to break the traditional democratic-hierarchical structure of departments, has not prevailed. Equally important, tensions and ambiguities of value in the ideals promoted by the reformers have remained unresolved.

Although "politics," in the sense of venal manipulation of law enforcement and protection of corrupt or violent policemen could be minimized, politics could not be eliminated from police work. Every time a top police administrator makes a decision to undertake a program, the decision is political; even the overarching decision to emphasize the "anticrime" approach to the job, in which the primary effort is to respond rapidly to calls about crimes in progress or immediately past, is a political decision because, when it is made, other possible tasks, such as patrol and service, are neglected. The reformers' effort to narrow the very definition of police work was not successful because most of the range of functions that the police had done before the reforms were not taken over by other actors in society. So it became clear that the police job did not have a fixed and narrow definition, but rather continued to be a collection of jobs, among which administrators and political leaders had to choose.[144] Thus police administrators had to be sensitive and reactive to political demands, or they could not respond to political and social change; the artificial insulation of the police chief from politics, such as occurred in Los Angeles when the chief was given civil service status, resulted in a department that was perpetuated in the image of the chief. At the same time, the decision to emphasize one approach rather than another frequently leads to political criticism, because all the approaches—patrol, prevention, anticrime, and investigation and apprehension—are interconnected, and one of them cannot be chosen without affecting all of them.

The moralism of the reformers, which drove the campaign for cleaner and more regularized government, itself created conflicts that have undermined the success of their efforts. Some reformers thought that if the police enforced all the laws systematically, including the laws against vice, the result would be better cities and better citizens, as well as honest police. But large parts of the population did not care to see the morals laws enforced; they did not consider gambling, drinking, and prostitution to be wrong, or in any case not wrong enough to want to do anything to stop them. And many police agreed with those views enough to be willing to take a little graft to protect vice. As early as 1884, Clubber Williams, who commanded the precinct in New York's "Tenderloin," a synecdoche he himself coined for the luxurious life afforded by the bribes available from the brothels, complained about the attempt to eliminate prostitution: "The true policy would be to localize the evil rather than spread it over the city. I take a liberal view of the matter, and don't believe it can be suppressed. There are 40,000 strangers in the city every day, and these all go to the places in my precinct, and not from curiosity I am sure."[145] The campaign against immorality thus led to corruption, as well as to an atmosphere of prurient hypocrisy in political life. In the long run, it interfered with the reform effort to make street police into "professionals." Commanders were unwilling to give patrolmen the discretion to be professional, partly because they feared corruption; instead, they surrounded patrol people with regulations, like soldiers in the military.

The military analogy has proved particularly misleading. If it were used to imply no more than a rigidly honest, dedicated bureaucracy, as it sometimes was in the early days of reform, it would be relatively harmless; unfortunately it has often been used instead to create the image of an embattled army fighting a "war on crime." Armies are organized and trained for killing an enemy, usually more or less well-defined, and not for service and law-enforcement among a civilian population to which they themselves belong, in situations for which they have to make fine-grained legal and social distinctions about what action is required. One police force in the United States that was literally like an army was the Pennsylvania State Police, deliberately organized in 1905 on the model of the constabulary that had been used to subdue insurgents in the Philippines; like that constabulary, it was a fearsome body, uncompromisingly brutal to strikers to the point where local police expressed their opposition to it.

When the "war on crime" analogy is combined with the professionalized, anticrime approach to police work, the results distort and poison police relations with citizens. The police think of themselves as an occupying army, and the public comes to think the same. The police lose the connection with the public which is a principal advantage to local policing, and their job becomes progressively more difficult, while they become more unpopular. It seems that is exactly what happened in Los Angeles before the infamous Rodney King incident in 1991.[146]

The police and the reformers have come to see that the insulation from politics effected by the anticrime and the military models has cut them off from the public. The police are not "professional" in the sense that lawyers, doctors, or, for that matter, military people are, because they do not have a defined role for which they can set their own standards; they are instead reactive to the changing needs of the city, as expressed, sometimes very obscurely, through politics. The police reformers have come full circle; they now seek better and closer relations with citizens. Mark Moore, a leading proponent of community policing, puts the disillusion with older reform measures succinctly:

> Problem-solving and community policing are strategic concepts that seek to redefine the ends and the means of policing. Problem-solving policing focuses police attention on the problems that lie behind incidents, rather than on the incidents only. Community policing emphasizes the establishment of working partnerships between police and communities to reduce crime and enhance security. The prevalent approach that emphasizes professional law enforcement has failed to control or prevent crime, has failed to make policing a profession, and has fostered an unhealthy separation between the police and the communities they serve . . . [147]

POLICE AND THE USE OF FORCE IN U.S. CITIES

At all times, the police have carried out a great deal of social control through the force implied in patrol and in checking on and sometimes acting against apparent deviants in the streets and public places. They have acted mostly against lower-class offenders and vagrants, identifying them and enforcing their subordinate status.

The reaction of local police to lower-class urban life was complex, partly because the police themselves were often lower class. On the one hand, class distinctions and conflicts were much sharper before the 1930s than they are now. There was a virulent fear of revolutionary ideas that often resulted in outright vigilantism. In 1875, the Chicago *Tribune* editorialized: "There is no people so prone as the American to take the law into their own hands when the sanctity of human life is threatened and the rights of property invaded in a manner that cannot be adequately reached and punished by the tortuous course of the law. Judge Lynch is an American by birth and character.... Every lamppost in Chicago will be decorated with a Communist carcass if necessary to prevent wholesale incendiarism or prevent any attempt at it."[148] For decades, big-city police followed an impulse only slightly less bloodthirsty, harassing radicals and labor agitators. As we saw in chapter II, mounted police charged a peaceful group of unemployed demonstrators in New York's Tompkins Square Park in 1874 and "rode down and clubbed anyone who was poorly dressed and in the way." In 1937, the police killed ten picketers and wounded dozens in a strike at a Republic Steel factory in Chicago.[149] Vigilantism was common throughout the nineteenth century and well into the twentieth. People were impatient with criminal justice, which they thought corrupt and inefficient. They were not embarrassed to recommend or even undertake a lynching, and they were even less embarrassed to think that a policeman might do it for them.

At the turn of the century, the respectable public did not make a clear distinction among radicals, vagabonds, and ruffians and criminals; they were all viewed as criminals or as part of a potentially criminal class. Thus the police in large cities gave nightly shelter to vagrants, not only as a humane measure, but in order to obviate a vague danger; that service function passed away as attitudes to the police job as well as to vagrants changed. Eric Monkkonen says, "Social welfare reformers, and some police chiefs, began to differentiate the components of the 'dangerous class,' and tramps became, to them, the unemployed rather than dangerous." But as late as the twenties and thirties in Los Angeles, which had a consistently antilabor administration, the conservative *Times* indiscriminately praised actions against vagrants and labor organizers.[150]

At the same time, the police contrived to protect diverse habits in urban life, whether of the rich or poor, and whether they involved liquor, gambling, after-hours clubs, or almost anything else. The police were tolerant, sometimes at the price of a little graft. In fact, the localism of the police was a force that preserved pluralism in the United States. The police have generally ceased to harass labor picketers, as labor organization has been accepted and the police have themselves become unionized.

DEADLY FORCE

Carrying firearms has been so prevalent in the United States that the police originally carried them not as equipment required by the departments, but just as other citizens carried them. The "fleeing felon" rule, which prevailed until recently, permitted a policeman to kill a person fleeing from a felony charge, if the arrest was lawful and the person might otherwise escape. Nevertheless Americans were ambivalent at the outset about police carrying weapons as part of the job. The *New York Times* grudgingly accepted the arming of the city police in 1857: "The objections to an armed police are patent to everyone; the danger of placing deadly weapons in the hands of men who may use them with impunity at their own discretion, is too great to be lightly incurred; and it is only as the choice of a lesser evil that such a measure could be recommended." New Yorkers, at least those who were not likely to be among the ones shot, did seem to think that the use of the weapon was the lesser evil in many cases; a year later, the *Times* again editorialized that: "[t]here is absolutely no safety but in summary and even lawless measures,—that the police are our sole reliance, and that they must have power to shoot down every ruffian who resists arrest or attempts to escape."[151] Middle- and upper-class people recognized that once the police were armed, they were not going to be punctilious about due process, and thus when the police cut corners in killing people, the respectable public did not object; when a patrolman shot an unarmed sailor who resisted an arrest for being disorderly, the coroner's jury charged the patrolman with homicide, but the grand jury, composed of more substantial citizens, cleared him.[152]

There have been times, from that day to this, when police chiefs confronted with spates of crime have used a military or Wild West rhetoric about deadly force. During the draft riots of 1863, the New York police commissioner advised the police in confronting the mob, "Take no prisoners." In Los Angeles, which was pretty close to the Wild West until quite recently, the chief said in 1927 that he wanted gunmen "brought in dead, not alive," adding that he would "reprimand any officer who shows the least mercy to a criminal." And as late as 1990, Daryl Gates, then the chief in Los Angeles, told a congressional committee that he thought that casual users of drugs ought to be shot.[153]

There were few effective restrictions on the use of deadly force before the 1960s. As recently as the seventies, the Police Foundation found that 43 percent of its sample of those shot by the police had been unarmed; at that time, of course, the fleeing felon rule could have made most of those shootings justified. Aggregate figures for shootings by and against police after 1970 are now not so difficult to obtain for large cities, but figures for the much earlier period, before World War II, are rare; government agencies did not release them, and counts from newspaper stories are few. We do have some interesting figures from a survey of crime in Chicago in 1926 and 1927:[154]

	1926	1927
Murders, manslaughters, justifiable homicides	485	471
Killed by police	43	46
Police, deputy sheriffs, watchmen killed on duty	11	9

The survey commented that while most of the killings by police were justified, "in others it would seem that the police were hasty and there might be some doubt as to the justification, but in every such instance the coroner's jury returned a verdict of justifiable homicide and no prosecutions resulted. From this we may conclude that the police of the city of Chicago incur no hazard by shooting to kill within their discretion." Chicago, which had a population approaching three million in the twenties, had a great reputation for criminal violence at the time, which might well have prompted violence by the police. The figures cited in the survey, however, while high, do not imply any massive effort to dispose of criminals deliberately by police guns.

There were reports of deliberate killings to eliminate criminals. In Los Angeles in 1927, "Mile-Away" Thomas, a suspected hijacker who had succeeded in establishing his alibi that he was a mile away from the scene of thirteen crimes of which he had been suspected, was killed while breaking into a storehouse, by a detective who was alleged to have told him the location of the storehouse. Such cases do not seem to have been usual however, and sometimes caused a scandal. In 1938, the head of the Los Angeles political-spying squad was convicted of planting a bomb in the car of an investigator for a local reform league. But crimes such as this are calculated matters of protecting graft at a high level and are very far from dispatching suspects in the streets.[155]

Later chapters will show that the use of deadly force has been profligate in Brazil, Jamaica, and, to a lesser extent, Argentina. We might pause to think about why, in the United States, the use of firearms against suspects, although it has certainly been often abused, never reached the level it has in some other cities in the Americas. Certainly some of the social elements that contribute to such systematic killings were present: strong class conflicts between the poor and the better-off; impatience with the courts and a willingness to resort to extralegal means to punish and deter, combined with a disinclination by the governments to put a stop to vigilantism; a weak sense of citizen participation by many, as reflected in machine politics. But there was not the sense of frightening economic crisis, the constant threat of poverty with no apparent exit, that haunts the Third World. There was not the near-panic fear of crime, abetted by the mass media and political leaders, that often prevails at the present time, both in some U.S. cities and elsewhere in the Americas.

Under the surface, the population of U.S. cities was becoming more pacified. Moreover, the police were not strongly disciplined along military lines, despite the occasional talk to that effect; they shared instead a generally democratic attitude.

Although as time went on they were increasingly cut off from the public, it seems unlikely that they would have been inclined to shoot suspects under circumstances that went beyond the already permissive fleeing-felon rule. A growing appeal to the rule of law was struggling to overcome vigilantism and complaints about the ineffective criminal justice system in the United States. Class conflict was tempered by an egalitarian sense of rights; even though much of the public in Los Angeles, for example, approved of or was indifferent to the harassment of vagrants, there was always a faction that was critical of the jailing or removal of people who had committed no crime.[156] Citizens were already doubtful about the police use of firearms, and shootings by police were questioned, even if they were not ultimately disapproved. From the beginning there was some sense that the police, like the rest of the government, ought to act within the bounds of the law.

VIOLENCE WITHOUT FIREARMS

In the cities of the United States, the pattern of police violence, and much of the protest against it, has centered on nondeadly force, typically beatings of people who are "threats"—that is, perceived as criminal or in some way deviant. This seems to be the essence of the use of force for social control: deviants are out of control when they fail to comply with police orders, doubly so when they are disrespectful or defiant. Since the early days of urban policing, people who are defiant have run a substantial risk of being beaten up. "There is no remedy for insulting language," a captain in New York opined in 1866, "but personal chastisement."[157] Much of the abuse of deadly force, in the Third World as well as in the United States, has also fit this pattern; the fleeing-felon rule itself can be viewed as an expression of an underlying idea that defiance of arrest for a serious crime may be punished by shooting. Nevertheless, the paradigmatic abuse in the United States has been a blow as punishment.

Police beating extended to torture of suspects who defied questioning for confessions or evidence, or just to make sure they were punished. Cornelius Willemse, who was a captain in New York City before the turn of the century, recounted how his sergeant told rookies they were supposed to beat suspects in serious cases, lest those they arrested might later in turn "beat" the charges through politics or law; there was usually no effective complaint against a beating, unless the police chose a victim of the wrong class. Inspector Thomas Byrnes, who commanded the detectives in New York after 1880, used the "third degree," as coercion of suspects was called, systematically. Suspects were held incommunicado for interrogation, even though the law required them to be taken before a judge, in New York and Los Angeles as well as other cities. Innocent people were tortured and sometimes confessed to crimes; in two of the most famous murder cases in the history of Chicago, the Bobbie Franks murder by Leopold and Loeb in the twenties and the Susan Degnan murder by William Heirens in 1941, the Chicago police tortured suspects who turned out to be innocent.[158]

Coercion, combined with greed, produced in the investigative work of detectives abuses similar to the pattern in Latin America, discussed in later chapters. Detectives extracted money from suspects in return for reducing or dismissing charges. They "solved" crimes by finding and returning the proceeds, without ever charging the criminal; in this way, they collected a reward and kept thieves in business. They played favorites, keeping some criminals in business and driving the others out by harassment and prosecution. Inspector Byrnes in New York was particularly adept at finding the proceeds of thefts committed against prominent people; he kept a stable of informers to let him know who was responsible for such crimes. In Los Angeles in the twenties, detectives took bribes to reduce charges against suspects and to steer them to particular lawyers. Detectives, who had originally been organized separately from the preventive police, continued to be "rogue" policemen, close to the underworld they were supposed to control, masters of their own secret methods. Inspector Byrnes had that reputation, and, in Los Angeles in the twenties, among many examples, Richard Lucas, the detective who was said to have lured "Mile-Away" Thomas to a storehouse to be shot, was forced to resign after having participated in a complex scheme to frame a reform city councilman on a morals charge in which the woman supposedly "involved" was a relative of one of the detectives.[159]

Throughout the 1920s, coercion of suspects was routine. In Los Angeles in 1924, when an assistant district attorney who could not identify himself was beaten in an interrogation cell, the famous reform commissioner August Vollmer failed to take any action. By the time of the first national commission on crime and law enforcement in 1930, prosecutors surveyed agreed that coercion of suspects occurred in most of the jurisdictions in the country. The commission's concise account of some of the worst and most well-documented cases, *Lawlessness in Law Enforcement*, initiated the long process of inducing prosecutors and judges, including the U.S. Supreme Court, to take action to exclude physical coercion from the process of interrogation.[160]

The Contemporary Situation: The Decline of Torture and Deadly Force

The minimization of the use of coerced confessions and the decrease in police use of deadly force are among the success stories of human rights in the United States.

The exclusion of physical coercion in confessions has been primarily the work of the judiciary, joined sometimes reluctantly by prosecutors. From the thirties to the sixties, the Supreme Court expanded the concept of "voluntariness" in confessions, until finally, under Chief Justice Earl Warren, the *Miranda* decision held that the confession has to be shown to be fully voluntary, in the sense that the accused has knowingly waived his rights to remain silent and to have counsel. Although the burden of proof is on the prosecution to show that the confession is voluntary, the constitutional requirements about confessions work as well as they do principally because the state court judges, who hear most of the cases in which confessions are offered, have generally been conscientious about applying the burden of proof and excluding confessions that appear to be tainted. Prosecutors also are increasingly reluctant to offer confessions that may cast doubt on a conviction.[161]

What the situation used to be like—and what it could be still, were it not for the systematic changes effected through the power of the courts and backed by the other elements of the criminal justice system, including the police themselves—can be seen in pockets where the third degree has recently been used. In Chicago, after a conviction for the murder of a police officer was thrown out by the state supreme court in 1987 because the defendant's confession was coerced, his lawyers brought a federal civil rights case for damages; shortly afterward they began to receive tantalizing anonymous letters from an apparently knowledgeable police source, directing them to other witnesses. It developed that detectives in Area 2 of the Chicago police had been torturing suspects for twenty years. As one of the lawyers for the victims said to me, "When [reform police commissioner] O. W. Wilson tried to drag the Chicago Police Department into the twentieth century, Area 2 refused to come along." After years of pressure, the police disciplinary body brought charges against some of the officers, in which allegations in fifty cases were investigated, involving torture instruments such as plastic bags over the head and a field telephone mechanism that can be attached to the victim's body and cranked to vary the current (a device used so much in Brazil that it has a nickname, the *pimentinha*). It is not clear that torture has ended in Chicago, since there were many officers involved and complaints were being made as late as 1992.[162] Torture is difficult to stamp out once it starts because it seems to be almost habit-forming; it is an easy way to clear cases, and it punishes the suspect as well.

Some cruel uses of excessive force in the streets may be regarded as torture when they are used to punish people; thus the stun gun or the taser or canine units are sometimes used, as we saw in Los Angeles, to inflict pain. The third degree, however, is largely a thing of the past even where street abuses are at their worst, because, it seems, we have developed a societal norm against coercing confessions; police in New York who tortured prisoners with a stun gun were sentenced to long prison terms. Even the most severe police critics no longer complain of the problem; for example, the NAACP's 1993 national report on police brutality, *Beyond the Rodney King Story*, scarcely mentions coerced confessions. The interest of the *Dirty Harry* story, for example, in which the protagonist policeman makes a decision to use violence to force a kidnapper to reveal the whereabouts of his victim, lies in the conflict over this contemporary norm; in the days of Thomas Byrnes and Cornelius Willemse, it would have been a very short and uninteresting story.

The decline in the use of deadly force is not so well known a story as the end of the third degree, perhaps because, except at the very end of the process, it has not been a matter of dramatic judicial decisions. It has resulted chiefly from a determination on the part of police chiefs and their commanders to enforce tighter regulations on the use of weapons through training and discipline, and through prosecutions in some jurisdictions. Although the American Law Institute had recommended in its Model Penal Code as early as 1962 that deadly force should be used for arrest only when an officer believed that there was substantial risk that the suspect would cause death or serious injury, the major change in the thinking of local police came in 1972 after New York's reform police commissioner Patrick V. Murphy adopted a policy allowing the use of deadly force only as a last resort, against persons believed to pose a threat of immediate serious injury.

In an article aptly called "one of the most influential pieces of research in the history of policing," James Fyfe, a former New York policeman, reviewed almost five thousand incidents of shots fired before and after the regulation was imposed, finding that the number of civilians shot dropped dramatically after the new rules took effect, without adversely affecting the crime rate, the safety of officers, or the arrest rate. The research was later replicated in other cities; Fyfe found that after the notoriously tough Frank Rizzo left office in Philadelphia and the police were forced to adhere to restrictive laws on the use of deadly force, fatal shootings by police declined by 67 percent, while injuries to officers declined at the same time. In 1980, the International Association of Chiefs of Police adopted a policy limiting the use of deadly force to situations reasonably posing a threat of death or serious injury. A consensus had been reached, and later studies of the forty years between 1950 and 1990 show that police shootings peaked in about 1971 and have declined since then by about half. By the time the U.S. Supreme Court decided in 1985 that shooting a felon who presented no threat of physical injury, such as an unarmed burglar, was unconstitutional under the Fourth Amendment as an unreasonable seizure of the person, several police authorities appeared in the case to urge the Court to take that final step.[163]

The change in the rules both reflected and reinforced a change in public tolerance of the use of deadly force on the streets. It is hard to realize now how great the change has been. As late as 1967, during the uprising in Newark, *Life* magazine ran photographs showing a man, who was fleeing with a pack of looted beer, being shot in the back by police; at the time, it no doubt seemed to many readers a photographic coup more than a violation of human rights. In many minority communities, however, such acts of violence caused outrage; indeed, those reactions had the greatest influence in inducing police chiefs to require more caution in using firearms. Blacks and Hispanics experienced the shooting of one of their number, at least when it was not required for the defense of life, as a terrible discrimination. And there is evidence that they were right: Fyfe's research on shootings in Memphis, for example, showed that when police were permitted to shoot unarmed fleeing suspects under the old fleeing-felon rule, they were much more likely to shoot blacks than whites. He concluded "that Memphis police used their broad authority to shoot in elective situations when their targets were black, and that they typically refrained... when white subjects were involved." This is, indeed, the worst form of discrimination, one of the great evils of the segregated world from which blacks had struggled to escape. It is a statement, in effect, not only that the life of a black person is not as valuable as that of a white person, but that the assertion of the authority of the government to make an arrest is more important than the life of a black person. The suspicion of wrongful use of police firearms spilled over onto all shootings, whether they were justified or not; in the sixties and afterward, police shootings, as well as other acts of police violence, provoked enormously destructive rebellions. The discrimination in the shooting of unarmed persons deprived the old fleeing-felon rule of whatever legitimacy it might have had; instead of acting as an extreme deterrent to crime, it was likely to incite more violence. Under these circumstances, since the old rule apparently did not reduce crime or protect the lives of police or citizens, the chiefs saw that there was no remaining reason not to restrict the use of the gun to situations where there was virtually no alternative.[164] Furthermore, the figures suggest that the killings were numerous enough in the early seventies, as contrasted with what they had been earlier, that senior police officials may have been apprehensive about their ability to control the police shootings, not to mention the public reaction, if the figures were allowed to climb still higher; in New York, for example, the police killed eighty-seven people in 1971. The alternative was to find a way to regulate the shootings.

Both of the changes in police practices—the minimization of physical coercion in interrogations and the great drop in the use of deadly force—seem to me to be late products of the very long process of pacification and change in the consciousness of urban Americans, reflected in their institutions; unnecessary killings and tortures became offensive to the sensibilities of many. This was accompanied by an increasing interest in and commitment to equitable legal procedures; shootings and physical coercion are doubly disturbing because they fall especially on the poor. Although people in the United States have long been frustrated by how slow and technical the legal system is, and even though we know that a person who has money will get better counsel and ultimately a more complete hearing than a poor person, it continues to be important to us to have a residual sense that the system is open to all and does not discriminate on the basis of class or race. A poll conducted for the American Bar Association in 1994 found that most Americans believed that equal justice prevails in the courts only "some of the time," but a majority thought it could be achieved.[165] Even that qualified confidence is more than the criminal justice system enjoys in much of Latin America. Thus prosecutions of middle-class and rich people, however unusual, are important to the legitimacy of the system and provoke enormous public interest, among many other reasons, because people want to see whether the system can do justice in such cases.

Changes in police procedures were part of the "due process revolution" in criminal procedure, through which the courts tried to assure, among other things, that every accused person would get a chance to assert his or her rights to remain silent and to have counsel, and that the police would adhere to constitutional protections against searches and involuntary confessions. It is significant that the symbolic leader of the revolution was Earl Warren, who was originally thought to be an unlikely candidate for such a role because he had been a notoriously tough progressive reform prosecutor in California. The key for Warren, I suspect, is the identification "progressive reformer," which in his case as in many others marked a person who was incorruptible and also self-righteous, allowing his moral and anti-Left convictions to color his prosecutorial decisions. His staff made use of some of the police practices prevalent in the thirties, including incommunicado detentions and intimidation. But more important in his case, it seems, was his determination to free the prosecutor's office as well as the police from corruption and party influence. He came on the scene in California when it was still close to the vigilante past from which he tried to help it emerge. More than others, he knew the connection between corruption and violent police work, and he ultimately came down against the use of the third degree and for the assurance of due process, by way of the logic of his commitment to reform.[166] Having been an agent of the pacification of the cities in California, he became an agent of pacification of the country through the rule of law. The due process revolution, however, was in a sense too late politically. It was the work of those, like Warren, for whom the pacification of urban life was important; it actually occurred, however, with a time lag of some thirty years, after the sense of pacification had passed from much of the population. Thus the reversal of the revolution became a politically appealing project for conservatives after the sixties.

THE CONTINUING PROBLEM OF POLICE BRUTALITY IN THE UNITED STATES

The control of deadly force, like the control of interrogations, is still uneven in American cities; in Newark, New Jersey, for example, where rampant car theft provoked public fury in 1992, there is evidence that the police summarily shot car thieves in an effort to deter the crime.[167] The principal problem of police violence for the present day, however, is nondeadly force—beatings of civilians in the streets. One reason that reformers have been slow to come to grips with it is that it is difficult to isolate and easy to conceal. Torture usually occurs in a station house, as part of an investigation, so that it is often not quite so difficult to isolate, and it can be controlled partly through control of the trial process. A shooting is very difficult to conceal and often attracts a great deal of notice; it is true that an unjustifiable shooting may be claimed to be in self-defense, but that is always somewhat risky because it may require the cooperation of other people or the manufacture of evidence. In any case, the use of firearms can at least be detected and tracked by superiors, so that their oversight acts as a control. But less well-defined uses of force are more invisible; as everyone knows, the Rodney King beating became a scandal only because it was recorded on videotape by a chance witness, and even so, as the trial process revealed, the "excessiveness" of the force was somewhat ambiguous. If there had been no videotape, Rodney King would have been just another name on a long list of police complaints. Although the incidence of police brutality has very likely decreased in the twenty-five years since I wrote about it in New York City in *Police Power,* visible or not police abuses still occur frequently and police administrators still do not face up to all the problems presented by them.

Police violence in the street is easy to cover by criminal charges against the suspect, such as disturbing the peace and resisting arrest, which put the injured person on the defensive and automatically supply a motive to have manufactured a complaint against the policeman. I described the anatomy of these "cover charges" in detail in *Police Power,* but they should not have been a new discovery. The charges are a perennially successful device because the power to use force is a defining characteristic of the job and the line between excessive and justifiable force is difficult to draw; well back in the nineteenth century in New York, an inspector told Cornelius Willemse, "When you use your stick, always make a collar with it because you understand...you can always use force to overcome unlawful resistance. Don't forget that 'unlawful resistance' covers a multitude of sins." Furthermore, the code of silence, of backing up your fellow officer, is virtually ironclad, so that an officer can rely on his partner and others to substantiate the charge of unlawful resistance.[168] Those old lessons certainly are still being learned and followed in Los Angeles and New York, as well as in other cities.

Police lying is an endemic problem now in U.S. police departments, just as it was twenty-five years ago when I wrote that "police lying is the most pervasive of all abuses." In shootings, for example, police sometimes plant weapons to make it appear that the victim was armed; in a case that is perhaps unique in its revelation of duplicity, the federal courts found that in the city of Houston, Texas, in the 1970s, there was a practice of planting "throw-down" guns in the hands of persons who had been shot, that was so well known and widespread that the city was held legally responsible for it.[169]

The pattern of street abuses has changed little since *Police Power;* some people are beaten as a form of punishment when they are arrested for crimes that seem heinous to the police, but much of the abuse of violence arises out of defiance of the police. Police on the streets perceive themselves to be in a situation of potential danger, in which they must take control; some of them think that if they cannot get control any other way, they must use violence. Some police perceive the threat posed by defiance no differently than the threat of an assault; it is dangerous because the loss of control is dangerous. Although we may say, then, that the cover charge that makes up "contempt of cop" is as false as the testimony that buttresses it, for the police it has an emotional truth, because a person who defies the police seems to present a danger just as a criminal does.[170] Car chases, like the one that resulted in the beating of Rodney King, are extreme cases of defiance that actually are dangerous to the police and the public; they commonly result in an enraged reaction by the police.

Nevertheless it is clear that many acts of defiance against the police do not lead to use of violence; many police are much cooler than the rest of us in situations of anger and chaos. This raises the question as to how situations of defiance escalate into police brutality and how individual officers could avoid them. In studying the psychology of the use of force and how to control it, Hans Toch found, not surprisingly, that fear was the key; if officers were fearful in a situation and could not admit to themselves that they were afraid—thought they shouldn't be afraid—they tended to react with an anger that was difficult to control. Thus, those who could not admit their fears were most likely to use excessive violence.[171]

The control of police use of force is obstructed not only by the code of silence and lying about charges, but also by the corruption that persists in many cities. If fellow patrolmen or superior officers have something to hide, or if they suspect corruption and are afraid that investigation may reveal it, then they will be very cautious about inquiring into any sort of misconduct, for fear that some investigation may unravel a scandal that will involve everyone. That was one lesson of the Mollen Commission report of 1994 on corruption in New York City.

All the contemporary interlocked problems—excessive force, systematic lying, and corruption—have a common root in the conflicting demands made on police. Graft, particularly money taken in connection with vice crimes, persists because the public is hypocritical about morals offenses. While they do not want to say outright that these should not be crimes, they do want to go on indulging in those offenses; the result is that the police are sometimes paid off. The brutality and lies, as I pointed out in *Police Power,* also arise from conflicting demands. The police are asked to keep order and control pariah groups that the public fears; at the same time, the public wants to believe that the police act lawfully. One result is that the police harass those who are "out of order," and then try to make the actions look legal. And although there are periodic scandals about police brutality and corruption, on the whole the public is not too dissatisfied with their police. The authors of *Beyond 911* quote a Philadelphia police officer saying, "For the police force to be willing to do the job of 'shoveling shit,' they had to be allowed to sleep on the job, be rude, harass defendants, and extort bribes." In the eyes of the public, police work remains a tainted occupation.[172]

Hypocrisy and conflicting demands, operating in a semimilitary and anticrime framework, have shaped police culture. The police often have a "bunker mentality"; they are suspicious of outsiders and confident that they must protect their own interests because no one else will. They are secretive because they are confident that whatever they say will be used against them. In fact, until recently most departments, including New York, had a rule restricting members from "unnecessary conversation with the public." Thus they are highly regulated, with a complex of rules surrounding what every policeman does. Yet the discretion of individual officers and teams on the streets is and always has been enormous; the regulations cannot encompass the ways of dealing with the problems. Rank-and-file police are very nearly as suspicious of their superiors as they are of the public. The police have been increasingly losing contact with the public, through the military analogy, corruption, and abuse, for generations.[173] And it is out of this situation that the demand for more public accountability, discussed in the last chapter, has grown.

PATTERNS IN LATIN AMERICA AND THE CARIBBEAN

Although policing in Latin America and the Caribbean is as different from policing in the United States as the societies are different from one another, several patterns of urban police problems are recognizable throughout the Americas. All the six locations, north and south, have in common the urban problems of the New World, brought about by immigration, colonialism, social dislocation, and mobility. Clientelism, which interferes with citizen control of official abuses, is a perennial characteristic of politics, especially in Brazil, Jamaica, and Mexico. Where the voters are poor and politicians have often had control of such scarce resources as there are, relations with leaders have frequently taken the form of dependency—on the distribution of jobs and political favors, including, in some cases, jobs and promotions on the police force.

Thus politics in the most direct sense plays a role in the police. Police obtain preferment through political leaders, and in some cases, such as in Jamaica and Mexico, the leaders have expected support from the police against the opposition.

Corruption takes all its multifarious forms. When rackets are under the protection of officials, the police take the graft and distribute it throughout the political system. Alliance with the rackets leads to "hard crimes" such as kidnapping and drug dealing. The prevalence of corruption, combined with the increasing alienation of the police from the rest of society, contributes to impunity for all police misconduct, for hard crimes as well as the abuse of citizens in the station houses and on the streets. Detectives, who form police bodies separate from the preventive police in Mexico and Brazil, turn the process of criminal investigation into a racket in which they form alliances with criminals and extract payments from victims in exchange for returning their stolen property. That racket feeds into the coercion of suspects for information and thus directly into the use of torture.

The public fear of crime is widespread and growing, combined with an impatience with the criminal justice system that in some places amounts to disgust. Increasing numbers of people say that the courts and even the prisons do not deal harshly enough with criminals; prosecutors are accused of being lenient in pressing charges and recommending sentences, defense lawyers of having cases delayed or dismissed, courts of being slow and hypertechnical. Critics everywhere complain that only a small percentage of those arrested, even for what appear to be serious crimes, are sentenced to substantial incarceration. The impatience has resulted in a judgment, sometimes by police officials themselves, that the other actors in the criminal justice system—the lawyers and judges especially—have to get out of the way of the police.[174]

The mounting anger at the criminal justice system, combined with the military analogy for the police and the call for a "war on crime," makes an explosive brew of state power and vigilantism. Police may take it upon themselves to obtain evidence of crime by violent means and even to bypass the rest of the system and punish by violence in the streets. Following the logic of the military analogy, police units may be specially created to do the dirty work, while being insulated from criticism by their special status; we see such developments at least in Los Angeles, Buenos Aires, São Paulo, and Jamaica. The effects of the war on crime and impatience with the justice system reach their nadir when police as well as supposedly respectable citizens justify attacks on those who are merely marginal. In the most uncontrolled situations, the police may use violence, including deadly force, against the merest petty criminals and those who are poorest, in an effort to intimidate and deter crime and thus to create a semblance of order in an increasingly miserable population.

Such a version of the war on crime is a temptation for governments as well as for their citizens. On the one hand, it rallies support for the government through the common fear of crime; on the other, it creates an image of decisive action, simple to grasp, through vengeful violence. It deflects attention from complex social problems that are among the causes of crime and turns it to quieting peoples' fears, thus creating a sense of "order." It is a way of controlling all strata of society by concentrating on one set of problems that creates fear across the societal spectrum.

Yet everywhere, and especially in countries in transition to democracy, such policies are recognized to be risky. In all the places in this study, government officials, as well as citizens who think about the issue, know that the police have no legitimate power to bypass the justice system and punish summarily. Civil society has limited the legal powers of the police precisely because people mistrust and sometimes fear them. In city after city, it is clear that people know that they are asking those they fear to free them from the fear of crime. They sense the dilemma, and governmental officials are aware of it; thus officials, including the police, try to conceal arbitrary police violence, to assimilate it to the requirements of the law. The bunker mentality of the police is strengthened, the alienation of the police from the public is increased, and the cycle of demand for official accountability is set in motion.

CHAPTER V
São Paulo

INTRODUCTION: POLICE IN URBAN BRAZIL

Although Brazil occupies almost half the land mass of South America, it has a relatively small national police. Most of the police in Brazil are organized on a statewide rather than a national or municipal basis; thus, in a pattern that differs from the United States, the city of São Paulo, as distinguished from the state, has little control over the police. In the Brazilian states, the police are split functionally between the military police—the PM—who do the work of patrol and order keeping, performing service functions, making summary arrests, and stopping persons for questioning, and the civil police, who run the station houses and investigate crimes. The PM is under civilian control, although there has been a military impulse in their organization; for example, their ranks are divided into officers and lower ranks, and the two are separately trained.[175] The civil police appear, at least on paper, to be very well organized. Each station is run by a chief (*delegado*) who is expected to be a lawyer and has agents working under him. Much of the work of investigation, including interrogation, is nominally carried on as a function of the courts but actually by the civil police. In 1992, there were about 70,000 PMs in the state of São Paulo, of whom about 28,000 were working in the metropolitan area of the city; there were some 30,000 civil police, of which half were in the metropolitan area.[176]

During the military dictatorship that began in 1964 and lasted, with a gradual easing of repression toward the end, almost twenty years, the state police bodies were taken over by the armed forces. The civil police and the PM, which was formed out of earlier protomilitary units, were reshaped by the magnet of the military dictatorship, fighting both crime and subversion through torture and deadly force.

Although Brazilians were not permitted to vote directly for a national president until 1988, the dictatorship loosened its grip earlier at the state level. In 1982, some reform governors dedicated to eliminating the excesses of the dictatorship were elected, including André Franco Montoro in São Paulo. The torture and killing of political dissidents ceased, indeed had virtually ceased before the new administrations came into office, and has never revived. The Montoro administration went further, to try to eliminate the torture and shooting even of ordinary suspects. Those reforms were never popular with the police, and they turned out to be unpopular with much of the public as well; as the issue labelled "human rights" became highly politicized, the reform government lost out after one term, in 1986.

In succeeding years, São Paulo elected governors, such as Orestes Qúercia and Luiz Antonio Fleury, who dismissed many of the police reformers. The new administrations took an increasingly hard line on law enforcement, while at the same time they were surrounded by disaffected reformers and human rights advocates ready to criticize any increase in violence. These changes and continuities in the abuse of deadly force, mostly by the PM, and torture, mostly by the civil police, in the decade after the dictatorship and in the light of the past, are the subject of this chapter.

THE PROBLEM: CONTEMPORARY SÃO PAULO AND POLICE VIOLENCE

The distribution of income in Brazil is radically unequal and has become more so in recent years.[177] The regions of Brazil are also unequal in wealth, with the states of the north and northeast mired in poverty. By contrast, São Paulo is the economic giant of Brazil, producing almost half the national industrial product and acting as a magnet for the poor and landless from all over the nation, especially from the north and northeast. By 1990, metropolitan São Paulo was thought to have more than fifteen million people, the vast majority of them poor. During the 1980s with the burden of international debt and runaway inflation, the condition of the poor grew worse; the proportion of families whose economic circumstances were characterized by the government itself as "miserable" (as distinguished from merely poor) rose from 11 to 19 percent.[143]

The city is a sprawling place, spread out into many districts. In a fashionable section like the *Jardins*, near the center of town, stores and restaurants are located in elegant small buildings, formerly the townhouses of the wealthy, that have been redecorated in startling postmodern fashion. In the heart of town, where the shopping is not so fashionable, modern storefronts are put up on the facades of older buildings, with goods thrown into bins in the front, and street vendors working in front of them—hardly distinguishable from low-price districts in cities in the United States. In the *favelas*, people live in shacks of wood and roofing tin, often near noisome sewage ditches. Although there is a system of inexpensive public transportation, the air is always fogged with the exhaust of cars inching along the main arteries. This is the city, often very poor, but on the whole ordinary in appearance, that, together with its environs, is patrolled by twenty-eight thousand members of the PM, a group about the same size as the New York City police. Despite the relative modernity of São Paulo, its problems with police use of deadly force and torture are similar to those of many other Brazilian cities.[179]

During the decade before 1993, the PM killed an increasingly large number of suspects. (See chart on following page.) It is difficult to convey a sense of how astoundingly large these figures are; in 1992, more than four people a day were being killed. That figure for one year, as well as the smaller figure for 1991, represents more deaths than all the deaths and disappearances for partisan political reasons documented during the more than fifteen years of the dictatorship.

For public relations purposes, the PM claims that almost all the killings are legally justified as armed reactions to "shoot-outs" or other life-threatening confrontations.[180] Quite apart from the large number of interviews and studies that tell another story, more fully recounted in a moment, the data from the police themselves suggest that, in a large number of cases, their explanation is not correct. The number of persons killed is

CIVILIANS KILLED AND WOUNDED BY POLICE AND
POLICE KILLED, STATE OF SÃO PAULO, 1983–1992[181]

Year	Civilians Killed	Civilians Wounded	Police Killed
1983	328	109	45
1984	481	190	47
1985	585	291	34
1986	399	197	45
1987	305	147	40
1988	294	69	30
1989	532	n/a	32
1990	585	"	21
1991	1074	"	57
1992	1470	"	n/a
Metropolitan Area Only			
1991	898	251	21

so much larger than the number wounded as to suggest strongly that many of the killings were deliberate; a pattern of shootings in real confrontations would be expected to show a larger proportion of civilians injured in relation to those killed. Conversely, the number of police killed in such confrontations is undoubtedly inflated; the newspaper *Folha de S. Paulo* revealed in 1991 that 70 percent of the reported deaths of police occur in accidents or off duty. Thus the proportions show that in 1991 the police must have shot dozens of civilians for every policeman who was shot. According to official figures, moreover, there are between four thousand and five thousand homicides a year in the metropolitan area of São Paulo; thus the police account for at least 15 percent of them.[182]

It is nevertheless significant that the police continue to cling to the claim that substantially all the shootings are in self-defense. They owe at least that much allegiance to the rule of law; to admit that a large number of the shootings are of unarmed suspects would put the PM on a collision course with the formal system of justice and would be embarrassing for the government. When much of the public finally became convinced at the end of 1992 that the killings were not in self-defense, as we shall see, the change in public opinion did indeed cause difficulties for the São Paulo government.

During the same period—that is, after the dictatorship and throughout the eighties—the civil police routinely tortured suspects in the station houses. The extent of the mistreatment cannot be quantified even roughly, as can the killing by the PM, but it was in fact a more open policy. Reformist civil police officials complained to us during our first visit in 1987 about how widespread the practice was. The police used beatings with their fists and feet, electric shocks from the *pimentinha*, a device made from a telephone mechanism that can be cranked to increase the current, and especially the *pau de arara* (parrot's perch), the method of choice because it does not leave marks. On the parrot's perch, the victim is hung over a horizontal pole inserted behind his knees, head down, with his hands tied to his ankles; there he may be subjected to other tortures or just left to contemplate his sins until he has had enough. Guaracy Mingardi, a sociologist who spent the years 1985–87 working in the São Paulo civil police, reports that it was standard procedure to hang a suspect from the parrot's perch to see whether (or rather what) he would confess. He quotes a chief investigator breaking in new agents: "When you go to a district, you don't have to know the bums of the place. You can start with those the PM drags in every day. When you have a thief with a past, you give him the perch until he gives up some crimes. He names others, you grab them, give them the perch, and start all over."[183] A group of progressive judges told us in 1987 that there was truth in the common saying that "there is a parrot's perch in every station house in São Paulo."

VIOLENCE, THE LAW, AND CITIZENSHIP

São Paulo's citizens, squeezed by the economic crisis, are very concerned about the high level of crime in the city, even though the crime rate began to decline in the last part of the eighties; the homicide rate is lower than it is in many cities in the United

States.[184] It is not difficult to see why the police took a hard line in recent years on law enforcement; what is difficult to see is why the notion of a "hard line" included so much killing and torture, and why, after the end of a military dictatorship, that line was acceptable.

Brazilians have traditionally had very little faith in the equity and fairness of their justice system. Interviews and public opinion surveys are larded with striking condemnations, such as "In Brazil justice only functions to favor the rich," or, more simply, "It's a joke!"[185] The opinions of criminal lawyers I interviewed were more measured, but not in essence very different. They point out that a middle-class person, with property and roots in the community, will almost always be released while awaiting trial, even for a very serious crime, and that middle-class defendants, through one device or another, virtually never serve time in jail even if they are convicted. Similar discriminations against the poor are a subject of complaint in every modern system of criminal justice; in Brazil, however, they are widely perceived as making the system hopelessly inequitable.

Brazilians generally have relied less on the formal legal system than on personal relations and informal networks to solve their problems. A classic type in Brazilian sociology is the *homem cordial,* the man who acts from the heart, and for whom social relations are, like those of the family, patrimonial. In the family one is a full "person," enjoying important reciprocal and often hierarchical relations; outside it, one is merely an individual, an impersonal citizen no better or different from the next. Many Brazilians never ceased searching for patrimonial relations; thus political and economic life became personalized and clientelistic, and the powerful were expected to show their power by helping their friends and supporters. Conversely, vengeance could be as direct as personal support. As the sociologist Buarque de Holanda said, "enmity can be as cordial as friendship, because both of them rise from the heart, and come, thus, from the intimate, the familiar, the private."[186]

The effect on the notion of citizenship, which is in other polities a place for the political equalization of individuals, has been characteristic. Citizenship in Brazil, at least until recent years, tended to be hierarchized; there was an unspoken belief that some citizens were better than others. The anthropologist Roberto Kant de Lima tells the revealing story that when the government of Rio de Janeiro ordered the police to refer to every individual as *cidadão* and not to use derogatory terms, the press began a solemn dicussion about whether citizens are indeed all the same, and the police actually began a slowdown to reverse the order.[187] The tradition of hierarchy contributed to a political system in which voters followed particular leaders and were dependent upon them for favors—a system that was personal, and in which citizen participation was not encouraged. Corruption was encouraged, and violence was always possible as a way of maintaining the power of the boss.[188]

In this worldview, those who are low in the hierarchy, the poor, are different, more subject to the influence of evil, which may lead to crime; by the same token, education and reason may protect people from the temptation to crime. By a very slight extension, the educated are seen as radically different from the downtrodden; the citizenry is divided into *feras e doutores,* the wild and the cultivated.

Attitudes about the poor and uneducated are rooted in a history of mistreatment against the dispossessed. The civil police traditionally beat poor suspects in the station houses to force them to confess. The militias, which were predecessors of the PM and organized during the years of slavery to keep order in the streets, had always tried to control the poor by violence. In 1899, an Italian diplomat in São Paulo complained to his home office that the police were guilty of acts "insupportable in a civilized country...the old tradition of beating the slave has unfortunately not disappeared." As he saw it, what the São Paulo police did to the poor was what the authorities were ceasing to do, or at least doing less of, in Europe: punishing publicly, by physical means. In the first part of this century, the São Paulo police acted particularly harshly against striking workers and their organizers; it was characteristic of them, moreover, not to distinguish between workers, common criminals, and "vagabonds."[189]

Thus the conditions of police work that existed before 1964 created an atmosphere that was hospitable to the dictatorship, although, after gaining control of the police, the military regime pushed the repressive tendencies in law enforcement to extremes. Under the tutelage of the United States, for the purposes of the Cold War, the Brazilian military, having no external enemy, had been mobilized to fight the subversive "enemy within"—the left-wing radicals among its own citizens.[190] The PM was organized to fight the war against the domestic enemy in the form of common criminals as well as subversives; as they had for generations, they continued to lump together radicals and ordinary criminals as "undesirables." Crimes that the PM might commit in their work were to be judged in a new system of military justice. Special squads were formed, heavily armed and quick to react like military assault teams. The best-known in São Paulo was the ROTA, a few hundred policemen who called themselves an elite, wearing a special armband and beret, with the motto, "The ROTA is reserved for heroes." In the first nine months of 1981, near the end of the dictatorship, the ROTA shot 136 people and killed 129 of them. Civil policemen were recruited to torture political suspects; under the impunity of the dictatorship, they formed a death squad to eliminate suspects, criminal as well as political. It proved to be so murderous and corrupt that it was gradually eliminated, at least in its original form, before the dictatorship ended.[191]

The violations of human rights during the dictatorship, especially the tortures and murders, were particularly shocking in Brazil because they were visited on middle- and upper-class people, who had scarcely ever experienced them before. The abuses, moreover, were more severe—the tortures more ingenious, the executions more numerous—than they had been before. When the dictatorship ended, the violence largely passed from the political opponents of the regime. But the violence was not, as events turned out, to pass from the traditional targets of police work.

Law, Order, and Society in São Paulo After the Dictatorship

The experience of the dictatorship exposed the effects of Brazil's hierarchical traditions and brought home the importance of equal citizenship. It dragged into the open the conflict in Brazil between the ideal of the rights-bearing individual and the "person," with his net of influence and connections. As the dictatorship ended, the Catholic Church sought to strengthen the sense of shared humanity through human rights, while the newly formed Workers Party and reform administrations like that of Montoro in São Paulo sought to strengthen the sense of citizenship, especially among the poor. Montoro's ministers tried to improve the lot of prisoners and prevent them from being abused. In the civil police, they replaced the leadership at the top with *delegados* who hoped to increase efficiency and do away with corruption, and reformed its system of administrative discipline. In the PM, they tried to scatter the ROTA and dismiss the most violent members; more than eighteen hundred members of the PM were dismissed between 1983 and 1986.[192]

The police succeeded nevertheless in resisting fundamental change in the way they treated citizens. Torture continued in the station houses because, for the investigators in the civil police, it was an integral part of the entire investigative process. Under Brazilian procedure, which on paper is very restrictive of police discretion, the police are not authorized to arrest anyone for a crime except on the orders of a judge, or when the crime is in progress or immediately afterward (in flagrante). The police are, however, authorized to detain people to verify their identity; in fact, a large part of the work that the PM reports every year consists of such verifications. When suspects were detained for identification, the civil police, in turn, were not supposed to keep them for interrogation, although they did so with great frequency.[193] In 1987, we were told by disaffected members of the civil police that in serious cases, such as kidnappings, the suspect might be taken to a secret place of detention, left over from the dictatorship, to be interrogated.

This was the way that police investigators not only solved crimes, but made deals with suspects and victims; for the police, who were poorly paid, it was intertwined with a system of corruption. Civil policemen sometimes took a bribe to ease up on the torture of a suspect. After they obtained a confession, the investigators often took a bribe from the suspect to release him or reduce the charges, and a bribe from the victim, in property crimes, to return the proceeds. Yet the police never tortured middle-class people or anyone who was likely to have political connections, except in cases (such as a number of notorious kidnappings) when they were desperate for evidence. Middle-class people, when they were accused, would get a lawyer to negotiate with the police. As a policeman said to Mingardi, "The one who gets beaten is poor; the white collar doesn't get beaten, he makes a deal."[194]

Most of the civil police, then, systematically resisted the reforms early in the Montoro administration, because it was a matter of money for them as well as the accepted way of doing the job. In 1987, when I first visited São Paulo, some civil police reformers who had served under Montoro were infuriated by the widespread torture; they said that the practices made both criminals and police more violent and cruel. The disciplinary officer of the civil police, a long-time reformer, was reluctant to make such direct claims, although he did give us the figures of the number of charges of torture pending in his office:[195]

TORTURE CASES — DISCIPLINARY OFFICE OF THE CIVIL POLICE, SÃO PAULO				
	1983	1984	1985	1986	TOTAL 1983–86
New Cases Opened	45	48	67	64	224
Officers absolved	76	78	94	100	348
Officers guilty	37	46	74	61	218

These were by no means all the cases of torture; in many cases, victims were afraid or thought it useless to complain. As late as 1992, I found one of the civil police reformers sitting alone in a bare room at the top of the forbidding police headquarters in downtown São Paulo, isolated no doubt for fear that he might contaminate others with his uncompromising honesty. He delivered to me his final pronouncement that "a corrupt police is always violent."

Torture was used by the civil police for the most ordinary crimes, especially when poor people and property were involved. In August 1987, Jairo Fonseca, a well-known human rights and criminal lawyer, called us to his office to meet a suspect, a seventeen-year-old who had been working as a sales clerk in a large office. With his mother sitting by him, he told us how he and other youths had tried to steal some typewriters from the office and he had dropped his ID card as they ran away. The police caught him and beat him to confess and to name his accomplices. When he refused, they tied him in a chair, with his bare feet on the floor, wrapped exposed wires around his fingers, and cranked up a machine (to which the wires were attached) to increase the current running to him; his bare feet on the floor also increased the shock. He confessed. He showed us where the wires had gone around his fingers, but he said he was not going to accuse the policemen officially, because he had made a deal with them in return for being released in his mother's custody. Nonetheless, we thought it likely the story was true, partly because he did not deny the underlying crime to us, and partly because it would have been surprising for him to have invented the torture instrument described, the *pimentinha*. Jairo Fonseca told us that he himself had caught the police using the *pimentinha* in 1985, when two of his clients, brothers from a *favela*, were tortured with it in the central criminal investigative station in São Paulo; Jairo rushed to the station accompanied by a commercial television crew, burst into the room where the two had been mistreated, pulled open a cabinet that the brothers pointed out, and revealed the field-telephone mechanism while the cameras were running for the local news.

An underground ideology, straight out of the Old Regime, was used to justify the use of torture. Afanásio Jazadji, who ran a popular radio call-in program centered around crime, and who was elected a representative to the state legislature with the largest majority in the history of São Paulo, said that the police used torture only against the guilty; it was the job of a good policeman to know who was guilty and make him confess. Sometimes, he said, the policeman is not sure just what the criminal has done, but he beats him, just as a man beats his wife: he knows she has done something wrong, even though he may not be sure what it is. The important thing about torture, said Afanásio, is that it is the only way to get the truth. This view paralleled a suspicion on the part of some policemen that the "human rights" objection to torture was literally hypocritical; they believed that torture was used everywhere, that its use was inevitable, and that police work was impossible without it.[196]

In the trial of criminal cases in São Paulo, the use of confessions was considered routine and essential to the system; neither the police nor the judges had a better means of investigation. Some judges confided to lawyers that they thought the use of coercion to get confessions was justified, because otherwise the cases would not be solved.

In São Paulo in the eighties, where the social crisis was deepening, the traditional police were thus able to claim that the reforms were making them less effective in solving crimes. And Paulistanos were ready to give that claim a sympathetic hearing. The metropolitan region continued to grow rapidly, swollen by poor people, many of whom were black. The standard of living was dropping while economic inequality and the crime rate were increasing. The combination touched a nerve of racism and fear in Paulistanos. Those who could afford to do so isolated themselves from the poor in new neighborhoods, in high-rise buildings or behind high walls, often with remote-controlled gates and private security.[197]

But the fear and anger about crime was not restricted to those who could afford to segregate themselves from it. There were a great many people in São Paulo who were hard working and skilled, who indeed might work more than one job, and who were nevertheless very poor. There was a constant danger, fueled by the inflation rampant at the time, that they would be still further reduced, and that danger was only increased by the possibility of being the victim of a serious crime. People such as these, just as much as those who were better off, felt a consuming resentment against those who commit crimes.

No government had ever contained that spirit of revenge by obtaining a monopoly of force or by governing through respect for law. The informal institutions of security confronting Paulistanos are, like the civil police, arbitrary and intimidating. Vigilante justice by lynching was and still is common throughout Brazil, in the cities as well as in the countryside. In a study of 272 lynching incidents reported in major São Paulo newspapers from 1979 to 1988, the sociologist José de Souza Martins found that "[i]n the lynchings that occur in capital cities, the poor and working class demonstrate their will; they are their own judges—rendering decisions about the crimes to which they are subjected, demonstrating the importance to them of recovering a predictable system of formal justice."[198]

A great many people, including some public officials, express approval of lynching, and the police, although they sometimes rescue the victim, rarely make an attempt to arrest the perpetrators. They might run the risk of being lynched themselves, because the rage of the mob is partly against the officials of the state.

Vigilantism is slightly organized in the institution of gunmen hired at a small price by storekeepers and other businesses in the Brazilian cities to kill thieves and other petty criminals. Some state governments have struggled hard to control these gunmen; in 1988, Luiz Antonio Fleury, then the minister of public security, claimed that the São Paulo state government had eliminated them, and the government of Rio de Janeiro, where they are particularly common, has had a special prosecutor and investigators trying to control them for a decade. Nevertheless, this sort of vigilantism is still very common and receives widespread public support; in a poll taken by the national public-opinion agency in 1990, 30 percent of the population expressed support for the *justiceiros,* as they are called in São Paulo. These groups of gunmen are usually staffed or sponsored by off-duty police or former policemen, and they often threaten or kill witnesses against them; there is even a name for the elimination of such witnesses: "burning the records."[199]

As their name implies, the *justiceiros* make the claim, which many people accept, that theirs is a real system of justice, necessary because the government system has failed. After the government campaign against the *justiceiros* in São Paulo in the early eighties, the sociologist Heloisa Fernandez interviewed one of them, a former military policeman convicted of murder, who said:

> I preferred working in the slums. I preferred the outskirts, the poorest barrios. There are already a lot of police on the asphalt [i.e., the paved streets outside the *favela*—ed.]. It's the slum-dweller, the worker, who needs police, because the poor *aren't protected* at all.... The rich person, if he's robbed, is going to lose a little bit of what he has, but life goes on. But if somebody earns a pittance...no matter how little is stolen from him, that makes a big difference. I was class conscious. I went there to protect the slum-dwellers.[200]

Although this seems to be a self-serving statement—the *justiceiros,* after all, act on behalf of those who can pay—the *favelas* are indeed very poorly policed, and their residents have developed a parallel system to punish predators in their midst. Where a bandit who victimizes outsiders may be viewed as a hero, a bandit who preys on local people will be dealt with internally by lynching or by gunmen. The slum dwellers say, "If there are no police, the people have to act."[201]

In the last few years, in the face of the fear of crime, the use of private security guards for businesses and private homes has also been growing. This process, which is widespread in contemporary society, produces a special apprehension in Brazil. It is clearer to Brazilians than to people in the United States that the use of private security tends to cede the power to use violence to private industry.[202]

Vigilantism and other informal methods of resolving disputes, as well as private security, all partake of the general mistrust of the government system of law as inadequate and unfair. Confronted with such public attitudes, the promotion by the government of something called "human rights" created an explosive conflict between the hope for equality and the tradition of hierarchy. Many Paulistanos did not distinguish clearly between civil and political rights and the general array of social needs; to be underpaid, for example, was seen as a violation as much as being attacked by the police. While this commingling of rights and needs may have its good side in driving people to press for satisfaction of their needs, one of its effects in the short run is that rights are viewed, not as something automatic, shared by all, but instead as scarce, even maldistributed.[203] As part of a formal system of law, rights were viewed with suspicion, as special privileges—only in this case, they were thought of as privileges for criminals. Talk of rights produces on the part of many, including some civil police, an increased fury against the legal system. In July 1992, some teenagers reported to the human rights office of the São Paulo bar association that they had been arrested after one of them had brandished a gun at a bus conductor. Even though none of the boys arrested had the gun, the police beat them with a club to tell the location of the weapon. Along the length of the club were written the words: "human rights."[204]

The presence of violent crime, combined with the sense that the police not only do not control it but actually participate in it, and with the burden on citizens to use self-help to solve their problems, produces what one former member of the Montoro administration described to us as a "psychosis of fear"—a vengefulness and a conviction that lawful solutions are a waste of time. By playing on the fear of crime, vengefulness is directed at criminals instead of more powerful actors in society. Because of the public's frustration and rage at the threat of increasing poverty, those who commit crimes, or are even in the class of those who commit them, are increasingly dehumanized and even demonized. Afanásio Jazadji, the radio journalist who gave us the philosophy of torture, said in a broadcast in 1984:

We have to take these incorrigible prisoners, put them all up against the wall, and burn them with a flame thrower. Or throw a bomb in their midst, BOOM, the problem is over. They don't have family, they don't have anything, nothing bothers them, they just think about and do evil, and we should bother about them?... These bums (*vagabundos*), they are costing plenty, millions and millions a month; let's make hospitals, nurseries, orphanages, asylums, to give dignity to those who really deserve to have that dignity. Now, for this sort of person...person? To talk about a "person," we are insulting humankind.[205]

VIOLENCE IN THE MILITARY POLICE

It was in an atmosphere of such public feeling that the reform Montoro administration was turned out of office, replaced by ever more security-minded governors, notably Luiz Antonio Fleury in 1990. It was as secretary of public security—administering both police forces—in the previous administration that Fleury had optimistically announced in 1988 that *justiceiros* had been stamped out in São Paulo. The number of killings on duty by the PM began to rise dramatically after he became governor in 1990 (see statistics above), and it is apparent that there was an element of "delegated vigilantism" in the use of deadly force by the PM. Fleury's secretary of public security, Pedro Franco de Campos, vigorously defended the violence with a phrase that became famous or notorious, depending on one's politics. "In these cases," he said, speaking of police shootings, "the police must respond with force, and is not expected to give a rosebud to the *marginal*."[206] In the rhetoric of São Paulo law enforcement, that was an encouragement to the police to shoot; undoubtedly officials thought that to have the PM do the shooting was superior to having freelance vigilantes doing it. In August 1992, I heard a colonel high in the PM give an oblique but profound illustration drawn from a training talk for PM officials. He projected a transparency on a portable screen, showing the trademark mushroom cloud of a nuclear explosion, with a ghostly caricature of a "tough guy" face outlined in it. In the First World, he said, violence is technological, at a distance, abstracted from individuals, like the atomic explosion;

in the Third World, for example in Brazil, the violence comes through direct, personal contact, as in a stabbing with a knife. He did not need to spell out the implicit last step: that punishment, or even deterrence, should be direct, swift, and physical as well.

In 1991 and 1992, PM officials were claiming that eliminating criminals through shootings was the way to reduce crime and to show the public the police were efficient. In August 1991, I asked why they did not try to show their efficiency, for example, through the arrest rate. The arrest rate proves nothing, they replied, because the criminal justice system is so inefficient. They cited a state study from 1986 showing that the number of those arrested who were eventually incarcerated was extraordinarily small; as one colonel put it, crime was an occupation "without risk." The PM, furthermore, could scarcely affect the conviction rate, much less the rate of incarceration, because they did not process arrests; they were obliged to turn their suspects over to the civil police. The civil police, they charged, turned few of the the arrests into criminal cases, because of inefficiency and corruption. Thus the awkward division of the police job between civil and military police was used to explain the violent, summary style of the PM.

The conflict between the PM and the civil police is bitter. The PM claim that the civil police are corrupt, a charge that, as we have seen, has considerable substance; the civil police claim, in response, that the PM make poor-quality arrests and fail to collect evidence. It is impossible to resolve the relative responsibilities; the point is, rather, that the criminal justice system suffers. Although it is not clear how well the system as a whole performs, because the courts and prosecutors do not keep a record of the conviction rate, the sketchy evidence suggests that the rate is low.[207] Brazilian criminal procedure does not provide for plea bargaining or other informal dispositions of cases. Once a case is brought, furthermore, it can be disposed of only with the consent of the judge. The result, as a respected prosecutor told me, is that relatively minor cases require almost as much attention as major ones, and the courts are unable to dispose of cases rapidly.

In the nineties, the PM were bypassing the civil police and the courts to prove their own efficiency. In an interview with me in September 1992, a senior officer of the PM proudly claimed that the PM's policy of becoming more aggressive with criminals had been successful in reducing the crime rate. He showed me a chart, based on the first six months of 1992, as compared with the same period in 1991, to prove that general homicides were decreasing while killings by the police were on the rise, with these figures for metropolitan São Paulo:

	1991	1992
General homicides (per day)	9.2	7.6
Civilian deaths in confrontations with police (per day)	2.4	3.7

The chart showed that the PM were expected to kill almost half as many people as were killed in general civilian homicides. The point was that the PM were eliminating suspects, and the officer claimed that the policy was successful in reducing the homicide rate.

The policy could not be justified on the grounds that the PM would actually be killing murderers, rapists, or armed muggers, because those killed were for the most part the most peripheral of offenders, when they were criminals at all; PM officials told us in 1991 that they realized that for the most part it was not the violent criminals who were being shot. In 1992, Caco Barcellos, a TV journalist for the O Globo network, in his bestselling study of over four thousand killings by the PM over twenty years, found that the majority of those who could be identified had never had any contact with the criminal justice system at all before they were killed. Of the minority who had a criminal record, most of them were mixed up in theft, drug dealing, or the like; very few were connected to the violent crimes the public most fears, such as robbery or rape. The majority were colored (*negro e pardo,*) in a city where more than 70 percent of the population is white.[208]

The unstated standard behind the killings was roughly that

"a thief must die." As a prosecutor who had formerly worked in military justice explained it to me, "The PM believes he is allowed to kill when the person is poor, black, and a thief." The standard could be expanded to include anyone who was a *marginal*—a potential criminal or a person in the criminal class. The theory that lay behind the shootings as a means of reducing crime, if there was a theory, had to be that the killings would create a generalized sense of caution and fear of the police and would eliminate some of those who might go on to commit more serious crimes.

The effects can be seen in some of the rare cases where the acts of the police could actually be proved in military court, rather than just strongly suspected. In one case, the PM killed a youth, apparently because he was black and had a toy gun, which might have made him at least a potential thief.

Toy-Gun Case

On the evening of May 25, 1989, Márcio Moura da Silva, a black youth of seventeen, was walking with friends who were white. According to his acquaintances, Márcio, who had found a plastic toy gun, was lagging behind the others and examining the toy. Military policemen, who apparently saw Márcio with the gun, stopped and detained him. His friends, who were standing separate from him, saw him picked up and taken away.

The police took Márcio to a cemetery, where they put out a call that there was "an exchange of shots" at that location. A young PM lieutenant, who was not part of that command but happened to be nearby, upon hearing the call rushed to the cemetery, thinking there was an emergency. In the cemetery, the lieutenant heard four shots, ran toward the sound, and found a group of PMs standing around a corpse, the body of Márcio. The police explained "that at that time they tried to approach the individual next to the wall of the cemetery, he drew a gun and ran into the cemetery, when the shoot-out occurred." They showed the lieutenant the plastic gun, whereupon he asked how there could have been any shootout. He directed them to take the toy and explain the matter to their commander. He later learned that the policemen, thus warned, had presented to their commander a real .32-caliber pistol.

No residues of gunpowder were found on Márcio, and the young lieutenant testified against the accused policemen, who were found guilty and sentenced to twelve years.[209]

In many cases, people who behaved in a suspicious manner and defied the police by running away or driving away were shot. A PM official told me that a majority of PM shootings occurred after car chases, when the victim was finally stopped by the police. A car chase, as the police in every city know, is an act of defiance that endangers both the police and the public and tends to make the police angry, excited, and sometimes violent; in the United States, the driver runs a substantial risk of being roughed up. In São Paulo, the driver runs a substantial risk of being shot.

Even lesser acts of defiance could provoke the use of deadly force. In 1991, Eloi Pietá, a member of the state legislature, investigated the conduct of the PM in the periphery of metropolitan São Paulo, where the PM were apparently less punctilious about giving a legally valid explanation for what they had done than they were elsewhere in the area. A report of one of the encounters, filed by the PM with the civil police, reads:[210]

> A witness pointed out two youths who were supposed to have robbed a pedestrian. On being approached, they ran away. One was taken prisoner, the other dead. The prisoner was released as the victim of the supposed robbery was not identified.

And another:

> The military police had knowledge that individuals unknown had robbed or stolen some days before. In making investigations in the area, they encountered, days later, two unknown persons with characteristics and clothes similar to the thieves, who tried to flee; one of them was killed.

The flimsiness of the pretexts for shootings points, I suspect, to one reason why so many of the victims of police shootings are minors; they are afraid of the PM and sometimes have the bad judgment to bolt, when adults might stand still. Such was the case of Enéas da Silva, selected by human rights groups for special attention because it involved a teenager, although many similar cases might have been chosen.

Enéas da Silva Case

On October 14, 1989, at around 10:30 P.M., Enéas da Silva, black and sixteen years old, was looking at a pornographic magazine with several other boys. They were sitting on a water tank in their *favela* neighborhood when they saw a military police car approach. Scared of what might happen if they were caught with a magazine prohibited to those under the age of eighteen, Enéas and three of his friends ran away from the approaching car. The two policemen got out of the car and followed them with their revolvers drawn.

Enéas ran down an alley, until he was caught in a dead end. There he was surrounded by the policemen, who shot him several times. Enéas, according to his friends and neighbors, had never been seen carrying a weapon and at the time of the shooting was unarmed. One witness, a woman who lived in a shack near where the shooting occurred, testified that she was in bed when she heard someone yell, "Stop and put your hands up." She heard a voice say, "Don't shoot me, I'm not a bandit," and then heard approximately eight gun shots.

Several people in the *favela,* including Enéas's aunt, saw one of the policeman go to the car and use the radio. According to the PM, the officers reported "a shoot-out with outlaws (*marginais*)." The policeman ran back to the scene of the shooting, firing his gun in the air. Witnesses saw the two policemen drag Enéas's body from the back wall of the shack where he was shot, dump it at the opening of the alley, and go back to the dead end, firing their revolvers again. They left a .32-caliber revolver by Enéas's left hand.

After the radio message, another police car arrived and a policeman who got out of the car warned Enéas's aunt to get inside and mind her own business, pointing his pistol at her. According to witnesses, the police lifted up the back seat of the police car, threw Enéas's body in the back, lowered the seat and drove away. They took Enéas to the hospital, where he was pronounced dead.

Military justice prosecutors at first found this case difficult to solve, having little to go on except that the gun had been found by Enéas's left hand, while Enéas turned out to have been right-handed. Upon reinvestigation after the case became notorious, witnesses were interviewed and the officers were found guilty of homicide.[211]

One of the prosecutors told me that Enéas's was a "very common" type of case. It is common not only because the victim was a poor, black youth whose only crime was to run away, but also because the police followed their standard pro-cedures for covering themselves. They planted a weapon by the victim and had him taken to the hospital after he was already dead. Through these means, which critics of the PM have reported repeatedly, they suggested that they did not mean to kill the victim, and, not incidentally, effectively interfered with the forensic investigation of the scene of the shooting.[212]

The attitude of the rank and file of the PM to the abuse of deadly violence was not simple. The majority of the PM did not shoot people except those who offered violent resistance to the police, and many PMs opposed the aspects of the system which encouraged violence. In 1983, at the height of the Montoro reforms, there were protests by the enlisted men in the PM about its rigidity and violence. In 1991, I interviewed an officer in the PM who was opposed to the system. He explained what a great deal of other evidence has confirmed, that the wide-spread use of deadly force grew out of the military's "national security" policy of action against an internal enemy, which is translated now into paramilitary anticrime actions in the streets. Although the extreme example is the rapid-response unit, the ROTA, whose commander once spoke of it as "a state of the spirit," the same spirit—of violent action—is prevalent throughout the PM. Through the moral transmutation that permits criminal suspects and those who refuse to obey the police to be seen as an internal enemy, actions that are taken against such people are transformed into something heroic, provided that they are done as part of a PM's duties rather than for personal reasons. The rank and file are trained to think that violence against "criminal elements" is justified, even in cases where the victim is not actually armed.[213]

A PM major, formerly a commander in the ROTA, explained the thinking to Heloisa Fernandez:

> Heroic figures turned out to be those who always went out to events where there was shooting. The officer, the sergeant, the enlisted man came to have value when they...came out of the event *alive* and *injured*. Thus they set up a way of coming out injured because it looked good. It appeared in the headline: "The hero is *x*, and the hero is injured." That is what I call the system. They did not need to do away with the ROTA, but with the system that it used and others wanted to imitate.... The system encouraged the hunt for confrontations (*ocorrencias*). Sometimes, if it did not find them, it had to invent them....
>
> There is no way of measuring preventive policing. How are we going to measure the work of a battalion? It's not a liter, not a kilo, not a meter.... So, we are looking for something measurable to compare the battalions. For example, the ROTA killed *x*, the other battalions killed less than *x*....
>
> And that is what I call the system that feeds the thinking of the PM. The person has to risk death to be valued.... He wants his wife, parents, neighbors to see. He wants to be seen and praised.
>
> The point is, dangerous work does not just exist. The state of danger does not exist; it is we who make it.[214]

In short, the violence continued because the command of the PM glorified and rewarded those who were violent. A relatively small number of men accounted for most of the killing. For example, I was shown a file in which a lieutenant had been investigated in connection with twenty-two killings between 1989 and 1992; Gilson Lopes of the ROTA had participated in forty-four killings as of September 1992 and had risen to the rank of major, amid the constant praise of his evaluators.[215]

Some in the PM command made the violence difficult to resist. Disaffected enlisted men (*soldados*) from one of the PM battalions complained in an anonymous letter to the São Paulo bar association in April 1992, that the commander had formed a "uniformed extermination squad." He demanded killings, saying to new recruits, "See if you can give me at least one little knockover (*tombinho*) in your first day on the street to show you have heart," and granting five days' leave as reward for a killing.[216] As the resistance of the enlisted men indicates, this is no doubt an extreme case, but it is nevertheless part of life in the PM.

THE MEANING OF THE VIOLENCE

Politicians in São Paulo were always aware that a "tougher" policy of the sort that Luiz Antonio Fleury pursued, as secretary of public security and later as governor, was likely to bring about an enormous amount of violence. As early as 1983, Manoel Pedro Pimentel, a minister of security in Montoro's government, said that it was "ironic" that "[t]he same people who today accuse us of inertia, if we act, will accuse us tomorrow of killing. Because if a heavy force such as ROTA goes out, it is clear that it will kill."[217] Nevertheless it was also clear that a majority of the population was in favor, in an undefined way, of a tougher policy. When Fleury was questioned, in 1989, about some particularly suspicious police killings of people with no criminal records, instead of directly defending the police actions, he said that "what the population wants is that the police act boldly." It seems that he read the popular perception accurately; people know that the police are very violent, but they believe that some arbitrary violence is inevitable in the control of crime.

The São Paulo state administrations made the policy work, in part, by labelling those who were the victims of PM violence as "*marginais*"—the dispossessed, who have no influence. During the dictatorship, and for generations before, the police had acted against labor with violence. At the present time, however, they handle strikes with the greatest care; the PMs sent out to keep order at labor actions do not even carry firearms. Fleury carefully expressed his policy of separating "us" from "them" on an occasion in 1991 when the ROTA received a new supply of vehicles: "The philosphy is what we always try to teach. A police that may be the friend of the worker, the householder, and of students, but very hard in relation to bandits. For the bandits there is to be no mercy, no, and the ROTA is going to continue on this path, confronting criminality."[218]

The level of the police killing by the PM, as well as of the torture by the civil police, seems inexplicable except as a way of controlling the poor. It is true that the level of violence that prevailed in São Paulo in the late eighties and nineties could not be said to be necessary for the purpose; there are other cities with masses of poor people that have lower levels of violence. In this hierarchical and unequal society, nevertheless, the elites continued to rely on violence as they had traditionally done. There is no question that at least some of them recognized what they were doing; in 1983, when the secretary of public security in the reform Montoro administration reluctantly agreed to let the ROTA patrol again in the poor areas of the city, he said that he did so in part because he feared that the administration was "sitting on a powder keg" adding, "Poverty is not the cause of crime, or else all the poor would be criminals. But it is a factor and, insofar as this factor pushes those who do not have strong internal controls, they may give in and commit crimes." Thus the violence is a system of intimidation. At the end of the dictatorship, in 1982, the commander of the ROTA said, "We—ROTA—are the only thing that the criminals fear. And as the old saying goes, fear leads to respect, which is tranformed into admiration and leads to love."[219]

If it is a function of ordinary police work to reproduce and represent a social order, then the police work in São Paulo, the treatment of suspects in the station houses as well as the street violence by the PM, reproduces an order that is, and is expected to be, imposed by violence against the dispossessed and the poorest. While Governor Fleury tried to soften the effect by saying that the police would attack only bandits and would protect workers and students, there was evidence apart from the police killings of actions against the poor as a group. The PM engage in "blitzes," as they are called, in which they systematically sweep through an entire *favela*, searching houses indiscriminately for weapons or wanted persons; in an interview in August 1991, the governor's secretary of public security specifically justified the practice and said he meant to continue it.[220]

The hierarchical nature of the social order is reflected in the organization of the PM itself. Officers are trained in a special academy, separate from the lower ranks and isolated from the larger society as well. A teacher at the academy wrote in 1991, "Only through the bonds of coordination and subordination that characterize the...hierarchical power that is instrumental to public administration, is it possible to assure the harmony and efficiency of the adminstrative apparatus."[221] The lower ranks, most of whom have themselves been poor, experience the discipline from their superiors for minor infractions as severe and arbitrary. But the discipline does not teach that violence itself is subject to discipline; instead it teaches that violence is appropriate against those who are subordinate.

ACCOUNTABILITY AND IMPUNITY IN RIO DE JANEIRO AND SÃO PAULO

Despite the long traditions of hierarchy in social relations and the imposition of order by extralegal means, the desire for more equitable and participatory government is strong. In 1992, Brazilians impeached their president, Fernando Collor de Mello, specifically for crimes of corruption identified with discredited paternalistic politics. A drive for government accountability is always contesting with the old ways of resolving problems.

Control of Torture

The pressure for change in law enforcement was particularly powerful against the use of torture, as a symbol of the abuses of the dictatorship. It was slow to take effect; after the reform *delegados* of the civil police were driven from office in the Montoro administration, it seemed to me in 1987 that torture was so deeply rooted that it would never decrease substantially. But federal law and the actions of some local officials gradually changed the situation. In 1988, the new constitution declared torture a crime not subject to bail or executive clemency, and Brazil subsequently ratified the U.N. Convention against Torture and other Cruel, Inhuman or Degrading Treatment or Punishment.

The criminal procedure of Brazil has not dealt adequately with the problem of coerced confessions. Although the 1988 constitution guarantees a defendant's right to remain silent and to the aid of a lawyer, and excludes unlawfully obtained evidence from trials, the criminal procedure code not only does not exclude a confession made to the police, but it also provides that a defendant's refusal to answer questions may be used against him.[222] The rigidity of the procedures for investigation and trial, moreover, have reinforced the dependence on confessions for the solution of crimes. Because there is no plea bargaining, nor any provision for granting immunity in return for testimony, it is very difficult for the prosecutor or the judge to compromise cases. Thus there is little that the system can offer a defendant or a witness, once a case has begun. The bargaining is pushed back into the station house, before formal charges are filed in the case. This was a situation that could, and did, lead to pressure on the defendant to confess and to shape the case before it was given to the prosecutor and the judge; as we noted earlier, it also contributed to a lot of corruption in the station houses.

Despite these weaknesses, in recent years the criminal justice system worked hard to minimize the use of torture. By 1992, all my sources, including those who were most critical of the civil police, such as Guaracy Mingardi, thought that the incidence of torture in the São Paulo station houses had dropped. Relatively activist judge-inspectors (*juizes corregedores*) in São Paulo took advantage of a 1989 change in the criminal procedure law providing for temporary imprisonment for investigation up to five days, pursuant to a judge's order, to try to get control over interrogations. They required a simple request in writing, a physical examination of the prisoner at the beginning and end of the period, and they listened actively at all hours to complaints from prisoners. Prisoners arrested in the act and not for investigation were supposed to be presented to a judge within twenty-four hours. Cooperating with the judges, the attorney general established an office to investigate complaints of abuse of power by the civil police; when we studied it in 1992, the office was investigating the complaints, although it was not bringing many charges. These bureaucratic structures, combined with the constitutional protections and the threat of criminal sanctions, blended with a change of public attitudes through which torture ceased to be taken as the norm; in the public opinion poll concerning human rights taken in 1990, a large majority of the sample in São Paulo thought torture was a serious violation of rights.[223] By 1992, according to the disciplinary officer of the civil police, he no longer had dozens of complaints and proceedings pending for torture as he had had in 1987. Certainly there are cases in which torture is still used against poor suspects, those who are likely to be too intimidated to complain, or in property crimes, when the police want to find the culprit and recover the property. The judge-inspector in Osasco, a working-class town in the periphery of the city, described a case from 1992 that he had been able to authenticate. The victims recounted an interrogation in which they were suspended on the "parrot's perch" and then were further tortured by having electric shocks applied to them through wet cloths, which spreads the effect and makes it more difficult to detect after the fact. The judge heard complaints of the same pattern in three different cases of property crime, occurring in the same station house late at night, after it was supposedly closed. Upon being questioned, the station chief did not deny the practice, but tried to justify it. The difference from the old days is that the judge suspended the police involved and started legal proceedings against them.[224]

Control of Extrajudicial Killings

Until 1993, it was difficult to picture what form the control of deadly violence in São Paulo might take; it seemed that there was no important political actor that had any interest in control. The PM command is itself a potent social and political force standing in the way of external accountability for its abuses; Gov. Luiz Antonio Fleury was a product of the training academy for officers of the PM, where he had been educated before becoming a prosecutor.

In the English-speaking world, we would expect some attempt at control of official violence through the civil judiciary. In São Paulo, tort claims against the state for injuries and death by the PM indeed can be brought to the courts, but they have not been a major avenue of redress. Judges in the courts to which the claims are assigned told me in 1992 that they believed less than one hundred cases were filed each year for all types of police abuse. In death cases, the damages are usually small, consisting of a pension based on the expected earnings of the victim, and even at that, the state is slow to pay; the courts have the power to award larger damages, but they rarely do so. A human rights law office of the Catholic Church in São Paulo, the Centro Santo Dias, systematically brings such actions in all of its police abuse cases, but their work is a drop in the bucket; the lawyers have no illusions that their work acts as a deterrent to the shootings by the PM. In 1993, there were some signs of change; lawyers in the office of the state attorney general itself brought damage actions against the state on behalf of prisoners killed by the PM in a notorious 1992 massacre at the Casa de Detenção (house of detention), of which more in a moment. Still the courts were reluctant to grant substantial damages.

Administrative controls over the violence of the PM were negligible. There is a system of administrative discipline, but it is rarely used to dismiss policemen who have committed serious assaults; the records of the PM showed that five people were dismissed for the abuse of deadly force in 1990, a year when 585 civilians were killed.[225] Instead such offenses are usually presented as criminal matters in the military justice system, from which I selected the two cases I described in detail above, the toy-gun and Enéas da Silva cases. Those two cases are typical in some respects and exceptional in others—typical because the crimes are similar to many others reported in the newspapers and charged in the tribunal, and exceptional because the facts were established through a conviction. Military justice is funded and administered in such a way as to make it nearly impossible for the prosecution to win more than a few cases involving acts of violence. In the vast majority of cases, there are no independent witnesses who can say whether there was a shoot-out or not. And, again according to prosecutors, the police will often, if not usually, corroborate the claim of self-defense by producing a weapon, as they tried to do in the toy-gun and Enéas da Silva cases. As the PM has grown in size and the violence has increased, the military justice system has become more choked; although the number of new cases keeps increasing, the number of cases decided has actually dropped. As of the end of 1992, the system had fourteen thousand cases pending, in four trial sections, each with one prosecutor, or some thirty-five hundred cases for each prosecutor.[226] A homicide case sometimes lasts a decade, during which the accused policeman is usually retained on duty. A prosecutor reported to me that the officers on trial seem hardened to the killing; they joke about it and do not seem to think that they have done something wrong so much as that they have made a bureaucratic error.

The problems with military justice are epitomized in the work of Dra. Stella Kuhlmann Vieira—"Dra. Stella," as she is called—who had come back to Brazil after years of exile in France. She returned, she says, because she felt that there was little she could contribute to the world in France; to her it was, as she said, a "completed" society. But there was something she could do for Brazil, as a society still being formed; she found it in pressing for justice at the military tribunal, fighting delay and other sources of impunity. In strong cases, she asked for preventive detention against the accused, which results in a decision within ninety days, thus keeping the policemen out of the community and avoiding the usual delays; she used the device, for example, in the toy-gun case.

She found that military policemen will sometimes stop at

nothing to fight the prosecution. In one of her cases, dating back to 1983, two policemen, searching for thieves of car parts, ordered three youths to stop. When they failed to do so, the PM shot at them and hit Alexandre Camilo, ten years old, in the back, killing him. The police took the other youths into custody, and, with the aid of other PMs, tortured them to try to force them to testify that there had been a shoot-out. Fortunately, the youths were able to stick to their story, and, with the aid of the Centro Santo Dias, the two policemen were charged with homicide. In defense, the investigators from the battalion produced a gun supposedly taken from the boy, as well as a medical report showing that he had been injured in the front of his head. Ultimately, the prosecution had the body exhumed and found that the medical report had been falsified; Alexandre's spinal cord had been severed by a shot from behind. In 1992, nine years after the shooting, the killers were finally convicted of homicide.[227]

The obstructions can be even more direct. In 1992, Dra. Stella brought homicide charges against a PM, Daniel Viana, who had worked in his home neighborhood as a *justiceiro*, using his police pistol to kill a supposed thief; Viana was identified by threats he had made to the victim and by the fact that cartridges at the scene of the killing matched his weapon. That case led into an even more serious one, in which Viana was found to have been part of a kidnapping ring. After that case began, the prosecutor in charge of it, together with Dra. Stella and other justice officials, were followed by PM cars and by cars without license plates, receiving death threats both in person and by telephone. As this is written, one of the prosecutors has resigned from the military justice system.[228] The episode tells us that the police get serious about resisting accountability, and the stone heart of impunity is reached, when investigation finally touches on the corrupt connection between the police and crime. There is an echo of the old *delegado* sitting alone atop civil police headquarters who said, "A corrupt police is always violent."

The efforts at accountability and control in Rio de Janeiro

contrasted strikingly with São Paulo. In 1990, at the time that the hard-line government of Luiz Antonio Fleury was elected in São Paulo, the voters in Rio—somewhat more liberal—chose the veteran populist Leonel Brizola, who offered a program for reforming the police and strengthening the protections for human rights. The aims of the commander of the PM and the secretary of public security, both veteran human rights activists, were chiefly to change the attitudes and practices of the PM for the future, rather than to punish past violence through discipline. According to their thinking, violence had been so prevalent, and at the same time so difficult to prove on a case-by-case basis, that it was more useful to change the incentives than to accuse and try the perpetrators. The commander of the PM told us that he had not emphasized the dismissal of abusive police officers, but instead tried to rehabilitate them; he found that those who were dismissed too often wound up working with the vigilante killers. PMs were to be decentralized into community citizenship centers, which would offer social programs and even legal advocacy in addition to police services. In the fall of 1992, a program of education in human rights and social problems was being offered at the university to all police. The commander was establishing a council of ethics in each battalion to advise on problems of violence and corruption, together with a complaint committee that would deal with civilian complaints, with citizen participation. But as compared with São Paulo, his methods of discipline seemed to be relatively strong. According to his own account, he did not leave discipline to the military tribunal, but dismissed officers for serious crimes through administrative means. According to their records, the PM administratively dismissed fourteen policemen for homicide in 1991.

The underground resistance to the extraordinary reforms was correspondingly uncompromising. In 1991, a reformist major in the PM was gunned down after he criticised the work of an enlisted man in the street. The PM who killed him took his wallet to make the shooting look like a robbery, but fortunately a person standing nearby who knew the major was able to identify the killer.[229] The work of vigilante extermination groups, which has been much more widespread in Rio than in São Paulo, seemed to come to a crisis in 1993, when gunmen in civilian clothes killed eight teenagers sleeping in a square in the center of the city and another group later killed twenty-one victims in a *favela*. The killings raised a scandal throughout Brazil, provoking an investigation at the federal level as well as in Rio. The investigations revealed that the killers in both cases were mostly military policemen acting for motives of revenge—in the case of the teenagers, because some youths had supposedly attacked the wife of a policeman, and in the case in the *favela*, because four military policemen had been killed there. More important, the investigation revealed a network of police working in extermination groups and a "shadow administration" of police seeking to maintain connections to corrupt enterprises; it appeared that the four policemen killed in the *favela* had been trying to sell weapons and that negotiations had collapsed. Once again, violence and corruption worked together to preserve impunity and resist accountability for the police; the shadow administration was fighting the reforms by violence.[230]

In São Paulo as well, police violence finally provoked a crisis—not in reaction to official reforms, as in Rio, but in reaction to a crescendo in official violence, the massacre at the state Casa de Detenção in the fall of 1992. One of the many jobs of the PM in São Paulo has long been to put down prison rebellions. Since the underground philosophy of the PM holds that a principal job of the organization is to clear the city and state of thieves and criminal types, particularly when they defy official orders, it is easy to see that sending the PM against rebellious prisoners is an invitation to extrajudicial executions. That is exactly what has happened, with increasing carnage from year to year. Finally, in October 1992, at the Casa de Detenção, the PM, many of them from the special squads armed with automatic weapons, killed 111 prisoners, none of whom had a firearm. Even though 41 percent of the population in São Paulo expressed their approval of the assault and a state representative, a former captain in the ROTA, said that the police should have killed more, the massacre ultimately contributed to a national and international scandal that finally slowed down the killings by the PM in São Paulo.[231]

A number of different factors converged to create pressure on the PM. The military police investigation of the massacre claimed that it was unable to find who was responsible for the killings, and finally a commission from the federal Council for the Defense of the Human Person was forced to report officially that the prisoners had been summarily executed. Culminating years of complaints by international human rights groups, it was an embarrassing situation; lawyers for the families of the dead made a complaint to the Inter-American Commission on Human Rights at the Organization of American States. The massacre came hard on the heels of the publication of Caco Barcellos's best-selling *Rota 66: a história da polícia que mata* (Rota 66: the history of the police who kill), which focussed attention on the flimsiness of the argument that the shootings were eliminating "criminals," by showing that most of the victims did not appear to be criminals at all. Perhaps worst of all for the PM, a constitutional convention was looming, including a proposal to have the military police tried for their crimes in the ordinary courts of justice, instead of their own military system.

In 1993, the official count of the number of killings by the PM dropped to 409, according to the state government—still a huge number, but only about a third of the 1992 total.[232] The police claimed that they were trying to get closer to the community, being trained in human rights, and being sent to psychological counseling; sergeants in the ROTA were transferred and "community policing" became a byword as it was in Rio.

The drop in the violence relieved the pressure from the federal government and the international community on the PM and the state administration, but it proved little, finally, except that police commanders can reduce the killing if they choose. There is still no institutional control to prevent the violence from rising again. As if to prove it, the week after the massacre in the Casa de Detenção, Caco Barcellos received word from important politicians that the PM was "preparing something for him"; he departed for a quiet stint reporting for the *O Globo* television network in New York. The proposal to have the military police tried for crimes in the ordinary courts of justice was finally rejected.[233]

Nonetheless, the international and federal intervention did dampen the abuse of deadly force. It is not hard to see why the Brazilian federal government would be concerned to put some controls on police violence; human rights, after all, was a source of legitimacy for the democratic transition government. Politicians had been elected, as well as defeated, over issues of human rights. Moreover, opinion polls and interviews showed that the public was aware of and frightened of the arbitrary violence of the police; in the 1990 poll in São Paulo, more than 80 percent of those interviewed said that they believed that the police arrest and kill innocent persons. Under such circumstances, the presence of the police increases, rather than alleviates, the sense of insecurity; the widespread approval of violence against "criminals" is rather like a desperate gesture, approving vigilantism because there seems to be no alternative. That state of mind cannot contribute to the legitimacy of the government; the federal government seemed to realize at least faintly that, in a society such as democratic Brazil, arbitrary violence cannot promise order.

CHAPTER VI

Buenos Aires:
City and Province

The police tend to look for easy ways to fight crime. During the military regime it was torture. Later it was trigger-happiness and the pretense of confrontation. Why did this happen? The police felt protected during the military regime because repression was permitted. Then, with the coming of democracy, the police grew inactive. Today in police circles there is a sense that crime must be combatted by very tough methods, not strictly within the confines of the law....

Today the police feel that they can go back to acting in those old ways. They have reverted from inaction to the pattern of tough action, which seems to come more easily to them. And this is happening in a context in which society is perhaps moving toward conservative positions; the death penalty and other repressive measures are being discussed.

I don't know whether the police are taught to be trigger-happy, but in the face of crime, no doubt what comes most easily is arrogance. It is like an anticipatory penalty that the police give the criminal. Faced with a criminal, the police think, "I'll punish you just in case the judges don't." They believe that they will avoid the risk, for example, that they will be charged with illegal coercion. For its part, the institution does not reproach them at all. Often, it rewards them when they kill a criminal in a confrontation. The need to make "good" statistics is part of the problem.

But I have to make clear that not all police set out to kill people. Even if a policeman kills a presumed criminal in a presumed confrontation, he still has a problem with the courts. Furthermore, a policeman can be charged for not getting a search warrant or for detaining a person longer than is appropriate.

In addition, I believe that the esprit de corps of the security forces is weakened. In order to protect one another and to preserve the public image, they hide serious crimes of corruption, like bribes in the streets, assaults and kidnappings. They are hardly ever indicted.

— GUILLERMO LEDESMA[234]

INTRODUCTION: POLICE, SOCIETY, AND AUTHORITARIANISM IN BUENOS AIRES

Scandal about violence and crime by the police is always simmering in Buenos Aires; for many Argentinians who suffered under the last dictatorship, exposure or impunity for official violence is a barometer of the success or failure of democratic government. At the end of 1991, when the scandal boiled over following the discovery of a police kidnapping ring, the newspaper *Clarín* asked for some informal thoughts about the police from Guillermo Ledesma, a distinguished jurist who had been one of the judges at the trials of the discredited commanders of the dictatorship. He gave the unsparing comments that are the epigraph to this chapter. The thread of those remarks is strong enough to enable us to interpret much of the recent history of the Buenos Aires police, both in the city and the province.

Judge Ledesma's sketch could be read to describe police problems in São Paulo as well as Buenos Aires; and indeed there are parallels between the situations of the two cities, although, as I·shall show, the problems are not as daunting in Buenos Aires. Both are huge metropolitan regions in the southern cone of South America, in countries that emerged in the mid-eighties from long military dictatorships; Argentina's was the bloodier repression, in which thousands were tortured and "disappeared." Both countries have been making the transition to democracy in the past decade, although torture and extrajudicial killings have been used by police forces in Buenos Aires, as in São Paulo, since the end of the dictatorships.

Argentina has had a weak democratic tradition. The Radical Party, which spearheaded the move to universal male suffrage in the first quarter of this century, never seriously challenged the underlying hegemony of the landed oligarchy. At the onset of the Great Depression, in 1930, the Radicals were cast aside in a military coup, which stunted the growth of constitutional government in the country. There was a succession of elected governments and dictatorships in the following fifty years, frequently marred by corruption, culminating in the long "Process of National Reorganization" (*Proceso*) from 1976 to 1983, in which the military and its allies tried systematically to tear the shallow liberal tradition up by the roots. The *Proceso* collapsed following the defeat of the Argentine army in the war with Great Britain over the Malvinas (Falkland) Islands.

In Argentina the problem of poverty is not so great as it is in Brazil, and conditions are, relatively, even better in Buenos Aires. People are politically mobilized, with a high literacy rate, and party organization is relatively strong. Even though many owe allegiance to a repressive and corporatist political past, thousands of others recognize the importance of democracy and the rule of law.

The government led by Raúl Alfonsín following the *Proceso* was the first Latin American government that was able to convict and jail any of the former dictators for their crimes against human rights, even though most of those condemned were ultimately released for political reasons, much to the disgust of Argentinians who wanted to call them to account. Impunity and its obverse, accountability, for contemporary police abuses as well as the crimes of the *Proceso,* has become a touchstone of political discourse for Argentinians committed to democracy.

Argentina was a rich nation at the beginning of this century, but is now still an underdeveloped one. The landed elite was frightened of and opposed to industrialization, with the attendant formation of a working class, and modern development has never fully taken off. Industrialization during World War II and the corporatist policies of the Perón era in the forties and fifties did develop a strong and organized working class while industrialization was largely protected from foreign competition. When the protection passed, some of the industries were unable to compete successfully, and many members of the landed elites did not want to see them succeed. During the *Proceso* there was a policy of deindustrialization, in which the size of the working class actually shrank by a quarter and a large informal economic sector grew up, similar to that in many other countries, such as Brazil. For decades, then, less fortunate Argentinians have faced a prospect of increasing economic depression that threatens a loss of status.[235] It has always been tempting to look for simple and forceful remedies for the long economic malaise.

The city itself is not so large, with a population of perhaps three million, but it is only a fraction of the Buenos Aires metropolitan area, which is home to more than twelve million people. The city is the jewel of the society, the capital of the country, and one of the most elegant cities of Latin America; although the sidewalks are often cracked and the services slow, there are still hundreds of blocks of luxury stores and handsome old houses like those in the European capitals generations ago. Surrounding the capital are some rich suburbs as well as enormous *conurbanos,* some of them working-class cities like Quilmes, and some of them no more than *villas de miseria,* shantytowns.[236]

The province is governed separately from the federal capital at its center, a situation that gives rise to a division of authority in the police for the metropolitan area as a whole. The capital is policed by the federal force, who number some twenty-eight thousand, while the province as a whole has a separate police, numbering thirty-five thousand; while I have not been able to find out the number of each force that is assigned to the capital or to the metropolitan region, it is clear that there is a more concentrated police presence in the capital than in the province. The administration of the forces, federal and provincial, is structurally similar; each is managed by a chief, who functions under a minister appointed by the president or the governor. Although each force is unitary—it does both investigative and preventive work—its structure is hierarchical. Each has a body of ranking officers, who are the administrative officials of the force, recruited and trained separately from the subofficers and agents, who do the work of patrol and investigation. The pay is low at all levels; in 1991, we were told that a policeman at the first level was paid about U.S.$300 a month, while a *comisario,* a station chief, received a little over U.S.$800 a month.[237]

A series of coups has been attempted against the national government in the last decade, and an atmosphere of menace prevails for journalists and others who try to expose official corruption and violence. Despite that atmosphere, extralegal violence, either as common crime or as vigilantism, is much less prevalent in metropolitan Buenos Aires than it is in São Paulo. Thus the continued police violence in Buenos Aires, as in other places in Argentina, is a political puzzle that accompanies the economic puzzle of the continued underdevelopment.

The history of police brutality in Argentina is well documented, a tribute to the tradition of critical journalism in the country. The historian Ricardo Rodríguez Molas traces the use of torture in the twentieth century to the onset of the modern dictatorships in 1930. And in 1968 the radical journalist Rodolfo Walsh was able to describe ironically a pattern of the use of deadly force that is still recognizable in contemporary Buenos Aires: "None of the experts consulted has been able to give a satisfactory explanation for the efficiency of the provincial police [in killing ten suspects for every policeman shot], but three hypotheses are offered: a) the use of automatic weapons in every encounter; b) the order to shoot at anyone unknown or suspect who flees; c) the simple execution of captured gunmen."[238] Police violence in Buenos Aires is not simply a hangover from the *Proceso,* as Judge Ledesma suggests, but instead shares with the dictatorship common roots in an old authoritarian tradition, derived from political ideas that predate modern practice in criminal justice. The nationalist ideology in Argentina opposed rationalism and liberalism as secular creations of the Enlightenment, and idealized authority as it was before the destruction of the Old Regime in Europe. The nationalists glorified the military as the best of citizens, lauded its "civilizing mission," and urged the armed forces to watch the "internal front" against indigenous radicals. Although, in its pure form, the nationalist ideology never had, and was not intended to have, a mass appeal in Argentina, it had a strong attraction for some of the powerful, including many in the military. It encouraged police practices that were antiliberal, rooted in the power of authority, even terror, rather than law; the tough, even the rogue, police were glorified. The ne'er-do-well son of Leopoldo Lugones, a preeminent nationalist writer of Argentina, became the head of a notoriously cruel secret police after the military coup of 1930.

Arguments in favor of arming for national security against the enemy within, promoted by the United States in the 1960s, fell on fertile ground in the Argentinian armed forces. The *Proceso* was triggered in 1976 by the election of a leftist government, but it rapidly expanded into a war for authoritarian hierarchy and against liberalism. One of the reasons that the *Proceso* killed so many was no doubt that its program was to destroy the social and ideological bases for modern political life. The police were recruited into the *Proceso*, to use for political purposes the methods, including torture, that they had used in law enforcement for decades. In some cases the connection to the older authoritarian tradition was obvious; when Miguel Etchecolatz, a tough *comisario* who served as right-hand man to the provincial chief of police during the dictatorship, was later convicted for his responsibility in dozens of cases of torture, he denounced the new democratic regime as "an Argentina without God."[239]

When the dictatorship was swept away by the debacle in the Malvinas Islands in 1982, the perennial Argentine economic insecurity remained and deepened. In 1989, the Alfonsín government disintegrated in the face of its inability to guide the economy. The level of unemployment has been very high, and the brakes put on inflation by the Menem government in the nineties produced high prices for durable goods. Economic inequality increased, and wages were often so low that people, including policemen, often had to work two or even three jobs to make a living. Crime apparently did rise during the eighties, and there was a strong sense of anger and vengefulness against criminals. The sale of private weapons and the use of private security by the well-to-do was increasing. The physical insecurity of Argentinians in the face of crime was virtually assumed by the media.[240] Many in Buenos Aires, accustomed to the idea that order must be imposed directly, by force, were not surprised that the police went on disciplining the poor and troublesome by shooting and coercion.

TORTURE

Some were indignant at the idea that the police might not be as tough as they had been. In 1985, in a letter to the editor of the newspaper *La Nación,* a reader complained that she had been robbed in her home, and that, while the police had caught the robbers, they had recovered very little of her property. She went on to say, "From so much time spent in police stations I learned that, however much the minister of the interior meets with police officials to counsel them, the obsessive respect of this government for human rights prevents the police from dealing with criminals with rigor, to avoid charges of illegal physical or moral pressure."[241]

Although the police might pretend to a citizen, as an excuse for not being able to recover stolen property, that the government's human rights policy tied their hands, it was clear after 1983 that torture was still being used in the station houses, mainly in crimes that involved property or produced public indignation, like the robbery described in the letter to the editor. The terrifying methods identified with the dictatorship—electric shock and even burns to the skin—were still used, although apparently not as often as in the past. In the nineties we heard and read in the newspapers constant reports of beatings and the use of the "dry submarine"—a plastic bag placed over the head until the prisoner nearly asphyxiates. In 1991, the Dirección Nacional de Derechos Humanos at the Ministry of the Interior reported 698 complaints of illegal coercion (a euphemism for torture) made to the courts from 1984 through 1986. Medical evidence corroborating the fact of injuries was found in 267 cases; of these, ten showed evidence of electric shock. No convictions were reported. A later report for the years 1987–89 did not yield much better results.

While some Argentinians took torture as routine, it was at the same time so much the symbol of the *Proceso* that stamping it out was of primary political importance to the newly democratic administration of Alfonsín in 1983; as in Brazil, human rights were a source of legitimacy for the government as well as a bone of contention. New legislation ratified the U.N. Convention against Torture and made torture a serious felony under Argentine law. The Alfonsín administration also sought to change characteristics of criminal procedure that were thought to encourage police coercion of suspects. In 1987, the Congress amended the federal code of criminal procedure to provide not only that a prisoner's statement had to be taken before an investigative judge, but, more extraordinarily, that a confession made to the police "shall be devoid of evidentiary value and shall not be used at the trial."[242]

Almost all our sources agreed that the 1987 laws were successful in decreasing the use of violent coercion, but even police sources agreed that the problem continued. It was difficult for the police to change the habits of a lifetime; besides, they could hope that suspects might be too frightened or think it useless to repudiate before a judge a confession made to the police. Torture, furthermore, as the author of the 1985 letter to *La Nación* well knew, is a way of finding the proceeds of a property crime, regardless of the confession's admissibility at trial. And torture does not have information as its sole aim; it is also a way of punishing and degrading suspects. Thus it is used especially against the poor and anonymous.

One of the torture cases that arose after the procedural reforms of 1987 assumed special symbolic importance because it was also one of the rare cases of a person's "disappearance" in the hands of the police after the end of the dictatorship. In September 1990, Andrés Nuñez was picked up in the city of La Plata by the Buenos Aires provincial police, who were investigating a minor theft. Prisoners in the police station heard his screams and even saw the lights dim with each application of the electric shocks; subsequently, the witnesses said that the police became agitated and fearful about something that had happened in the station. Nuñez was never seen again, and for years the police stonewalled the criminal investigation of his disappearance, claiming that he had never been in the station. Finally, in 1994, under pressure from the legislature, the trial got under way against policemen in the unit, many of whom were by that time fugitives.[243]

In an effort to put a stop to torture, reformers in the national legislature continued to narrow the discretion of the police. Overriding President Menem's veto, they voted in 1991 to limit the time a person could be detained for purposes of identification and without charges to ten hours, reduced from the traditional twenty-four. Finally, the legislature went still further, passing a sweeping reform that prohibited the police from questioning a suspect, except to establish his identity, and required the police to inform him of his right to counsel and to remain silent.[244]

ABUSE OF DEADLY FORCE

The Buenos Aires press, voracious for copy, reports police killings regularly. As in other urban areas in the Americas, the police claim that the killings are in self-defense, an explanation that is always viewed with suspicion by the public and the press. In some cases, as Guillermo Ledesma makes clear, the police excuse is a cover for extrajudicial killings of poor people. Such shootings occur, just as in São Paulo, when people defy the police, particularly when suspects are caught after a car chase. And sometimes the police outright assert their power to get rid of troublemakers and thus to control others.

Case in José C. Paz

On the afternoon of January 8, 1988, a workman complained at the provincial police station that he had been attacked by four youths, who had escaped in a Ford Taurus. A mobile police unit pursued and finally caught the Ford on the dirt roads in José C. Paz, a poor district outside the capital. According to the initial police reports, all four youths, ranging in age from eighteen to twenty, were killed in a shoot-out in which the police used automatic weapons.

Eyewitnesses later said that there had been no shoot-out, but that the police had planted a weapon and had even fired a shot into their own vehicle to create the illusion. Forensic investigation showed that many of the police shots had been fired point-blank at the youths. The police were charged with murder by the investigating magistrate, who said: "The police car stopped three meters from the Taurus; when the four occupants of the vehicle started to get out of it with their hands behind their heads, complying with the police order, the police pushed them back into the interior of the car and shot them."[245]

Gonzalo Herlán Case

In February 1987, Gonzalo Herlán, twenty years old, was killed in the city. Five years later, the courts finally determined that the federal police had murdered him.

According to his mother, Gonzalo Herlán had begun to take drugs during his teens. Finally, with his own consent, he received treatment; but when he was released, his family thought he was still in bad shape. He was accused of an attempted robbery, and he was again detained in his local police station at the beginning of February 1987, for being drunk. His mother remembers him telling her that the policeman in charge had said to him: "Drunk, drug addict! Aren't you ashamed, you bum, that your parents have to keep supporting you? While your father is busting his tail to support you, shit bum, and your mother is screwing the boss to give you something to eat." Gonzalo said that he grabbed a stick to hit the policeman, but the police threw him out of the station, warning him to get out of the neighborhood. When his father went to the station, the police renewed the warning that the young man should get out of the district. Frightened, Gonzalo visited the magistrate in his own criminal case, to ask him for protection.

On the night he was killed, Gonzalo was taking a walk with a friend. They were stopped by the police from the local station; the friend ran, but Gonzalo was caught. His body was found with ten bullet wounds, some at very close range; a .22-caliber pistol lay near his hand. The police claimed that he had been killed in a shoot-out with three policemen.

Witnesses had seen Gonzalo Herlán arrested and securely in the custody of the police the same night, before he was shot. When his body was found, no residue of powder could be detected on his hands, and he was wearing clean shoes, although the shoot-out had supposedly taken place in a muddy lot on a rainy night. The case against the police was at first dismissed, but on appeal the charges were reinstated and the police found guilty. By that time, the policemen, who had been at liberty, were fugitives from justice.[246]

Control by violent repression seems to have been policy in the eighties in some districts, where police shootings were particularly frequent; changes in management made the repressive policy clear. Comisaría 42 in the city of Buenos Aires had sixteen police killings in the year between July 1985 and June 1986, and six in the following three years after its *comisario* was transferred. Similarly, Lanús, a poor *conurbano* outside the city, had ninety-one killings in twenty-one months, before Lanús's tough *comisario* was eliminated in 1987, and forty-one (still a large number) in the next three years. A glimpse of life under the police in Lanús comes from Ingeniero Budge, a poverty-stricken district within Lanús that gave rise to the most notorious police homicide prosecution in recent years.

Ingeniero Budge Case

Juan Balmaceda was the self-appointed police "boss" of a neighborhood within Ingeniero Budge. He made deals to protect merchants and sometimes referred to local youths contemptuously as *negros delincuentes*. In May 1987, two local workmen had a running quarrel with the owner of a bar and may even have threatened him with a gun; the barkeep appealed to Balmaceda for help. When Balmaceda and other policemen found the two workmen with a third man, they shot all three. The police produced weapons that they claimed the victims had carried, but one of the guns, at least, came from another case, and many witnesses testified that the killing was an assassination. The case assumed the aspect of a test of the impunity of the police; the Ingeniero Budge community came together, with its lawyers, to organize the case and protect the witnesses. After a trial and appeals, the police were found guilty of murder in 1991.[247]

For Argentinians, these police shooting cases are political dramas about the three-way conflict among crime, law, and arbitrary authority. For many, the shootings are justifiable in the war on crime even if they are not really done in self-defense; for others, every investigation of a police shooting is a litmus test of the impunity of official violence.

Yet the dimensions of the problem of abuse of deadly force are not clear. The police, in the provincial as well as the federal system, do not release figures on the number of people killed, either by the police or by anyone else; a reliable count even of homicides in the general population is hard to come by. The Centro de Estudios Legales y Sociales (CELS), organized to resist the dictatorship and accustomed to government recalcitrance, made its own count by laboriously clipping the news stories of police killings over many years. And in 1991 the Dirección Nacional de Derechos Humanos at last collected some figures, culled from the morgue, for all homicides in the federal capital, including deaths in traffic accidents, during the years 1988–90. Finally, in 1992, the Ministry of Justice made a count of intentional homicides in the capital in the previous two years. The resulting comparisons of police homicides reported in the press with other homicides are these: [248]

	CIVILIAN DEATHS IN POLICE ACTIONS		HOMICIDES, ALL TYPES	INTENTIONAL HOMICIDES
	Capital	Province	Capital	Capital
1986	79	148	n/a	n/a
1987	33	102	n/a	n/a
1988	41	92	272	n/a
1989	41	72	329	n/a
1990	36	48	241	47
1991		83*	n/a	85

*This figure is for the Buenos Aires metropolitan area.

The number of police killings in Buenos Aires may not seem large to a reader jaded by the statistics of the hundreds killed in São Paulo. Nevertheless, the comparison with the general level of homicides is startling. Although the figures are suggestive at best, the data indicate that the police accounted for more than 10 percent of all homicides, including accidental homicides, during some of these years and that, if we look only at intentional homicides in the federal capital in 1990, the police accounted for a very large percentage.

The level of official violence, and its extreme arbitrariness, is dismaying in light of the fact that, by the standards of urban areas in the Americas, as reflected in the general homicide statistics, the capital or city of Buenos Aires does not seem to be a notably violent place. The use of self-defense by citizens against assailants is rising, but there does not seem to be a widespread problem of vigilantism in the form of lynching or gang attacks against suspects in ordinary crimes. CELS conducted a public opinion study in the metropolitan region in 1992 and found that 66 percent thought that life in the city was at least "more or less secure." Indeed, official statistics showed that crime had been dropping generally in Argentina since 1989.[249]

The sketchy figures renew the puzzle: Why do the extrajudicial killings continue? They do not seem to be the mirror image of private vengeance nor a direct response to urban violence. Is the killing just an old habit of the police, carried forward in an increasingly conservative world, as Guillermo Ledesma suggests? It is that, but it is more as well. The reasons for the continuing police abuses emerge from the failure of the government to call the police to account.

ACCOUNTABILITY AND IMPUNITY

There are several sources of accountability for the police in Argentina, including administrative sanctions or internal management controls by the police and criminal prosecution and civil liability before the courts.

The police have not disciplined their members by any system that would inspire a sense that the police are accountable. The methods of discipline continue to be opaque, both at the provincial and federal level. In the last few years, as the pressure to curb police violence has risen, officials have announced that some number of policemen have been disciplined; in 1994, for example, the secretary of security of the province claimed that eighteen hundred police had been dismissed; but we are never told for what offenses or upon what evidence.[250] It is apparent that discipline has been in large part a response to political pressures. When we asked federal police officials in 1991 what disciplinary action had been taken in some notorious matters, including the Gonzalo Herlán case, the answer was that there was no record of any action at all, whereas in another, less serious case that was under intense press scrutiny at the time, we were told that the *comisario* had been "suspended."

The discipline for individual officers in the provincial police was worse. In 1991, a case was under investigation from the poor district of Pacheco in which three youths had been killed by twenty-one policemen who fired 130 shots; there was a question, as usual, whether the matter really was a "shoot-out" or not. In a news interview, the provincial police chief replied stoutly that it certainly was a shoot-out, just as, he went on to claim, the Ingeniero Budge case had been a shoot-out—and this statement was made long after the police in that notorious killing had been convicted of homicide by the criminal courts. Ironically, it later appeared that the chief had been correct in a way he never intended: forensic evidence revealed that the youths in the Pacheco case had been shot at point-blank range.[251]

Police violence in Buenos Aires is often rewarded by superiors in the departments, as Guillermo Ledesma suggested and a policeman privately confirmed to us; a notorious example was the special Robbery and Theft Squad in the federal police. According to an analysis of news sources by CELS, the squad accounted for more than 30 percent of all reported police killings in the capital in the three years 1988–90. In those years, Robbery and Theft police killed forty-two suspects, left none wounded, and suffered two police injuries; four people were arrested at the scenes of the confrontations. It appears from the news accounts that the members of the squad lured the suspects, often led by an informer, into a trap where they were shot and killed. And these police were media "stars," often given special assignments in the glare of publicity.[252]

Under these circumstances, the avenue of redress most frequently relied on by human rights activists in Buenos Aires has been criminal prosecution, despite the fact that it is a slow and cumbersome process. In Argentina, a criminal case is investigated by a magistrate appointed for life, who has complete power to look into all the facts and can command the services of forensic experts to perform ballistics and medical analyses. The prosecutor's role has traditionally been limited; he has no discretion to refuse to prosecute a case in which the magistrate chooses to bring charges, and he has no investigative facilities apart from the police. Private lawyers representing the victim or his family, on the other hand, have the right to intervene in a criminal case, to present evidence to the judge, and to appeal if the case is dismissed—for example, for lack of proof against the accused policeman. Human rights lawyers in Buenos Aires make vigorous use of this characteristic of the criminal process in police homicides and sometimes in torture cases, regularly referring to the case as "my case," and ignoring the role of the prosecutor. In the Gonzalo Herlán case, for example, a lawyer from CELS pressed the successful appeal against the police. Every case presents a struggle between the perennial bureaucratic impunity and the tenacity of the victim's lawyers.

Police accountability through the criminal process has had serious limitations. Apart from the forensic services and their own clerks, the judges have no investigators at their disposal except the police. Furthermore, the society within which the magistrates work sometimes supports police abuse. An investigating judge in the province told us about a case in which, even though it was clear that the police had assassinated two suspects, people in the neighborhood told the judge that they approved of what the police had done. A poll taken in the Buenos Aires region in 1990 found that a bare 51.1 percent of the population opposed the use of torture, while 30.2 percent thought that its use "depended on the case" and 7.9 percent outright approved of it.[253] Thus a judge often had little incentive to devote his or her meager investigative resources to cases of police abuse.

Damage actions, which are theoretically available against the government and individual police, have been much less frequently used than criminal actions. In cases where criminal charges have been brought against the police, the civil case will usually be delayed pending the disposition of the criminal case, because a clear-cut finding in favor of the police may act as a bar to the civil claim. Even in cases where the failure of the criminal prosecution does not act as a legal bar that failure is powerfully discouraging to the victim or his family. Finally, Argentine lawyers explained that there is a cultural resistance to accepting damages from the government for its own misconduct, as if the impunity can only be breached and the wrong redressed by punishment. Nevertheless, damage actions are sometimes brought, particularly as part of the few successful criminal prosecutions, but the amounts recovered are usually modest.

Any legal action, criminal or civil, against the police takes place in an atmosphere of intimidation. Lawyers are frequently menaced; in the Gonzalo Herlán case, police cars surrounded the lawyers when they went to a forensic reenactment at the scene of the killing. Judges and their staffs are commonly threatened as well. In the Herlán case, threats were made to the judge's clerk, and in the José C. Paz car-chase case, the threats actually destroyed the case against the police. Former government officials told us that the investigating magistrate experienced such a campaign of harassment that he felt compelled to flee the country; the witnesses against the police then changed their statements.

The most chilling thing about the threats is that they are so routine. Everyone, including the judges, seems to take them as the norm and to realize that in most cases very little can be done. The judges have no investigative body to look into threats made in cases alleging police abuses; they do not trust the police to investigate their own officers, and they do not expect the federal police to oversee the provincial police, nor vice versa. And the fact that the threats are so brazen makes them more effective; it increases the impunity of the police. It is little wonder, in the light of the history of the *Proceso* and the continuing intimidation, that judges seem often to be subject to political pressure despite their apparent independence.

None of the weaknesses that I have just described in the system of accountability—not the haphazard administrative discipline, nor the reluctance of the judges, nor the intimidation—is entirely adequate to explain the continuing impunity of the police. Police superiors or the executive authorities could institute a better disciplinary system, and in some cases, at least, they could investigate and put a stop to the intimidation, if they chose. Something—or several things—in the system stop them from doing so.

One of the things, as Judge Ledesma saw, is widespread corruption. Some minor corruption contributes directly to violence; in 1993, for example, a federal police sergeant was convicted of killing a man who refused to pay him a bribe to overlook a traffic infraction. More generally, corrupt police take money from rackets and distribute it throughout the police departments as well as to civilian officials, forming a network that makes it all but impossible for any person to call another to account. The resulting impunity extends to every sort of crime, and torture and extrajudicial killing presumably constitute only a small part of illegal police activities. At the end of 1991, for example, the kidnapping scandal mentioned at the beginning of this chapter exploded, revealing that senior federal police officials and former agents had been using the skills at "disappearing" people and maintaining safe houses acquired under the dictatorship to run a multimillion dollar kidnapping ring for more than a decade.[254] Dozens of police must have known about the ring and kept silent, probably because they themselves had committed crimes known to others. Under such circumstances, it is all but impossible for the executive or the police to control police violence.

Furthermore, there is a lingering attitude among many officials, especially under the Menem administration, that the imposition of order without law is not entirely a bad thing. In 1993, a vice minister of defense was forced to resign after raising the question whether "sometimes torture isn't justified."[255] The characteristic ambivalence about "tough cops," as reflected in the judiciary as well as the executive, is revealed most clearly, however, in the case of Subcomisario Luis Patti, perhaps the best-known police scandal of the nineties in Argentina.

When he was appointed *comisario* in the conservative provincial town of Pilar in 1990, Patti came with a reputation as a tough cop who had been responsible for torture and killings during the *Proceso*. In October, a local investigative judge ordered the arrest of Patti for unlawful coercion (a lesser crime similar to torture) against two suspects accused of burglary and robbery of a residence. Living up to his reputation, Patti refused at first to surrender, justifying himself in a press interview: "To clear up a matter, the police have to commit no less than four or five criminal acts. If they don't, the police cannot solve anything. That occurs in Argentina and every part of the world. What are those crimes? Illegal deprivation of liberty, coercion (because to detain a person and interrogate him for two hours is coercive) and invasion of the home, among others. And there is no other way. When the *comisarios* don't solve crimes, it is because, as we say in our lingo, they aren't playing the game." When Patti finally surrendered, the judge charged him with torture, much more serious than coercion. The evidence showed that the suspects had been taken to a safe house in Pilar, where Patti had tortured them with an electrical device, used on the testicles of one of them. Medical evidence taken by the court's forensic experts, showing sores on the testicles due to the electric shocks, corroborated the charges. Despite persistent death threats, the judge adhered to the charges.

Defense lawyers moved to have the judge disqualified on the grounds that he was prejudiced against Patti, and powerful figures began to come to his aid. A popular talk-show host made fun of the charges, suggesting that Patti might merely have pushed the victims. The mayor of Pilar visited Patti in jail, and finally President Menem himself was quoted saying that Patti had "cleaned up crime" in part of the province and that he "does everything well." A higher court humiliated the judge by removing him on grounds of prejudice, an act that is rare in Argentina; after the case was assigned to another magistrate, it was quietly dismissed. Patti returned to Pilar in triumph and later was specially assigned to the federal investigation of a scandal in another province.[256]

The Patti case is a vivid example of the way the system not only perpetuates impunity but actually rewards the violent. If the result were a matter of lack of judicial resolve in the face of police threats, like so many other cases, it would be bad enough. In fact it is worse; the judge was actually punished for showing courage. The problem, then, is not just that the police are continuing in their old ways, as Guillermo Ledesma seemed to suggest; the problem is that much of the political system wants to foster "order" without fostering the rule of law that might encourage it. President Menem has exhibited something approaching contempt for the independence of the judiciary, for example, by packing the Supreme Court, increasing it from five to nine members "for purely political reasons."[257] The conclusion seems almost inescapable that the government is making use of the issue of "security" in order to increase its control. The fear of crime—fueled by the police and the media—in combination with a general fear of the police themselves, contributes to a demand for more security. The order reproduced and represented by patterns of police behavior and the approval of a "rogue cop" like Patti in Buenos Aires is both arbitrary and violent; it is social control through the very unpredictability of the authorities.

The distinguished Argentinian criminologist Raúl Zaffaroni has put his finger on the dynamics of security after the *Proceso*:

> When open political violence exists, the executive agencies of the penal system feel secure, because they are needed and there is no way to take away the power they possess. When this situation is not present, the efficacy of the agencies is not evident through the

exhibition of their so-called war deaths and these agencies try to recover their secure position by means of projecting another war; because open political violence does not exist anymore, there should be a war against ordinary delinquency.[258]

In 1994, in effect confirming Zaffaroni's insight, Menem proposed first to offer tougher legislation against crime and then to establish a "supersecretariat" for security, to include the federal police and other forces, to control crime as well as social unrest.[259]

The case of Buenos Aires is thus very important. It is tolerably clear that it presents a situation where the fear of crime, and the general sense of insecurity, has been artificially inflated, in part by the presence of police violence itself, with the purpose of maintaining control and avoiding accountability, especially for crimes related to corruption.

Fortunately, many in Argentina see through the artificial screen created by the government; the pluralism of society in the democratic transition is not so easily defeated. In the nineties, the pressure to curb police violence has increased, from groups like the Madres de la Plaza de Mayo that had been opposed to impunity for the crimes of the *Proceso,* and continued to oppose it in the democratic transition, as well as from the international community. In its *Country Reports on Human Rights Practices,* the U.S. State Department has been consistently critical of the lack of control of the police in Argentina. Relatives of those killed by the police have formed the Commission of Relatives of Victims of Institutional Violence to press for investigation and punishment; the commission has received extensive press coverage and has met with the minister of the interior. The numerous dismissals of police in the last few years, however obscure their reasons, are clearly connected to the national protest against police brutality as well as to international pressure. In 1991, the Dirección Nacional de Derechos Humanos began a campaign to get all the police in Argentina to adhere to the U.N. Principles on the Use of Force and Firearms. The legislature, as we saw in connection with torture, has continued to narrow the discretion of the police.

And the courts are becoming more vigorous in their actions against police. For the first time in the history of Buenos Aires, in an open public trial at the beginning of 1994, provincial police were convicted of the torture and murder of a prisoner, the most serious crime in Argentina.[260] The force of the demands for accountability and against the impunity of officials is still powerful long after the destruction of the dictatorship.

CHAPTER VII

Jamaica

Dem a loot, dem a shoot, dem a wail
A shanty town
Dem a rude boys out on probation
A shanty town
Them a rude when them come up to town
A shanty town
Police get taller
A shanty town
Soldiers get longer
A shanty town...

—DESMOND DEKKER[261]

Jamaica has a reputation as "the Violent Island" of the Caribbean; it is the performance of the Jamaican police in the face of—and as part of—the violence which makes it a significant case for this study. The problems with police violence are recognizably like those in São Paulo, and to a lesser extent in Buenos Aires, although Jamaica, governed under a system modeled on the British, has had no experience of a dictatorship (apart from the past colonial system, which does bear some similarity to a dictatorship).

Jamaica is a small nation with a population of two and a half million people, more than half a million of them in the metropolitan region of the city of Kingston. Although the population is over 90 percent black or brown-skinned, the small number of whites controls much of the capital. While overt racism of the sort found in the United States is rare, class conflict, often linked with distinctions of color, is endemic. Independent since 1962, Jamaica retains very close ties, both political and cultural, to Great Britain. The Jamaican governor-general, who represents the queen, together with the Jamaican prime minister appoints many officials, and many decisions of the Jamaican courts have an appeal of last resort to the Privy Council in Britain. Jamaica shares the liberal traditions of the United Kingdom, with a democratically elected bicameral parliament, a prime minister, and an independent judiciary. Proud of its reputation as a model for the transition from colonial to independent status, Jamaica has been ruled democratically since independence and indeed for some time before it.[262]

The police, the Jamaica Constabulary (JCF), comprises about eight thousand members: six thousand regulars, and nearly two thousand special constables, who are technically auxiliaries but work full time. The force performs all police functions, including investigation and patrol, and superior officers are not separately selected, as they are in some Latin American and other countries, but rather work their way up through the ranks, somewhat as they do in the United States.

In 1991, the Jamaican government retained a group of senior police officials from Great Britain to report on the work of the JCF. Their review, known as the Hirst report, was extremely critical—much more frank than one might expect from official consultants. Central to their work were their findings concerning the use of deadly force:

> Every Police Service, in the furtherance of its mission to serve and protect the community, has, on occasions to resort to the use of firearms. Alternative strategies developed by Police Forces in other countries to ensure that the use of firearms is an action of last resort only and not an immediate response is a measure of their professionalism.
>
> No such strategy exists in Jamaica and the continuing level of deaths attributable to firearms operations involving the JCF are undoubtedly produced by their use as an action of first resort. It is suggested that the development of strategies by managers is a key function in the discharge of their responsibilities.[263]

Coming as it did from British police, the report might have been expected to carry extra weight in Jamaica. Yet in the end, while copies of it circulate underground, the report has never been officially released, and although "strategies" suggested by it have been attempted, they have not been carried through consistently. While the situation has improved since 1991, political and social conditions have conspired to perpetuate the use of violence by the JCF.

Jamaica has had problems common to other postcolonial and Third World nations, shaped by the special history of the island. For generations before independence, the British used violent repression against a series of slave revolts and movements for independence, in a pattern that was carried forward to some extent in the JCF; the Hirst report characterizes the police as "semimilitary." In this century, a middle class developed, comprised mostly of brown-skinned Jamaicans, some of whom absorbed the patronizing attitudes of the British toward those beneath them socially. For them, a great source of authority and social distinction was education; they largely filled clerical jobs, including many in the civil service. As the political scientist Obika Gray says, the clerical class "placed great weight on decorum, proper manners and law and order." Respectable Jamaican society expects "discipline" in social relations, in the sense of personal self-control as well as public order; it extends even to the treatment of children, who are frequently subjected to corporal punishment by teachers and parents.

After the end of slavery in the nineteenth century, and even before, through the slave revolts, a peasantry with a strong sense of independence developed in the Jamaican countryside. Poor blacks retained some cultural characteristics from Africa, including a patois that was very different from standard English. A social chasm between the poor blacks and the middle class deepened over time. Rastafarianism, with its use of marijuana and its millenarian nationalist ideology, was one late manifestation of the rejection by some poor blacks of the British traditions of the middle class and the whites; by the same token, the middle class often scorned and feared the poor and the spirit of rebellion against colonial standards that the "Rastas" represented.[264]

After World War II, as independence came to the Caribbean, class differences became more acute in Jamaica. Peasants were forced off the land, crowding into the shantytowns in and around Kingston. Economic development tended to enrich those who were already well-off, marginalizing even those who had jobs; the number of unemployed was enormous. The distribution of income was the most skewed in the Caribbean.[265] The situation worsened over time, as Jamaica incurred foreign debt and the markets for its exports, especially bauxite, declined. The crisis created anxiety among those—working class and artisans as well as the middle class—who place great store by self-reliance but are only marginally above the unemployed. At the same time, some of the unemployed have come to form a black underclass that rejects middle-class life and sometimes turns to crime. Through colonial repression, then, as well as the defiance of it, together with persistent class conflict, Jamaica has become a place where violence is frequently used and a violent rhetoric is used to justify it. As Obika Gray says, "Aggressive and intimidating postures, looting businesses, and menacing ethnic-minority shopkeepers became poor people's way of protesting 'injustice' and their own status as outcasts in the society. As such, social-banditry-as-politics defined the ethics of the militant poor."[266] The lyrics of "Shanty Town" were typical of dozens of popular songs.

Since the Jamaican economy is not self-sufficient, and what it does produce is so unequally distributed, politics has been clientelist, with a hand in controlling and distributing such jobs as there are. One of the reasons for the political violence that surrounds elections is that adherents of the party that is defeated are liable to be deprived of jobs, with no sure way of finding other work. Given the explosive potential for class conflict in Jamaica, as well as the dependence of the economy on international capital, party leaders through the sixties were hesitant to mobilize the people and turn the parties into more than patronage and voting organizations. The paternalism of the leaders was borrowed from colonial relations, and the economic circumstances only reinforced it. As Terry Lacey put it, "The essence of 'Jamaican style' was the mobilisation of resources through charismatic leadership to build up a network of patron-client relationships with which to gather in and redistribute the wherewithal to administer a system of political rewards."[267] Thus, although there are well-defined parties, chiefly the People's National Party (PNP) on the left and the

Jamaica Labor Party (JLP), which is dedicated to free-market policies, participation has been based traditionally in personalistic, patron-client relations.

Both urban and rural violent crime rose in the sixties. Much of the interpersonal violence was and still is about matters that seem to an outsider at first to be relatively minor—quarrels between friends and the theft of crops, for example. The reaction to apparently petty thefts, however, is a reflection of how poor the victims are and how much they depend on the narrow margin of their property to keep them from sinking still lower. Their rage against those who steal is also a rage against the poverty in which they find themselves.[268]

Organized crime, particularly the drug trade, made matters worse. As criminals formed armed gangs, the fear of insecurity rose, while at the same time the dispossessed youth in the poor districts of Kingston often looked up to the gunmen as heroes. Before independence, the colonial government had never been punctilious about civil liberties, and in the face of the economic crisis after 1962, the government came to rely on force to repress threats from below, whether of political militancy or crime. The JLP government took draconician measures against crime and social unrest, especially after Great Britain shut off a safety valve for unemployment by imposing stringent limits on emigration from the colonies in 1965. Following a 1963 law that authorized flogging, criminal punishment was made even more severe in 1965, when, in an act reminiscent of the worst of the imperial past, the legislature approved the use of the cruel cat-o'-nine-tails. The government cleared shantytowns, replacing them with housing projects that were loyal to the JLP. In the fall of 1966, the government declared a state of emergency in Western Kingston.

The social conflict did not abate, and Hugh Shearer, the prime minister, claimed in 1967 that he had "given orders to the police to proceed without reservation and without restrictions to tackle the problem of violence and to bring the wrongdoers to justice in whatever way it can be done." A week later, speaking to the police, he coined a phrase still famous in

Jamaica: "When it comes to handling crime, in this country I do not expect any policeman, when he handles a criminal, to recite any Beatitudes to him."[269]

The underlying character of the government's domestic security policies was writ large in 1968, when the young Guyanese historian Walter Rodney delivered a series of lectures advocating black power and socialism, ideas that were anathema to the JLP. The government refused to allow him to return to Jamaica and used the police against a student demonstration in sympathy with him, ultimately provoking rioting and looting by poor youths and a violent reaction by the police and the army acting together.

The severity of the measures against what was at first peaceable and even academic advocacy revealed a government ready to fall back on the repressive habits of colonial rule—a government that did not have the confidence in the people or in its own legitimacy that would have led it to act in a less fearful manner.[270] It was, as Obika Gray put it, a hybrid between authoritarian colonial rule and democracy, unsure of its ability to draw on the people for support.

THE CONSTABULARY AND VIOLENCE

Violence in Jamaica was increased by the island's traditions and the fact that the government made only a hesitant attempt at a monopoly of legitimate force. Lynching of suspected criminals was common and was for the most part not punished; in fact, acts of violent self-help were seemingly accepted. Politicians began to draw for their own protection on gunmen, some of whom, identified as JLP or PNP adherents, were shielded from effective prosecution. The political protection of criminals led the island's chief newspaper, the *Gleaner*, to demand in an editorial in 1966 that the government "unfetter the police." Thus the police were thrown into an open situation, free of controls, where there was a great deal of violence in the society and demands on all sides for forceful police action, but no evenhanded application of the law. Sometimes the police acted summarily to get rid of a criminal who was protected by the politicians; more broadly, as Terry Lacey says, "the response of the security forces to a prolonged period of apparent impotence in the face of rising political violence was to direct their own frustrations and aggression against the more amorphous, not necessarily political, 'criminal element.'"[271] In the process, the police themselves became politicized, as party leaders wooed them to try to ensure that the police would not abandon them to gunmen loyal to the opposition.

Police were encouraged to act in a semimilitary way, often in concert with the army, as they had done in the Walter Rodney affair. The use of deadly violence by the police rose throughout the last half of the sixties, as shown by figures that Lacey collected from the press:

PERSONS SHOT DEAD BY POLICE, JAMAICA, 1960–69	
1960–65	33
1966	7
1967	17
1968	23
1969	59

Lacey also found that the police accounted in the latter years for an increasingly large proportion of all the casualties due to gunfire in the island.[272]

Having once released the whirlwind of official violence, the government was unable to bring it under control. While the precise figures for police killings in the seventies have not been assembled, everyone with whom I have discussed the matter takes it for granted that police violence did not decrease. Although the PNP, led by Michael Manley, tried to take a radically new road in Jamaican politics, embracing democratic socialism, the party was unable to escape the continuing economic problems. The international economic crisis caused by the scarcity of oil, combined with the hostility of the U.S. government to the Manley regime throughout much of the seventies, kept the dependent economy of Jamaica at a low ebb.[273] The problems of crime and unemployment grew worse, and there was little incentive to change law-enforcement policies.

The prevalence of firearms, moreover, dismayed PNP officials; in their view, a disproportionate number of the weapons were in the hands of gunmen ready to aid the opposition JLP. Since the police were traditionally more sympathetic to the PNP, the government relied on them as their protectors and found it awkward to criticize police policies that held out any promise of getting rid of gunmen. On the contrary, in 1974, the government adopted the Suppression of Crime Act, which can be used to relax standards for searches and arrests, and the Gun Court Act, which provides for expedited procedures and heavy penalties for firearms offenses.[274]

In 1980, after an election campaign marred by a great deal of violence, Edward Seaga, leading the JLP, took over the government, determined to pursue free-market policies and repair relations with the United States. Jamaica's social and economic problems, however, turned out to be structural rather than rooted in short-range government policy. The price of Jamaica's export products has never improved enough for the nation to escape from debt, although tourism has grown as the main industry and source of foreign exchange. The subsequent change of government back to the PNP at the end of the eighties has not altered the underlying situation; the distribution of income continues to be very unequal, and unemployment and crime are central concerns. Many Jamaicans are still just as frightened and angry at gunmen and "rude boys" in the Kingston ghettoes as they were when Desmond Dekker sang "Shanty Town." In a public opinion poll in 1992, 34 percent of the respondents said that the best way to control crime is to hang criminals. And people act on their convictions; lynching of thieves and other petty criminals continues. To take just one ordinary example: on July 3, 1986, in a news story collecting various items of violence, the *Gleaner* reported that "higglers" (stallkeepers) in the market in Kingston had set upon a robber and killed him. According to E. George Green, formerly the parliamentary ombudsman for Jamaica, 35 lynchings were reported in 1984 and 166 during the years 1986–92.[275]

The effect of the current economic dominance of tourism on Jamaicans is not completely clear. There can be little doubt, however, that it produces some tension and resentment of the tourists, so much more prosperous than even middle-class Jamaicans. In a speech to hotel workers in 1989, Michael Manley expressed his sympathy with them: "Even if you don't feel to smile, you damn well have to smile." Unquestionably, tourism generates increased criminal activity as well as fear and concern about crime. It has created a huge business in private security for businesses and tourist resorts; according to the sociologist Carl Stone, there were some thirty thousand private security guards at work in Jamaica in 1986—more than three times the number of police.[276]

In a situation where interpersonal violence, increasingly accompanied by the use of firearms, is widespread, where elites fear the poor and vigilante justice is common, the Jamaican police have been reckless of the lives and rights of poor people. The police frequently detain people for mere identification; the Hirst report found people who had been held without charges for "days or even weeks." Not surprisingly in an island where the cat-o'-nine-tails was used as a punishment for crime until less than thirty years ago, prisoners often charge that they have been beaten to confess to crimes, sometimes relatively minor ones such as theft of crops or livestock. In November 1992, John Headley died in a police station in St. James Parish; several other prisoners from the same lockup testified that they had seen police beat Headley three different times, trying to get him to tell where he had supposedly hidden a cow.[277]

But as the Hirst report recognized, the central problem continues to be the abuse of firearms and deadly force in the streets, which has increased enormously since the sixties. During the eleven years 1983–93, the police killed an average of 182 persons each year, although the number was declining over the period. For some of those years, we have data to compare those figures with the number of persons wounded by police, the number of police killed and wounded, and the number of general homicides in which the police are not involved.

POLICE AND CIVILIAN DEADLY FORCE IN JAMAICA, 1983–1993 [278]										
	1983	1984	1985	1986	1987	1988	1989	1990	1991	1992	1993
Civilians killed by police	196	288	210	178	205	181	162	148	178	145	120
Civilians killed by civilians	424	484	434	449	442	414	439	542	561	629	n/a
Civilians wounded by police	n/a	n/a	n/a	n/a	n/a	98	71	96	81	85	n/a
Police killed	7	20*	9	15	8	n/a	13	11	10	9	n/a
Police wounded	n/a	n/a	22	n/a	n/a	n/a	24	23	8	16	n/a

*See note 278.

Even in the year with the highest number of civilian homicides, 1992, the police accounted for over 18 percent of all homicides in the island, and in some years for more than a third. The police kill many more than they wound, according to the government's own figures, although the ratios are the reverse in cases of civilian shootings of police. These figures point toward a disproportionate use of deadly force by the police, and no doubt some suspects were being killed deliberately.

In a pattern that is familiar from other countries, the authorities claim that almost all the shootings are justified because the suspects were armed and shot it out with the police or at least displayed a weapon in a threatening manner. Although I do not believe that this claim can be sustained, as I will show more fully in a moment, it is as important in Jamaica as elsewhere that the government make the assertion, because it indicates how strong is the international norm that bars the use of deadly force except as a last resort. While the domestic law of Jamaica on the use of deadly force is quite vague, permitting the use of such force as is "reasonably necessary...to effect a lawful arrest,"[279] we were told in 1986 by senior law-enforcement people that police were not permitted to shoot unarmed persons. In 1990, furthermore, the police adopted "force orders" that specifically embodied the international standard: firearms are to be used only as a last resort and against armed resistance. The acceptance of that standard makes it possible, at least, for the police to be reformed in accordance with it; the outright rejection of the standard would give no leverage for reform.

As in other places in the Americas, people who defy the police in Jamaica run a real risk of being shot. In 1986, Patrick Locke was picked up at a gas station and taken to a Kingston station house for "questioning." Since the police placed no charges against him, he insisted on leaving the police station and was shot in the spine and paralyzed. Many unjustifiable shootings grow out of flimsy suspicions. For example, in the eighties, burglaries were said to be committed by criminals breaking in through roofs; as a result, there were several cases in which people who were repairing roofs were shot by the police.

Other cases grow out of the semimilitary tactics of the JCF; one well-known recent case is the killing of Sidney Francis in 1991. There was a very large crowd at the National Stadium on July 31 for a concert in honor of and attended by Nelson Mandela. Many police were present, including members of the Mobile Reserve, a strike force intended to be deployed against threats of violence. One man who climbed on a fence to get a better look at Mandela was roughly handled by the police. Some members of the crowd became angry and began to throw things at the police; members of the Mobile Reserve fired into the crowd, wounding a woman and killing Sidney Francis, a supervisor at a glass company. There are many similar cases, not so celebrated as this shooting, because they do not involve such a public event or such respectable victims. The JCF continues to conduct operations jointly with the army (the two together are always called the "security forces"), which results in unjustified shootings.

The worst abuses occur when the police, impatient with the

workings of the courts, simply dispose of suspects in bogus "shoot-outs." For example, Detective Corporal Alfred Laing, who appears in other similar cases, charged Eddie Hayle in court with possession of ammunition, but was never able to produce proof satisfactory to the judge. When Hayle left a court hearing in April 1985, Laing warned him to tell his mother "to prepare his burial suit." Almost two weeks later, according to neighborhood witnesses, the police staged a "shoot-out," in which Laing showed up at Hayle's house with other officers, heavily armed, in several jeeps. Neighbors heard Hayle begging for his life before several shots were fired, giving the aural impression of an exchange of gunfire; Hayle was then brought out dead in a plastic sheet. According to Eddie Hayle's brothers, the police took them to the station and beat them, to try to force them to tell where Eddie's supposed gun was hidden.

One of the most striking characteristics of the shootings is the callous cruelty exhibited by the police, showing that they expect to be feared and not to be held accountable. In 1984, Detective Corporal Laing chased a person into a house and fired into a room, hitting a teenage girl. When he realized what he had done, he cursed, calling the girl "bumbo-clat," a vulgar expression for a sanitary napkin, and explained, "I tink it was a boy I sight." In December 1991, police chased a suspect down a city street, firing at him but killing a bystander. One policeman involved in the chase encountered a youngster in the street and shouted, "Hey, boy, come outta me way before me a kill you." He did not kill the boy, however; he shot him in the foot.[280]

Officers like Alfred Laing present themselves as "mighty policemen," who hope to strike terror in the people but want also to be admired. In our investigation in 1986, we found that Laing had been involved in eleven different shooting incidents between 1982 and 1985, several of them apparently summary executions, such as the Hayle case. Yet Laing was famous for the parties he threw in the district where he worked, assiduously attended by the neighborhood people. An even more notorious officer was Keith Gardner, who had killed or shot a number of suspects; he wore a black outfit, sported three pistols, and called himself "Trinity," a name drawn from television. In the eighties he headed the personal security staff for Prime Minister Edward Seaga.[281]

IMPUNITY, ACCOUNTABILITY, AND REFORM

The response of Jamaican society to the abuse of deadly force has changed over the last decade. The reaction to the first Americas Watch report, in 1986, which squarely accused the JCF of unjustified extrajudicial killings, was revealing. After the report was serialized in the *Gleaner,* giving it maximum exposure in the island, newspaper columnists attacked it—not, however, on the ground that the conclusions about police killings were inaccurate. It was apparent that no one who knew anything about the subject took seriously the police claim that most of the shootings occurred in life-threatening confrontations. No, the columnists claimed that such shoot-to-kill tactics were appropriate under the conditions of crime and society in Jamaica and that it was none of the business of a human rights organization based in New York City to be complaining about them.

Regular columnist Morris Cargill pleaded underdevelopment as an excuse. "[S]ince the early Sixties," he wrote, "Jamaica has become a violent and anarchic society, with the incidence of robberies, rapes, murders (per capita) far in excess of any other country with even a vestigial claim to be civilized." He complained that the courts were understaffed, sometimes with prosecutors who were "not very bright." The police force, he said, was too small and staffed by people likely to be illiterate and venal. He concluded:

> So, my dear civilized friends of Americas Watch, what do you expect our honest citizenry, our authorities and the police to do to prevent us all from being robbed blind or being murdered in our beds?
>
> You are quite right. The police do shoot down known murderers and armed gangsters when they catch them, sometimes in cold blood. This is not the best way of justice, but in our present circumstances my only complaint is that they don't shoot enough of them. As Mr. Shearer once said, we haven't the time to recite the beatitudes.[282]

This is a classic piece of subaltern thinking, in which the violations in the ex-colony are excused because of its inferiority to the metropolitan center. Although the most important thing about these views is that they are advanced in Jamaica and are accepted by some of the public, it is worth pausing to respond to the argument on its merits, because I believe that versions of it feed an undercurrent in public opinion everywhere in the Americas, including the United States. It is always tempting to excuse violations of rights on the supposed grounds that the crime problem is dreadful, the culture is inhospitable to rights, or resources and "infrastructure" are lacking.

In the case of Jamaica, I think the evidence will not support the argument. It is true that the JCF is somewhat small; it is about the same size as the Los Angeles Police Department and polices a population of comparable size. While the LAPD has its faults, as we have seen, it is less violent than the JCF. The problem with the JCF, as the Hirst report found, was not that it was too small, but that the forces were not well deployed or well managed. The poverty of Jamaica does not seem really to account for the poor management. Jamaica, furthermore, was not so poor in security measures; if it is true, as Carl Stone asserted, that there were thirty thousand private security guards in 1986, then the problem was not poverty but an inability to channel resources to state-sponsored law enforcement. As for crime in Jamaica, the homicide rate in 1992, excluding police homicides, was about twenty-five per hundred thousand people (if police homicides were included, the rate would be almost thirty), which is quite high, but nowhere near as high as the most violent urban areas in the United States. If Jamaica is close to "anarchic" (and I do not think it is), it is partly because politicians have encouraged violence and the government has failed to act against lynchings.

The comments of Carl Stone, a leading social scientist in the Caribbean and a popular columnist for the *Gleaner,* were even more interesting:

> The average policeman in uniform cannot shoot straight enough to

handle the tough criminals with M-16 rifles and to protect you and me against serious criminals....

The much criticised Eradication Squad which wiped out many such criminals was designed for that purpose. Sharpshooting CIB [Criminal Investigation Bureau] men at various Police stations have earned the support of citizens by demonstrating a capability to shake down criminals and send them in flight from sheer fear of their awesome reputations and their daring deeds of violence....

...Even if this macho type Police strategy really does not work, it gives citizens a deep sense of confidence that there are tough cops who they think drive fear into the hearts of criminals....

Some way has to be found to reduce the incidence of killing of innocent citizens and to prosecute policemen who kill outside of circumstances when their lives are threatened. But tough macho cops the country needs to maintain a "balance of terror" in the streets.

The excesses must be curbed but there must be no removal of the frontline cops who strike fear in the hearts of the violent criminals and have the courage to confront them on the battlefield of violence.

To do that is to ensure that many citizens would have to fill the vacuum and become frontline men fighting crime in highly organised vigilante squads along the South American pattern.

It is significant that Stone believed that the alternative to the police violence was civilian "death squads." At another place in the article, he expanded on the relation between vigilantism and police violence:

Vigilante killings are popular and supported by a majority of Jamaicans because they feel that the Police are not able to control crime effectively due to inadequate manpower, guns and motor vehicles and because they fear that the court system does not work for them. To protect themselves they take the law in their own hands and seek to establish their own "balance of terror."[283]

Stone makes it plain that he sees the "mighty policeman" as the avenger of the citizenry; the fury of the wronged victim is the fury of the police.

In 1986, although ghetto communities were sometimes agitated by police executions, I was struck by how little protest there was against the abuses of the JCF; Cargill and Stone seemed to have carried the day. I was told that those poor people who were incensed by police brutality felt isolated and at the same time intimidated by the violence. In public opinion polls at the beginning of the eighties, Carl Stone had found that 66 percent of the sample thought that the police did not respect people's rights, yet 41 percent in another poll thought that the police did not use enough force and 10 percent said that "certain types...should not be brought in alive." Jamaicans felt themselves endangered by crime, and at the same time delivered over to police who were arbitrary.[284]

Jamaica has, nevertheless, a strong liberal tradition in the bench, bar, and public administration. Over the six years 1987–92, after the notoriety given the Americas Watch report and with constant agitation by the Jamaica Council for Human Rights and criticism from the U.S. State Department in its annual *Country Reports*, public opinion began to change. In September 1991, Carl Stone reported a poll showing that "public confidence in the police is now at an all-time low." The commissioner of police publicly criticized "brutality and corruption" and the minister of national security and justice said that there were "too many questionable police killings." The anger of the poor against the police was beginning to rise; there were frequent reports of civil disturbances, including roadblocks and fires, after police shootings.[285]

The courts, too, increased pressure on the police. In the four years 1989–92, forty-six policemen were charged with homicide. There were indictments for homicide for the death of John Headley, the man who had been tortured to death while being interrogated about a stolen cow, and for the killing at the Mandela rally. As in other places, however, the criminal process is a very blunt tool for reform, especially when the police are not themselves cooperative; many prosecutions have been unsuccessful.

Jamaican lawyers have been bringing civil tort actions for police abuses, in approved Anglo-American fashion, for many years. Several successful cases had been brought over the years for shootings by "Trinity." In the case of Patrick Locke, who was shot and paralyzed when he refused to be detained without charges, and in one of the cases in which a citizen was shot while repairing his roof, substantial damages were awarded. But according to Jamaican lawyers, the damages are usually not large, and they are smaller in cases where the victim has been killed than they are in cases where he has been permanently injured. The government reported to the U.S. State Department, for example, that U.S.$333,000 was paid in damages for police violence in 1991. This was not enough to make a difference in police policy; according to the Hirst report, government officials "on occasions simply 'write off' the costs rather than seek to sanction those involved."[286]

The government sought advice and aid from several quarters. A policy on the use of deadly force was formulated in 1990 with the aid of the International Criminal Investigative Training Assistance Program (ICITAP) of the U.S. Justice Department, and ICITAP also helped to formulate new regulations and training. In 1991, the Ministry of National Security and Justice received the advice of British police through the Hirst report, which affords a more unsparing and exact account of problems of management and accountability than I have seen for any other police force in the Americas.

According to the Hirst report, the JCF did not have an effective chain of command in which senior officers had management control over subordinates. The rank structure of the police was confused, with a proliferation of squads with overlapping duties, commanded by senior people who had made fiefdoms out of them. The lack of clear responsibility had led to indecisiveness and "buck passing." Some of the ranks, such as the rank of corporal, did not serve any clear function and existed apparently as a way to give promotions and better pay. Only 40 percent of the JCF was at the lowest, or constable, level (in a well-run police department, far more than half the personnel work at the patrol level), and the patrol work suffered. Some of the worst neighborhoods, where the police are the most unpopular but where a police presence is most needed, were not patrolled at all. The JCF, furthermore, was not well prepared for patrol but was primarily equipped to use force, which was, as the passage from the Hirst report at the beginning of this chapter notes, the instrument of "first resort." High-quality candidates for constable were not being recruited, in part, the report said, because many people viewed the police as "brutal and corrupt."

The report established that accountability at all levels had collapsed. Police, including those at the highest level, did not know what the regulations for discipline were. There were provisions for handling civilian complaints in the older regulations and other provisions set forth in 1991 as an appendix to the force orders drafted with the aid of ICITAP. They were not being followed. Although investigations were supposed to be completed within thirty days, 69 percent of the complaints filed between 1986 and 1991, a period of almost six years, were still pending in 1991. Complainants were supposed to be informed of the outcome of their cases, but they were not. Complaints that presented a basis for a criminal charge were supposed to be referred to the director of public prosecutions, but this was done in a haphazard fashion, and often not at all. There was, in short, no "system" of discipline.

The Hirst report had recommendations for accountability, derived from the British system, that could profitably be adapted to many cities in the Americas. They are:

(a) community accountability, through a democratically chosen council or committee;

(b) internal accountability through an inspector general;

(c) external accountability through a civilian complaints bureau.

The principles implied by these recommendations are, in my view, effective means to police accountability. External control of police is essential in a democratic society, but a police complaints bureau, however necessary it may be, is not enough because it is designed only to search for the facts about past abuses. A civilian body is also needed to set a direction for the force and make basic appointments. But even these strong institutions of external accountability, including both oversight and discipline functions, are not enough, because external bodies cannot ensure that police management is in harmony with policy. An internal oversight body must work with police managers and coordinate with the external bodies, so that police management, the complaint bureau, and civilian oversight do not work at cross-purposes. Such a complex of institutions does not exist in any of the places I have studied in this book, including the United States, as we saw in chapter III. Jamaica, of course, is no exception.[287]

Officials at the Ministry of National Security and Justice, in Parliament, and in the police, tried to put some reforms into effect. These related chiefly to training and promotion as well as investigation and discipline. Police were being specially trained, with programs even at the university level, and given special promotions for good work, in the effort to improve the management of the police. Discipline was being made more consistent and effective; the number of policemen dismissed by the JCF jumped from fifty-seven in 1990 to ninety-four in 1991 and ninety-seven in 1992. By act of Parliament, a Police Public Complaints Authority was established in 1993. It is independent of the police and has powers to subpoena evidence, to oversee police investigations or to start its own, and to refer cases to the director of public prosecutions. After its first ten months of operation, it had received 373 complaints, including 17 for shootings, and had disposed of two-thirds of them; as of this writing, its effectiveness is not clear, but observers have told me that abuses have continued to decline.[288]

Laudable as these changes are, they are probably not enough. The mismanagement and failures of decision making in the Jamaica Constabulary are too massive to be changed by these measures. And it is, in the end, mismanagement that permits the killing to continue; as commentators who were knowledgeable about the thinking inside the JCF told me, the disciplinary system is neglected and the killings enjoy impunity because officers at the middle command level believe that killing "gunmen" is good policy. As long as "most" of those killed are supposedly criminals, the abuses are acceptable. Thus police who kill people are retained on the force and wind up killing again. For example, the policeman who killed Sidney Francis at the Nelson Mandela concert in 1991 was found upon investigation to have killed an innocent person working on a roof three years earlier; if the first crime had been investigated in a timely way, the shooting at the Mandela concert might have been avoided.[289]

Finally, as a number of people with years of experience working with the JCF agreed, the Hirst report fails to set out a plan specifically for Jamaica. In its three types of accountability, the report sets forth an ideal, but does not tell us how to attain it, or even approximate it, in Jamaica. In fact it scarcely mentions the factor that has given rise to and perpetuated much of the muddle: political factionalism. Officers have attained preferment, their fiefs have been protected, and management has been broken down through long-term political preferment. Officers in the JCF do not expect successful reform, because they believe that politics plays a large role in promotions and tenure on the force.

Among the most notorious cases are those of Keith Gardner ("Trinity") and Alfred Laing. Far from having been disciplined by the JCF, they appear (at the time of this study) to have prospered. In 1990, Gardner shot and killed his wife and was later tried and acquitted for homicide. The weapon was never produced at the trial, because the assistant superintendent who had charge of the weapon had lost it; that officer was found to be negligent, but never punished, and the gun turned up in a police file cabinet in 1992.[290] Gardner, who himself continued in the rank of assistant superintendent of police, had private business interests as well. According to all accounts, Alfred Laing had opened a sideline promoting popular public dances. It is impossible to understand how these men could have escaped discipline and have made such successes without the connivance of their colleagues as well as support from the Jamaican political system.

Critics in Jamaica with whom I discussed the problem of politics in the JCF independently arrived at similar conclusions: they recommended that a bipartisan commission should oversee the police for purposes of appointment, promotion, and discipline. Only such a commission, it seems, could take the risk of dismissing and appointing and of insisting on competence in management, regardless of party. Without such a bipartisan body, Jamaican politicians will no doubt continue to interfere in the management of the JCF.

The Jamaican Police in Comparative Perspective

The order represented and reproduced by the Jamaican police is an insecure one; faced with persistent poverty and inequality, people fear crime from others in the society. The police have tried to suppress the violence, potential and actual, of the poor by means of official violence, applied in a way that does not seem evenhanded but instead arbitrary. It is, as Carl Stone implied, a kind of system of terror.

The comparison of Kingston (and Jamaica generally) with São Paulo and Buenos Aires is illuminating. All are cities where the population fears violent crime, a fear that is encouraged by the authorities. The fear is used by the government to justify its own violence and its continuing control. The use of the issue of "security" to strengthen government control is clearest in Argentina, where the serious threat of criminal violence does not loom so large.

The parallels between São Paulo and Jamaica are especially striking. Both places have intractable economic problems, giving rise to persistent poverty and maldistribution of income and wealth. Politicians have traditionally been apprehensive about the mobilization of their poorest constituents, while at the same time they themselves are responsible for allocating scarce goods. The result has been a personalist-clientelist politics. The elite and the middle class fear the have-nots and feel very little common bond in the society; they are little grieved by the death of a criminal, or a person in the "criminal class," at the hands of the authorities. The history of slavery and colonialism has contributed to the sense that such a death is an acceptable, even inevitable, response to crushing social problems.

People's fear and insecurity have led to furious anger in conflicts with others, including quarrels about petty crimes. There is a large amount of self-help and vigilantism, which the government does not successfully curtail or steer into a system ruled, at least nominally, by law. These are weak governments, that do not have a monopoly of legitimate force, under which the police often act like "delegated vigilantes," using violence arbitrarily or for personal or political reasons, much as private citizens do. The police torture suspects for information about, and shoot suspects over, the same sorts of matters for which citizens attack one another. In Jamaica, as in Brazil, some of the police killings blend into the lynchings; in 1991, after policemen in rural St. Mary's Parish repeatedly shot a man stealing coconuts and seriously wounded him, the coconut farmer commented that "the police should have killed him."[291]

The police certainly do reproduce order—an order that is violent, filled with personal vengeance, and socially stratified. The slapdash terror that the police have imposed has contributed, along with private violence, to making people feel powerless and dependent, and yet it is very different from the rule imposed by the police in a state that frankly imposes systematic control. Under an authoritarian government, control is not exercised through individualized acts of deadly violence at the discretion of the police, but by well-directed surveillance and repression; when an official act of violence occurs, however dreadful, it has been chosen as a matter of policy.[292] The sort of ill-controlled violence we see in Jamaica and São Paulo, thinly disguised as legally justified force, is the characteristic of policing in weak democracies.

The police in Buenos Aires act in a less desperate social situation, where there is less personal violence, vigilantism, and crime and the burden of poverty is not so great. Although there is less official violence in Buenos Aires than there is in Jamaica or São Paulo, there is still a disproportionate amount of it, fueled by authoritarian and antiliberal traditions and the vain effort of the government to strengthen its legitimacy through "security" measures.

In all the places studied, the abuse of violence is perpetuated through corruption and political interference in the police. These practices give political forces an interest in maintaining the status quo and also make them participants, so that it is correspondingly difficult to demand accountability.

The Jamaican example emphasizes that the police abuse of deadly force and coercion is not a consequence of dictatorship, but rather of more general historical, political, and economic forces. The causation is more likely the other way; the causes that perpetuate violent police abuses, including the legacy of colonialism and slavery in class relations, radical poverty and inequality of wealth, a weak liberal tradition and sense of citizenship, all can contribute to the breakdown of participatory government.

The danger for the government, as well as the hope for change, lies in its democratic-liberal character. Impunity for official abuses rarely works to strengthen the legitimacy of such a government, but rather weakens it. Violation of human rights becomes a fault line for political argument and conflict. The press, and ultimately the public, becomes suspicious of every claim the government makes for the propriety of official acts; because every police shooting is excused as justified, even when many of them clearly are not, the cynical suspicion is that none of them is justified. People believe that the acts of the police are, for example, socially, racially, or politically discriminatory. One of the things that seems to infuriate Jamaicans most about incidents of police violence is their lack of fairness; local people often see police actions as motivated by personal or party animus that spreads through the entire political system. It is this that has caused the civil disturbances against police violence in some cases. In 1992, Carl Stone commented acidly on the apparent mistreatment of a JLP (opposition party) councillor who claimed to have been beaten by the police:

> So soon after the Rodney King beating in Los Angeles and the angered tones of black protest there, we here have had our own

Rodney King with the beating of JLP councillor Desmond McKenzie. To be a JLP petty official feisty enough to demand your rights under a PNP government is like being a nigger in the Southern US who is fair game for police brutality. Rodney King at least had his day in court although the outcome was a shockingly dishonest jury verdict. McKenzie is not likely even to get that much out of our corrupt justice system.[293]

I cannot vouch for the accuracy of the facts in this account; the point is, rather, that a charge of partisanship in police work is accepted in Jamaica as routine journalism. This sort of charge, made regularly in the press, and believed by some in the electorate, should give rise to an effort by the government to minimize the damage of the charge. If the one who makes the charge cannot be eliminated, as in Jamaica he clearly cannot, then the dynamic pushes slightly toward less outright venality and arbitrariness in official life, including that of the police.

The hope is that politicians will recognize, sooner or later, that police terror and official impunity must be a source of increasing weakness, and will take action to strengthen the rule of law and accountability. It is not an entirely desperate hope, because even in a weak democracy arbitrary official action has not helped the legitimacy of the government and the politicians seem sometimes to understand that; the dynamic of political survival is in the direction of the rule of law. And the experience in São Paulo, Buenos Aires, and Jamaica confirms it; despite the terrible abuses that no doubt continue, torture and extrajudicial executions have decreased in recent years. The international standards that condemn the use of torture and require that deadly force be an instrument of last resort thus assume increasing importance, because governments first say they adhere to those standards and then find that they must make shift to try to adhere to them.

CHAPTER VIII
Mexico City, the Federal District

INTRODUCTION

At the "Deaths Foretold" conference in Bahia in 1988, concerning homicide in Latin American cities, the report on police killings of civilians in Mexico City was greeted with some skepticism. Like others, the report was based on a count drawn from news stories in the local papers, which was the only way that the organizers of the conference had at that time for getting an approximate total. Unlike some of the others, the report for Mexico City did not show a large number of police killings; it was proportionately one of the lowest in Latin America. The number of police killed, as reported in the press, was, on the other hand, rather high.

That result was a puzzle for some of us who were familiar with Brazil, for example, because Mexico City seemed roughly similar socially to other huge urban complexes, swollen by poor migrant populations, with insufficient housing, transportation, and other social services and great inequality of wealth; we wondered why Mexico City would not generate similar repression against the poor. We speculated cynically that the low figures might be especially inaccurate, perhaps a phenomenon of the Mexican press, which was notoriously hesitant to print news critical of the government. The difficulty with that speculation was that reports of police shootings do not necessarily imply criticism of the government; throughout the Americas such reports can be and usually are presented blandly as "confrontations." Finally we had to accept the figures for Mexico City provisionally and label them "exceptional," the way Mexico as a whole was labeled for purposes of human rights up to 1988.[294] In an effort to get at the truth behind the report made in Bahia, and to understand the reasons for it, I went to Mexico City in 1993 to investigate police violence.

227

ECONOMY AND POLITY IN MEXICO

Due to the vast expansion of government expenditures in the 1970s, in response to the development of its oil reserves, Mexico incurred an enormous external debt, which triggered an economic slowdown. The debt has been difficult to pay off, and the economy has not entirely revived; in the eighties, the downturn was severe enough to be called a depression. Economic inequality has increased, while the level of unemployment is high; in 1987, the announced unemployment rate was 18 percent, and it was no doubt in reality even higher.[295] The North American Free Trade Agreement (NAFTA) has certainly not solved the problem, especially for the poor.

There has always been insufficient land for those who want to work it. The population explosion of the last fifty years has led to a flight into the cities, especially Mexico City, which has grown as a metropolitan area from 1.5 million in 1930 to some fifteen million, fifty years later. The Federal District alone, as the heart of Mexico City and the capital of the country, has more than eight million, while the surrounding *conurbanos* have close to seven million. Of these millions, perhaps half earn the minimum wage, and a similar percentage live in squatter settlements, often without proper housing materials, sanitation, or electricity.[296]

Yet as a polity, the history of Mexico has been very different from that of Brazil, Argentina, or Jamaica. Although in legal form the country is a federation, in fact it has been one of the strongest and most centralized governments in the world. For decades after the revolution of 1910–20, in the classic description by Pablo González Casanova, the state sought systematically to wrest power, particularly the power to use violence, from local military leaders and bosses (*caudillos* and *caciques*) while at the same time protecting the country from foreign intervention:

> The presidential regime put an end to the conspiracies of the legislative power, the Army and the clergy. The dominant party put an end to the *caudillos* and their parties. The centralist regime put an

end to regional feuds. Intervention in local government not only eliminated free municipalities, but served to control the local *caciques*. The entrepreneurial state formed the basis for a national policy of economic and industrial development when large investments were needed for roads, dams, and centers for production, and when private initiative, both Mexican and foreign, was too backward and indifferent to invest. Limitations placed upon ownership effected agrarian reform and the oil expropriation, establishing the basis for an internal market and national capitalization in a country in which the number of customers was very small and national entrepreneurs practically non-existent.

The centralizing and pacifying work required the cooperation of the armed forces:

> The process of controlling *caudillismo* and *caciquismo*...depended partly on the professionalization of the Army, which sought to replace personalized norms of obedience with national norms of obedience. This control demanded a degree of energy and violence which often led to bloodshed.[297]

In the process, the army was itself subjected to the control of the central government. Although the army has a strong sense of its mission in national life, it is always at the command of the civilian authorities.

For the most part, however, the central government has sought to co-opt and absorb local sources of power less by violence than by offering positions in the Institutional Revolutionary Party (PRI) and its local administrations. Following the fragmentation and seemingly endless violence of the civil war, there was an overwhelming desire for political stability, for "peace and order."

Power has been centered in the president and in the PRI. In the past, the president has had control of the legislature, of governors, and even, more loosely, of the courts, although they are potentially independent.[298] While the president's powers are great, he has had to act through and with the cooperation of the members of the PRI, because under the constitution he cannot succeed himself. The PRI and its predecessor have won every national election since 1929, although since the mid-eighties opposition parties have begun to grow.

The PRI has largely kept control of economic and intellectual life; most collective endeavors of the sort we identify with civil society have had to take place with government encouragement. Labor and peasant movements were organized under the umbrella of the PRI, and potentially dissident leaders were mollified. Although newspapers in Mexico City, which has more than a dozen dailies, are numerous and free of formal censorship, the press traditionally has been very cautious in its criticism of the government, which has subsidized the papers and extended favors to reporters.[299]

Inside the shell of a federal, democratic constitution, then, Mexico has been an authoritarian, corporatist state. Although in the interests of the sovereignty of Mexico government rhetoric has had a loose orientation to the Left and against the United States, the style of governance, unlike that in many other authoritarian states, has not been strongly rooted in ideology or the exclusion of any class or group from society. Instead political relations have tended to be paternalistic and personal. There has been no civil service, so that government employees have had to depend on those above them in office for preferment and have often had to scramble for jobs every six years, just before the president goes out of office. The result has been a clientelist politics, in which both officeholders and private actors have had to depend on sponsors in the government or the PRI. Outside observers have remarked that the official manner is elaborately polite, even obsequious, in a way that sometimes seems hypocritical. There is a great deal of corruption, involving either money or personal influence; it has been persuasively argued that, given the centralization of government and the weakness of independent civil life, corruption in the conduct of affairs was inevitable.[300]

This style of government—in control of the legitimate use of violence as well as most other functions of society, but run by means of personal networks rather than by bureaucratic regulation—has been successful in Mexico. Despite the colossal social stresses of poverty and inequality, the country was relatively tranquil for many years. There is no continuing problem of vigilantism in Mexico City, and in my interview with the chief of police, he took pride in being able to say that crime was less serious than it is in many U.S. cities. Indeed, crime does not seem to be perceived as a social crisis in the way that it is in the United States and in some other cities in Latin America; an article entitled "Security in the Federal District" in a Mexico City magazine in 1992 emphasized this, citing comparative crime statistics with U.S. cities and a public opinion survey in which citizens thought that, while the city as a whole was dangerous, their own neighborhoods were not.[301]

This relative tranquility, together with Mexico's reputation for propitiating rather than destroying the discontented, created an "exceptionalism" for Mexico—an insulation from criticism for fraudulent elections and other violations of human rights, as though official violence were rare. In fact, it was not; as political scientist Roderic Camp remarked, "Historically, repression has been an acceptable rule of the game in Mexico."[302] But violence, when it was used, was often in the service of central policy; until the mid-eighties, the government was able to keep it quiet, partly because there were virtually no private nongovernmental organizations that were in a position to complain.

The "tranquility," then, was in part the quiet of the political tomb. There was nationalism in Mexico, but very little sense of citizen participation. As a member of the opposition remarked to me, the PRI's greatest success was in getting people accustomed to the idea that there was no alternative. There was a fatalism about it; in 1986, a majority of Mexicans polled thought that their country's situation would never improve.[303]

Even in its heyday, the centralist model never applied equally to all of Mexico; it was, and still is, strongest in Mexico City, the seat of government. Indigenous communities never owed strong allegiance to the national government, and there were towns where *caciques* still ruled, even if nominally in the name of the PRI. In the last generation, moreover, the authority of the central government has begun to change. A major act of official violence, the Tlatelolco massacre of student demonstrators in

1968, permanently damaged the reputation of the government among the middle class. The administrations of Presidents Luis Echevarría and José López Portillo, in the seventies, were particularly erratic and discouraging, and yet it was in those years that the national government intervened heavily in the economy, with attendant corruption. The succeeding years of economic crisis severely weakened the legitimacy of the government. In the eighties and nineties political movements in opposition to the PRI have grown, and civil society has been aroused from its slumber through nongovernmental organizations. Opposition parties on the left and right have criticized the rigging of elections and have forced electoral reforms that have both helped to maintain the PRI and to open the system somewhat to the opposition. The legitimacy of the centralist, interventionist state is ending even among officials of the PRI; the Salinas government tried after 1988 to decentralize some of the bureaucracy as well as to privatize state enterprises. It is widely accepted that the government's profligate corruption, particularly in the years since the discovery of Mexico's vast oil reserves, has slowed development and interfered with the improvement of the economy.

By the end of the eighties, Mexico's human rights record began to be aired, both by local and international nongovernmental organizations. The U.S. State Department, in its country reports on human rights, severely criticized Mexico and used the record as a bargaining tool in the negotiations over NAFTA; Mexican "exceptionalism" was at an end.[304] Human rights became a priority matter of state for the Salinas administration; as in Brazil and Argentina, issues of rights became a political testing ground for the government. In 1990, the government established a National Commission for Human Rights as an ombudsman for the police and other officials.

At the beginning of 1994, the uprising of a small, ill-equipped army of Indians in Chiapas caused a political explosion. Yet in many ways, the most remarkable thing for Mexico was not that the rebellion occurred; there have been other rebellions of the dispossessed in Mexico in the last generation which were crushed in silence and by the unmarked disappearances of their sympathizers. The difference in 1994 was that this rebellion occurred in the open, received notice and discussion, and, consequently, captured the national imagination.

POLICE VIOLENCE IN THE NATION AND THE CAPITAL

Mexican administrative practice makes a sharp division between the police's order-keeping functions on the streets, performed by a preventive police force, and investigative functions, conceived as deriving from the courts and performed by a judicial police body. Thus the capital, the Federal District (D.F.), is policed by a basic protection and traffic (*protección y vialidad*) force, by judicial police of the Federal District, who work only in the capital, and by federal judicial police, who have their headquarters in the capital but work throughout the country.

Preventive Police in the Federal District

The preventive police forces in the Federal District are enormous. According to René Monterrubio López, who was *secretario general de protección y vialidad* (chief of the PyV) at the time I visited in the spring of 1993, there were twenty-six thousand preventive police (PyV) who do the patrol and traffic work throughout the D.F. In addition, there are another twenty-six thousand auxiliaries who work chiefly guarding commercial establishments, and fifteen thousand *bancarios* who guard financial institutions. While the latter two groups are under the jurisdiction of the chief of police, they have very limited powers and are in fact paid largely by the enterprises that they guard. It is interesting that such security functions, which in other countries are now commonly performed by private firms, are a joint function of government and industry in Mexico City. While I have not been able to trace the administrative history of the development, I have little doubt that it is part of the history of the government's drive to centralization, mistrust of private centers of the control of force, and intervention in the economy.[305]

Citizen complaints about police abuses in the streets concern the PyV police rather than the auxiliaries, and the complaints usually arise out of the long-standing system of corruption. Patrolmen are paid the equivalent of about U.S. $260 a month, which is not enough to support a family in Mexico City. Out of that sum they have been expected to pay a "quota" to their superiors, to pay still more for choice assignments, and, on top of that, to purchase uniforms and gasoline for police vehicles. They also have to share with their superiors any additional graft they collect. The system is said to have reached its nadir during the tenure of Arturo "Negro" Durazo, the police chief who, during the late seventies and early eighties, turned the preventive police into a lucrative racket; so routine is the system that it is described even in the informal official history of the Mexico City police. Since the time of Negro Durazo, reforms have been attempted, but corruption persists.[306]

The untenable economic and working situation created by the system practically drives policemen to extort bribes from the denizens of the city. Cynical and frustrated, police sometimes beat up those who refuse to pay, or accuse them of crimes they have not committed. The recent case of Rafael Luviano Delgado, then a journalist for the newspaper *Excelsior,* is notorious.

On the evening of November 21, 1992, Luviano was driving home from a meeting, when a patrol car pulled him over. A policeman came up and asked for his documents, saying that Luviano had been "zigzagging." After examining the papers, the officer claimed that Luviano's license had expired which Luviano denies. Saying that Luviano would have to go to the station, the policeman drove Luviano's car, asking him what he did for a living and telling him that he ought to settle the matter with the police. Luviano said he would straighten it out at the station.

The policeman stopped the car in a dark street and returned Luviano's documents while another uniformed man pulled up in a patrol car. The first policeman addressed the other as "sergeant," saying that Luviano was a journalist from whom they would not get any money. The sergeant began to search Luviano's car, asking where to find the "arms" and the "drugs." When Luviano demanded to go to the station, the sergeant took from him his documents, together with about two hundred dollars in pesos. When Luviano demanded the money, an argument ensued, and the sergeant punched him hard in the face.

The police threw him, bleeding profusely, into his car, threatened to kill him if he moved, and fled. Luviano was able to hail a taxi and make his way home. When he finally arrived at a hospital, his right eye was so damaged that it had to be removed.

Luviano's case quickly became a cause célèbre, and a great embarrassment to the government. The officers were identified and jailed, and, even more unusual, the government made a large money settlement with Luviano.[307]

Some said that Luviano's case was typical in everything except the character of the victim the police chose to shake down. In 1992, the D.F. legislature received several complaints that followed the same pattern, and called the chief to a stormy meeting.[308] The system of corruption has made the street police a frightening body to all people in the D.F., regardless of their class. Whenever they meet a policeman, they are afraid that a payment will be demanded, and they do not know what else may happen; as they say about Luviano, "What if he had not been a journalist?"

Many low-ranking policemen hate the system of corruption, which forces them to work long hours under difficult conditions and scramble to find money to pay off their greedy superiors, who often abuse them as well. For years, police led by officer José Angel Pérez conducted a hunger strike in front of the National Palace to protest corruption by superiors.[309] During 1992, the D.F. legislature received some twenty-four complaints *from policemen* claiming abuse of authority and mistreatment by superiors. When Prince Charles of Britain visited

Mexico City in February 1993, the preventive police seized the opportunity to demonstrate against low salaries and oppression by their superiors; Manuel Camacho Solís, the mayor at the time, promised to do something about corruption or leave office.

Mayor Camacho Solís, working with René Monterrubio, his new chief of police in 1993, did take action to try to change the system of corruption. Salaries were now paid through a bank, rather than by the police department, in an effort to wrest control of the wages from superior officers and eliminate the "quota." Uniforms were now supplied from the same source that supplies the army, and repairs and gasoline for police cars were no longer administered by the department. Fringe benefits for the police were increased, and superiors began to be disciplined for corruption.

Nevertheless, the system has become so entrenched that the success of the reform measures is uncertain. The two predecessors to Monterrubio were relieved of office and have been under investigation for misconduct.[310] I was told that after a meeting between the police and Mayor Camacho Solís, the requirement to pay the "quota" had been lifted and that working hours had been cut. A short time later, superior officers passed the word that the political pressure was off and the "quota" would be resumed or else the hours would be raised again.

Under Camacho Solís, a new system of civilian complaints was established for the PyV police, with offices in public places such as subway stations, and staffed with civilian personnel. The complaints are investigated by a body outside the police. Policemen are encouraged to complain against their superiors, which they do with some frequency, claiming extortion, particularly through the imposition of bad working conditions when bribes are not paid to superiors.

Citizens complain especially about the bribes, but, so far as I can tell, almost never about the extrajudicial killing of suspects or other gross abuses of deadly force in the streets by the preventive police. Chief Monterrubio told me that 158 civilians were killed in 1992 by all police components under his command; that is a large number, but for combined police personnel numbering more than sixty-five thousand members, it does not seem astounding. In any case, it has not provoked complaints from human rights groups of a pattern of such abuse by the preventive police. It seems that the newspaper survey done for the "Deaths Foretold" conference was on the right track, at least as far as the preventive police is concerned.

The harshest critics of the Mexico City police would explain this result by saying that the preventive police are too busy with their extortion and bribery racket to be bothered chasing and shooting at suspects. Why abuse the citizen if there is no profit in it? I think, however, that the explanation lies again in the nature of the Mexican government, which has been at pains to get control of violence and to pacify the city. Although rising crime, especially organized crime, is a concern, the preventive police are not militarized; there is little rhetoric that pictures the city as embattled against criminal enemies, and none that analogizes the preventive police to an army. Killing a person, it would seem, is a serious political act, to be done for serious reasons. Almost all the complaints about spectacular police violence in Mexico are not made about the preventive police at all, but about the judicial police.

Federal Judicial Police

As a result of the centralization of the government, the federal judicial police (PJF) is a powerful presence throughout the nation as well as in the capital; the abuses characteristic of the work of the PJF set a pattern for judicial police in the Federal District as well as the states.

The PJF has tortured and killed, usually for reasons of policy. During the seventies, they participated with local judicial police and the army in the disappearance of hundreds of people thought to be connected with radical movements. During the eighties, they were implicated in spectacular cases of torture and killing in connection with narcotics cases throughout the country. In January 1990 in Mexico City, for example, PJF

antinarcotics police surrounded the house of Francisco Quijano to arrest him for the killing of another officer. When two
Quijano brothers, not including the suspect, came out of the
house to surrender, the police killed them outright and tortured
a third so brutally that he died. The Federal District medical
examiner initially found that all the brothers had been killed in
a shoot-out, but after Amnesty International was able to show
by an independent examination of the autopsy reports and
photographs that two of the brothers had probably been executed and the third tortured, the National Commission on
Human Rights (CNDH) ordered a new forensic examination,
which showed that the initial examination had been wrong.
The CNDH urged the federal attorney general to act against
the officers involved, but it does not appear that they have been
brought to justice.

In other cases, people have been killed when the federal narcotics police simply opened fire, sometimes with automatic
weapons, on automobiles that they suspected of being driven
by narcotics dealers. In a somewhat different sort of case, in
1989, federal narcotics police looking for drug traffickers participated in the invasion and search at gunpoint of an entire
town in the state of Durango, while hundreds of people were
forced to lie facedown in the village square. The federal attorney general explained blandly, "That's the way they work."[311]

The last phrase would seem to be the key. The war on drugs
was a matter of the highest state policy, being carried out with
funds from, and in cooperation with, the United States; under
such conditions, the judicial police were accustomed to carte
blanche. Here the rhetoric of war was used; the head of the federal narcotics police said that "drug wars had to be fought with
an iron fist and that drug traffickers...could not be 'collared with
caresses.'" The United States encouraged that view; when that
same head of the narcotics police was replaced in 1990, after a
storm of protest against the brutality of his officers, a U.S. official was quoted saying: "I think the human rights policy is going
to diminish [the Mexican police's] effectiveness at the street
level, but not at the program level.... You have to treat [suspects]

like you do in the United States now, which means they have all the leeway in the world to say nothing. Investigations will go more slowly."[312] Unfortunately for narcotics enforcement, the "anything goes" approach included corruption on the part of the PJF. The judicial police have sometimes been accused of killing people to cover up their corruption.[313]

Federal District Judicial Police

The three thousand members of the judicial police of the Federal District (PJDF) in Mexico City have operated very much like their federal counterpart, using violence for reasons of policy, and "solving" cases through coercion. In one noted recent case, the PJDF participated in the abduction of Braulio Aguilar Reyes, a union activist. Aguilar and his brother had been agitating for the democratization of the Oil Workers Union and for severance pay after a refinery was closed; the brothers had received threats from union representatives, who counted on a "security force" that included members of the PJDF. In April 1991, Braulio Aguilar was driving with his sister; they were cut off by two cars, front and back. Braulio was seized and carried off in one of the cars by two men in civilian clothes.

Occurring as it did in 1991, after official and nongovernmental groups had been formed to foster public interest in human rights, the case took a more favorable course than it might have taken in earlier years. Aguilar's family called on several of the private organizations, which immediately complained to the D.F. attorney general. Aguilar was finally released after forty hours incommunicado in a PJDF station and was immediately taken to a hospital, where he was found to have been badly beaten, resulting in spinal injuries and a ruptured eardrum. Two members of the PJDF were charged with abuse of authority and assault; according to the CNDH, both were convicted, although one has successfully appealed.[314] There are many cases of political intimidation in Mexico City as elsewhere in the country, but in most of them, unlike Aguilar's case, the perpetrators cannot be identified.

Although there was apparently no thought of charging Aguilar with a crime, the use of torture by the PJDF to obtain confessions was endemic, as it was in the federal judicial police and elsewhere in Mexico. Perhaps the most notorious case is that of Ricardo López Júarez, who was accused of kidnapping a ten-year old boy. Under the direction of a D.F. prosecutor, López was tortured for days in June 1990, to force him to tell where the child was hidden, until López finally died; his body was hanged in the jail in an effort to make his death appear a suicide, and his death certificate showed that he died of hanging. Fortunately López's mother, who had briefly been tortured in his presence in a final effort to get him to talk, was able to contradict the story; a further medical examination of Ricardo López disclosed that he did not die of hanging but of a horrible list of massive injuries. The prosecutor and several police agents were ultimately convicted of homicide. As in so many other cases, the point of the interrogation was lost in the grand guignol of police violence; I cannot find any record that the kidnapper was ever identified.[315]

Among the participants in the Ricardo López case were some shadowy figures, not actually officials but friends and relatives of police who did some of the dirty work. Such informal aides, known as *madrinas,* have appeared repeatedly in Mexican police work and may actually account for some unknown number of deaths and other crimes that cannot be directly traced to the police. In 1993, the federal attorney general forbade the use of *madrinas* by the judicial police.[316]

Mexican criminal procedure and practice traditionally relied heavily on confessions; they were the chief means of proof in most cases, and thus, according to Miguel Sarre Iguíniz of the CNDH, the police developed little skill in other ways of investigation. While confessions shown to be coerced are excluded from evidence, the suspect has the burden of proving the coercion. The courts, moreover, under a principle of "immediacy," give principal weight to the earliest confession, even if later statements contradict it. Under Mexican law, a suspect was supposed to be informed of his right to counsel and brought before a judge within twenty-four hours and released if no evidence was presented against him within seventy-two hours; nevertheless, confessions were not made inadmissible if these provisions were not followed. A great many confessions were coerced during incommunicado detention before taking the suspect before a judge.[317]

All the actors in the criminal justice system colluded to make confessions acceptable, regardless of how they were obtained. The prosecutors allowed the judicial police to violate the procedural rules in order to squeeze suspects, and sometimes, as in the Ricardo López case, prosecutors actually participated in the coercion. The courts, moreover, were and still are extremely reluctant to give any relief for coerced confessions; judges commonly do not release a defendant on account of such abuses if they believe for other reasons that the defendant is guilty. In the case of Maria Alicia Sánchez Cortés in 1990, the defendant was found in the trunk of a car by preventive police and taken to the office of the prosecutor, who turned her over to the PJDF. After interrogation for ninety-eight hours, during which the prosecutor did not insist that she be taken before a judge, given a medical exam, or permitted to see a lawyer, she confessed to participating in the murder of the driver of the car. She claimed in her first appearance before the judge that she was innocent and her confession had been coerced; although a medical examination showed no injuries, it should have been clear that during such a long detention psychological pressure or physical treatment that did not leave lasting traces could have broken down her will. Nevertheless, the court found her and those she implicated in her confession guilty. At the insistence of the CNDH, the police and agents of the prosecutor were disciplined, and some were prosecuted, but it does not appear that the courts ever acted to reverse Sánchez's conviction.[318]

The code of criminal procedure was amended in 1991 to try to put an end to the use of torture. Under the new law, courts are permitted to accept a confession only when it is made before a judge or a prosecutor, and the confession shall have "no probative value unless in the presence of a defense attorney or person of trust and, when appropriate, the translator of the accused." The suspect is to have a medical examination before and after the interrogation. In 1986, Mexico passed the federal Law to Prevent and Punish Torture, making torture a crime punishable by eight years' imprisonment. According to some commentators, it did not make any noticeable difference, and in 1991 the law was strengthened to make it a crime to fail to report torture committed by another official, and to require payment of damages to victims.[319]

The CNDH claimed that these measures reduced the incidence of torture, based on the fact that the number of complaints had declined. There is no question, however, that torture took place; in 1991–92, according to its own count, the CNDH received at least sixty-nine complaints of torture by the PJDF. As we know from Brazil and Argentina, reforms like those in Mexico do not have an automatic effect, because the police can try to terrify a suspect into repeating an involuntary confession in court, and because obtaining information is not the only purpose to torture; it also serves to punish and degrade the victim.

In an echo of Buenos Aires and São Paulo, coercion continued to be linked to a corrupt system in which officials, including prosecutors, extracted money from suspects. A classic example was reported by the CNDH. In 1991, Fernando Alpuing Ozuna and his wife sought the aid of the D.F. prosecutor to investigate a case in which they claimed to have been the victims of fraud. An assistant prosecutor solicited a bribe to expedite the case, the family paid the money, and Alpuing Ozuna went with a friend to a meeting to discuss the matter with the prosecutor. When they arrived at the appointed place, they were taken prisoner by judicial police at gunpoint and were tortured until they signed confessions implicating themselves in extortion. Fortunately they were found innocent and complained to the CNDH and the D.F. attorney general. In January 1993, the officials involved were dismissed.[320]

When I asked human rights advocates in Mexico City what they thought was the most pervasive problem in the criminal justice system, more than once I received the answer, "false charges, framing suspects." That is a chilling role for police to fill, and it raises again the question how the judicial police came to fill it. The answer, I think, is in part that they have represented an authoritarian state. If they used deadly force against a political enemy of the regime or against a narcotics dealer, they expected to escape punishment, because that was part of their job. If they tortured a suspect to confess, they found what the justice system required—a person to be accused of the crime. The judicial police, as well as other actors in the system, wanted to find someone who fit the charges and would clear the case; finding the truth was of less concern.

Corruption made the situation more complex. When the police extorted money from suspects or used violence to conceal corruption, they acted of course in their own interests. Traditionally, however, corrupt officials enjoyed impunity in exchange for payoffs to their superiors, providing they turned a blind eye to corruption by others and showed loyalty to the regime as a whole. Under these conditions, framing suspects had to be something that occurred frequently.

Impunity and Accountability

In the effort to control human rights abuses, President Carlos Salinas de Gortari adopted a typically centralist approach: he established the National Commission for Human Rights in 1990 to act as ombudsman for complaints throughout the country and named the distinguished jurist Dr. Jorge Carpizo as its president. The CNDH is an impressive organization, well-staffed and with the weight of presidential power behind it; many of those who work for the commission are dedicated human rights activists with years of experience. At times the CNDH has been unsparingly critical in its recommendations, calling for the punishment of publicly named officials, and has followed up by urging local and federal officials to complete their investigations.

On the other hand, the CNDH has only oversight power; it

cannot force an official to act on a recommendation; in particular, of course, it cannot interfere with the decisions of the courts. Some officials, even in the federal system, have been surprisingly recalcitrant; two federal attorneys general who failed to act in response to CNDH recommendations were dismissed. President Salinas finally moved the head of the CNDH, Dr. Carpizo, to the position of attorney general. The imperious force of such presidential pressure raises the question why officials fail to act, in the face of an outright threat of dismissal.

The reasons must lie partly in the personal nature of Mexican political relations, as well as in the corruption of the system. Those against whom the CNDH's recommendations have been made have friends and protectors who have some power to prevent them from being disciplined. Moreover, if the official who is ordered to act has engaged in corrupt acts or has himself participated in violations of human rights, he risks being accused if he acts against others. And it is likely that some of the commanders of policemen who have tortured or shot suspects do not fully believe that the policemen have done anything that was not part of their job. If the police acted in the interest of the government, they did what was expected of them, and no doubt to many commanders it does not seem fair suddenly to bring the police up on charges.

Thus those who have violated human rights are often not disciplined, but are instead shifted to another position or promoted. As of this writing, the men who killed the Quijano brothers as they were surrendering to federal narcotics police in 1990 have never been prosecuted, and one of them has been transferred and promoted.

The powers of accused officials to protect themselves through intimidation and retaliation are extraordinary and sometimes Byzantine. The killer of a muckraking Mexico City journalist, Manuel Buendía, turned out to be the very policeman who first rushed to investigate his murder and then carefully stole some incriminating files. He was convicted in 1993, nine years after the murder. As this is written, a PJF commander is on trial for masterminding the murder in 1990 of Norma

Corona Sapién, a lawyer who was the president of the Human Rights Commission in the state of Sinaloa; since the trial started, six prosecution witnesses have been murdered, some of them while they were in custody.[321] It is easy to believe that other officials would prefer to run the risk of losing a job, rather than the risk of accusing such people. Nevertheless, the criminal prosecution of these cases is proceeding and may ultimately have a deterrent effect.

An ombudsman body like the CNDH, however extraordinary, cannot do the job alone; no organization that acts solely by review and recommendations of discipline can reform an entrenched system in which thousands of people have a vested interest, some of them threatened with prison if the reform is successful. The CNDH, moreover, is no longer as powerful even as it was when it was created by presidential decree in 1990. The national legislature has accepted the CNDH as an institution of government, but in the process has limited its jurisdiction and transferred the oversight of local violations of human rights to state human rights commissions. Although this was no doubt part of the ongoing process of decentralizing the national government, the enforcement of human rights, which was never very well established in Mexico, is the last governmental function that ought to be given to local authorities.

The reform of the justice system to end impunity for police abuses as well as to minimize corruption, torture, and false charges requires more than oversight; it requires the participation of all the actors in the system. The 1991 reform in the code of criminal procedure, for example, provides that a confession is valid if taken in the presence of the prosecutor or a judge; that provision is not very useful unless the prosecutors and judges take action against the use of coercion. If the prosecutors refuse to countenance corruption and torture in criminal cases, the police abuses will drop off precipitately; if the judges monitor the work of the prosecutors and police, the abuses will drop off still more. The 1990 case of Maria Sánchez Cortes, described above, in which Ms. Sánchez was successfully convicted of murder after ninety-eight hours of interrogation, shows that in some cases, neither the prosecutors nor the courts have had any interest in preventing the coercion of suspects.

The public had little confidence in the will of the courts to give redress, and the courts were not being used to indemnify victims of false prosecution or police violence. Although the 1991 Law to Prevent and Sanction Torture provides for the compensation of victims, it appears to be used very little. If the courts cannot be reorganized to carry out this function, an adminstrative body such as the CNDH ought to be authorized to compensate the victims, a result that would be consistent with international law.[322]

Experience in other countries suggests that compensation by damages alone will not change abusive police practices; the police may be able to continue their abuses and treat the damages as a "cost of doing business." The management of the police has to resolve to condemn the abuses, reward and promote those police who do their work according to law, and dismiss and refer for prosecution those who do not. In the Federal District, in addition to the efforts of the CNDH, the attorney general has begun a campaign to upgrade the performance of the judicial police and eliminate abusive officers. There is a training program in human rights as well as proper methods of investigation, and, according to the attorney general, tighter control through discipline. More than four hundred disciplinary cases were brought against D.F. judicial police in 1992, and some seventy-five agents had been dismissed since 1988.[323] Because it is not clear why the agents have been dismissed, however, the disciplinary system remains of limited value as a means of accountability and restoring public confidence. Similarly, as we have seen, there have been efforts to cut corruption in the preventive police. All these policies will have to be carried out consistently over a period of years before they can be expected to change the police, not to speak of alleviating the almost complete public mistrust of the police.

CONCLUSIONS

With the strengthening of an independent civil society in

Mexico, the silent exceptionalism for human rights violations has faded in the nineties. As in the South American countries and Jamaica, human rights abuses, including police violence and the framing of suspects, have become a political battle-ground in which the legitimacy of the government is tested. The formation of the CNDH signalled the importance of the issue to the national government.

The situation of police violence in the Federal District in Mexico City presented a sharp contrast with São Paulo, Jamaica, and, to a lesser extent, Buenos Aires. The Mexican government has tried to control all sources of power—in the classic phrase, to get a monopoly of legitimate force—and in particular to subordinate the military to the civilian government, as well as to pacify the urban population. The government of the Federal District is not confronted with a major problem of vigilante justice, and the preventive police do not take a militarized approach to their duties. It is true that the judicial police have been implacable when they are crossed or when they think the government's interests are involved, and until recently there has been scarcely any accountability. But that is a very different thing from the sort of "combat" atmosphere that is found in the streets of some other cities.

My survey of the work of the judicial and preventive police in the Federal District of Mexico roughly confirms the conclusions drawn at the "Deaths Foretold" conference in Bahia. However dismaying the police work is in a number of respects, there is no persuasive evidence that deadly force is used in the streets as a form of semimilitary control by terror.[324] Deadly force is used as one would expect it to be used by a centralized, authoritarian state for which an atmosphere of tranquility is important: as an instrument of state policy, used by a relatively small group of people. And the CNDH is just the sort of agency that a centralized state would use to investigate official abuse.

The prevalence of corruption and impunity throughout the government has raised special problems for control of police violence and for criminal justice generally. Sometimes the police have killed those who try to uncover corruption. More often, they have manufactured cases for corrupt purposes or just in order to be able to say that the criminal justice system is "getting results"; unfortunately, prosecutors and judges have participated and encouraged those practices. The consequences for the system have been disastrous: everyone in Mexico seems to mistrust criminal justice almost completely, at least as cases are reported publicly, suspecting that every claim of guilt or innocence has some ulterior political purpose behind it. Any reform will require as a principal aim that all the actors in the system try to do the basic job, independent of the rest of the government, of relating the facts to the law, to yield honest and transparent results in at least some criminal cases.

The order represented and reproduced by the preventive police, in its day-to-day relations with citizens, is powerful and arbitrary. Although much police work undoubtedly involves the poor, as it does in every society, abusive police action in Mexico City seems to be just as intimidating to the middle class, probably because so much of it emanates from corruption. Thus police action tells people of all classes that they are subject to the whim of a venal government and that their problems can be resolved only by personal intervention, by payment or some other means. Police action also says that the venal system can be vicious if it is defied.

That same order has been more than mirrored—exaggerated—in the treatment of the rank-and-file preventive police themselves. The system is cruel to police, destroying their self-respect and threatening brutal working conditions as the alternative to extortion. It is not surprising that the police, desperate for money and frustrated as well, would show contempt for and mistreat citizens when the police themselves are despised and mistreated. The system of organized extortion in the preventive police has starkly illustrated the connection between corruption and the violation of human rights.

CHAPTER IX

Conclusion

Reports on human rights virtually never bring good news; characteristically they record the worst abuses in an effort to embarrass and badger governments into putting a stop to them. Yet such reports are also eternally, sometimes exasperatingly hopeful; the very fact that they are written and published implies a belief that there are human rights standards to which governments can be held accountable and that practices actually could be improved, under at least minimally democratic governments, such as those in Brazil, Argentina, Mexico, Jamaica, and the United States.

At the simplest level, this book continues in that tradition; in it I have tried to report the facts of serious police violence, particularly deadly force and torture, insofar as they can be known, in an effort to make a record—a witness—of the problems in six urban areas throughout the Americas. Through the comparison of the places and their cultures, moreover, I have tried to deepen the understanding of the causes of the violence, to see which practices are so widespread as to seem endemic to police work, and which are peculiar to a place and a time; the similarities and differences in the political and social characteristics of the places tell us something about the wellsprings of police violence and the conditions hospitable to human rights. The comparative method thus extends the transformative implications of reports on human rights violations; if cities that resemble one another in some respects have very different levels of official violence, that comparison suggests that there may be ways the violence can be reduced.

The comparison has shown a correlation between the sociopolitical structure of the places and the level of violence by the police; the departments reproduce and represent the relations in the social order. Where, for example, the order is one in which respect for rights is weak and private vengeance is not well controlled, the police tend to act with arbitrary violence. And in many cases, social relations of hierarchy or relative equality are reflected in the structure of the police department itself.

Police departments are not, however, mere passive mirrors of the social order, nor could they be, because such orders are complex and embody conflicting interests and values. Within the bounds of the politics of the city, the police can, to choose the extremes, emphasize regularity and law or act as delegated vigilantes. The characteristics of departments can encourage the use of violence; thus, for example, departments that represent themselves as similar to military forces, as the military police in São Paulo and the Los Angeles police have done, will use violence as an instrument of control much more than police who represent themselves clearly as part of civil government.

This book has also compared the methods of accountability for the police in the cities, as well as in some national governments. I have found these methods woefully inadequate in many cases, and it is clear that there are political barriers to making them more effective. But some accountability turns out to be a great deal better than none; it seems that a small reform, such as the spotty prosecutions of police in Argentina, in a situation where there has been little or no accountability, can reduce violence. In a few instances, a promising method of accountability has been neglected everywhere, as seems to be the case with damage actions as a source of policy. The comparison suggests not so much that the devices are useless, but that they could be made instruments for management and deterrence of abuse without substantial political change in the governments of the six cities. Beyond this, I have tried here and in chapter III to envision a system of management and accountability that might minimize police violence.

THE RHETORIC OF POLICE WORK

The differences among the police departments in the six localities are largely expressed in a common language. Rhetorical themes such as militarization, politicization, or complaints about the larger system of criminal justice are heard everywhere, so that they can be translated from place to place, although their meaning differs in practice.

The most general theme is the definition of roles (or the lack of it) for the police. In every city, there is a perennial debate concerning whether the police should devote their energies to order keeping, to even more generalized service functions, or to "law enforcement," a term that, in English, is ambiguous as to whether the police ought to turn themselves single-mindedly to chasing and perhaps even punishing criminals, or whether the police ought to look to the protection of the rights of citizens as well. The confusion continues just because it represents a basic tension in governance between order and liberty, a tension that government does not really wish to resolve, but rather wishes to leave ambiguous so that the police can make choices as the situation changes.

Complaints about "politics" in the police appear everywhere, and there are recurring efforts to exclude politics from the administration of police departments. In this usage, "politics" connotes the influence not of policy but of faction in police administration. For example, in Jamaica and historically in U.S. cities, police have found preferment through partisan influence. In some instances, political forces outside the police also protect favored suspects from prosecution, or, worse, try to see to it that some innocent party is prosecuted; such forces may also corrupt the police by demanding graft and protecting corrupt and violent people who are of their party. Proposals for reform of these abuses have been chiefly directed at insulating the police from party pressure in hiring and promotion, as well as in the administration of the criminal justice system. The growth of civil service status for police in the United States and proposals from reformers for a bipartisan police administration in Jamaica are measures intended to insulate the police from party influence and from "outside control." These reform measures have obscured the perception that police administration is by nature political, in the sense that decisions about whether to emphasize order keeping and social control on the one hand, or "anticrime" on the other, are not "technical" but are decisions about policy; such decisions ought not to be insulated, but ought to be at least influenced if not actually controlled by the larger polity "outside" the police. In recent decades, the intensely political nature of police work has been emphasized in another way by the organization of police rank-and-file benevolent organizations and unions; they have acted not only as labor organizations but as political groups to lobby state and city officials against reforms in policy.

Part of the reason some governments say they want to insulate the police from politics is that they want to insulate the choices for the functions of the police from criticism. In this connection, the enormous discretion that the police have, both on the street and in investigation, is a great relief for city governments. They can leave it to street officers and middle-level managers to emphasize direct action for social control if the police think such action is needed, and the city administration can to some extent avoid public awareness and even responsibility for the choice. In many cases, city administrations do not want to control the discretion of the police any more than they already have, and some would probably increase police discretion if they could. City governments can avoid effective "outside control" over policy decisions of the police by shunning "politics" in the police.

The long-standing debate about the proper emphasis for police work has led to a state of mind in which the various functions of police fuse together. In particular, the concept of law-enforcement work has come to include the order-keeping and social-control functions; law and order become one. Thus the police see a threat to themselves as a threat to order as well as a danger very like the danger of crime. In every city, defiance of the police gives rise to a sanction from the police; in São Paulo, the police might shoot the suspect who runs away, while in Los Angeles they might beat or slap him, although shooting is not unheard of.

At the extreme, the police become the embodiment of order and short-circuit the rest of the criminal justice system. They administer justice directly in the streets and the station houses, an impulse that is encouraged by the widespread impatience with the courts as slow, uncertain, lenient, and—not surprisingly—"legalistic." That impulse appears in the work of every department, even though the frequency of its appearance varies; the Mollen Commission report reveals the impulse clearly in New York, where corrupt police thought it was their job to punish neighborhood people as well as criminals, to "show who was in charge." In Buenos Aires, police sometimes try to boss a neighborhood directly; in the notorious case from the Ingeniero Budge district, the police killed some youths for crossing those whom the police protected. In São Paulo and Jamaica, the police shot poor men they thought to be thieves or gunmen, to avoid the trouble of taking them to court.

In São Paulo, the tendency was exaggerated by the split between the functions of patrol, vested in the military police (PM), and investigation, vested in the civil police. The PM, disgusted with the work of the criminal justice system outside its ranks, especially with the civil police, took it upon themselves to punish by the most effective means they could find: by killing suspects. They went to the limit, collapsing all the police functions into one, treating the order-keeping and control function as if it were anticrime, and killing those who were merely annoying and "likely" to become criminals. The PM's work reminds us that the functional division between preventive and investigative police is never complete; in São Paulo, the PM conducted massive raids into the *favelas* in an effort to find wanted criminals as well as to suppress crime.

Detectives, whose job is to investigate crimes, can also circumvent other parts of the criminal justice system, insuring a conviction by forcing a suspect to confess. By concentrating their efforts on suspects who are poor, they use the investigative function to reproduce an aspect of the social order. Sometimes, as in Mexico, they will work to make the system as well as the police look successful and emphasize the power of the state by picking out a suspect and framing him through coercion. Detectives usually have a symbiotic relation with criminals, in order to keep open their sources of information; this enables them, if they choose, nearly to eliminate the court process in property crimes, as the civil police have often done in São Paulo and as detectives once commonly did in departments in the United States. In such cases, the police coerce the suspect to give up the proceeds of the crime, then release the suspect in return for a bribe, and return the stolen property to its owner for a fee. In a history that is strikingly the same from place to place, detectives have taken on an organizational life of their own, which raises additional problems for the governments in controlling the detectives' violent tactics and corruption.

Governments and police departments never fully admit to taking shortcuts to social control and around the criminal justice systems. Citizens themselves are often of two minds about the police tendency to assimilate order to law and to administer direct punishment: on the one hand, they are impatient of crime and the criminal justice process; on the other hand, they are apprehensive about the police and even doubtful whether some crimes ought to be punished. The confusion of demands on the police and public ambivalence about law enforcement contributes to the corruption that appears in every city. The police are asked to enforce laws that a large part of the population, including many political leaders, do not really want to see enforced, and the police sometimes take bribes for themselves as well as for politicians. Corruption, especially when the proceeds are distributed throughout the political system, protects the police from accountability for any abuses. The resulting cloak of impunity that protects and sometimes encourages violence has been a serious problem in virtually all the cities, from New York to Buenos Aires. The old police reformer isolated atop civil police headquarters in São Paulo said the definitive words: "A corrupt police is always violent."

The confusion of demands made by society on the police and the ambivalence of public attitudes toward police violence and corruption consigns the police to the status of a "tainted occupation." Public opinion polls show that city dwellers recognize that the police may abuse suspects, for example, or may not be entirely honest; nevertheless, they do not expect the police to be much better, and they are fairly well satisfied with the results. People do not want to resolve the tension between social control and law; they often do not care whether the police use excessive force, unless the violence is thrust in their faces, as it was in the videotape of Rodney King. The public has a residual fear and distrust of the police, even while the public depends on them and expresses its satisfaction with them. Our dependence on an authority we fear increases our sense of insecurity in the cities, confused with our fear of crime. At the same time, the fear increases our sense of dependence on the police and our sense that we would not want them to be fully controllable and accountable, because then we would have to resolve our confusion about what it is we want the police to do.

The military analogy for police is partly rooted in the history of the development of departments from militias, as in the United States and Brazil; under colonial conditions, furthermore, as in Jamaica, the police did have a function similar to that of an occupying army. In contemporary terms the military analogy is easiest to understand as a way of bureaucratizing the police and controlling discretion while still encouraging some esprit de corps, as in Los Angeles. But the analogy, turned to the purposes of a "war on crime," waged by the police as army against an internal enemy, has distorted police work. Military forces are organized primarily to use violence against a well-defined enemy, and although they can patrol, they are ill-suited to turn to the police jobs of service, peaceable order keeping, or even arresting suspects for crime. A soldier is trained to solve many problems by shooting someone, and the police, if they think of themselves as an army, are likely to do the same.

The military analogy has contributed to the formation of "squads" or "teams" within the police, with specialized tasks, isolated from the public as well as from other police. Such squads set their own standards and sometimes adopt protomilitary goals. In Buenos Aires, the detectives from Robbery and Theft caught thieves in a cul de sac and shot them, while in a chilling parallel, the Special Investigations Section of the LAPD did exactly the same thing in California.

The special squads of the PM in São Paulo have been the most extreme case. There the ROTA took on a military mystique, which made them "heroes" if they shot suspects; they set a standard for other special squads as well as for the PM as a whole. Deadly force was so much encouraged that the PM thought they were justified even if they killed a person who was only a suspect or was in the class of those suspected. The "military" analogy has been strongest in countries like Brazil, where the armed forces themselves have believed it was their mission to take a role in domestic affairs; there the police have taken on some of the characteristics of an army. Although the analogy was not quite so strong in Jamaica, functioning on a war footing under emergency powers did lead the constabulary to abuses of deadly force. The military dehumanizes and demonizes its enemy, and the military analogy pushes the police to dehumanize the people they must work with, the poor of the cities. The dehumanization makes it easier to abuse those who are the enemy, easier even to kill or torture them.

In the United States the results of the confusion over police roles, the fear of disorder and the military analogy have not been quite so disastrous. In Los Angeles, the work of the police has been primarily directed toward anticrime measures and the rapid response of police units to reports of crime; the combination of that orientation with a "war on crime" has led to considerable police violence. The war had to be turned on an internal enemy, which turned out to be people, especially young blacks and Hispanics, in poor districts. The anticrime approach keeps the police in their cars, at a distance from the public; the military approach just increases the distance. The military analogy, in short, represents an order that is in effect at war with the poor.

THE GOVERNMENT AND CONTROL OF VIOLENCE

The amount of official violence, including torture and deadly force as well as less serious abuses, that accompanies the rhetoric of police work in the six urban areas varies with the nature of the polity. In São Paulo, for example, when the governor said in 1991 that the PM special squads would show "no mercy" to criminals, it signified to Brazilians that the PM was going to shoot a great many suspects. But in Los Angeles, when the chief of the LAPD said in 1927 that he would reprimand any officer who showed "the least mercy" to a criminal, that did not imply, as it turned out, that there was to be truly indiscriminate use of deadly force.

I argued in the introduction that the seriousness of official violence would vary with the "civilization," to use Elias's word, or, in contemporary parlance, the "pacification" of the populace in the cities, through a historical process that is now widely recognized.[325] One element of that process is the increasing revulsion against brutal and public punishment, accompanied by a growing desire for privacy, a desire to exclude even the awareness of violence from one's personal life. This may help to explain why the "third degree" and other forms of torture by the police have persisted so long and tenaciously; they are secret, hidden from view, even when we are aware at the margins of consciousness that they continue.

In the process, private interpersonal violence declined at the same time that public, official violence was waning. Through the regulation of industrial and bureaucratic life, as well as through literacy and public opinion, accompanied by the growth of the legal system, including the police themselves, urban pacification took hold, reinforcing the revulsion against official brutality as well as the desire for tranquility. Confidence in the government, combined with citizen participation, led to the increasing legitimacy of the legal system, reliance on rights as an aspect of citizenship, as well as a stronger sense of common humanity with other citizens, which in turn made official violence yet more unacceptable. There are variations of this very rough model in our six urban areas of the Americas. In societies that had colonial rule or slavery (commonly both) the revulsion against public and brutal punishment has never been complete. At the same time, the acceptance by elites of the poor as equal citizens in any but a very technical sense has been slight. Those characteristics of former colonial societies, while present in the United States, have been reinforced by the history of debt and dependency in Latin America and the Caribbean.

Brazil presents an extreme case among nations that now lay claim to being democratic. There has not been a strong tradition of participation and little effective recognition of the rights of others by Brazilians. The legal system, even as a means of settling of private disputes, has enjoyed little trust. The Brazilian anthropologist Teresa Caldeira has argued that the weak recognition of individual rights in Brazil has been accompanied by a correspondingly weak sense of the separateness, the integrity of the individual body. She writes: "On the body of the dominated—children, women, Black people, the poor or allegedly criminals—those who consider themselves to be in a position of authority mark their power."[326] Brutal punishment against the poor, the criminal, and the merely disorderly has been routine; torture has been used everywhere, almost exclusively against those who are "torturable," except during times of political repression, when it has been used more generally.

A similar but less radically hierarchical pattern appears in Jamaica, where generations of colonial rule left a gulf between the elite and the poor; across the divide there was little sense of shared citizenship. A stronger tradition of rights and respect for the law, however, has cushioned the conflict in Jamaica.

In both Jamaica and Brazil, the governments have conveyed only an uncertain sense that they "govern." Neither gave a strong signal that a principal purpose of the machinery of modern government was to exclude violent self-help, or that vengeance was really a crime. Under these conditions, modern weaponry and the rhetoric of a "war on crime" against an internal enemy made for a deadly police.

Most clearly in São Paulo, but to some extent in other cities, the authorities tried to lend some legitimacy to the violence by self-consciously minimizing the appearance of overt class conflict. Thus, under contemporary conditions, police rarely attack workers striking or demonstrating; the street violence is instead directed at those who are "marginal," who have few supporters in the society. In Brazil and Jamaica, the police reproduce a system in which outright violence is used to control such people.

In some ways, Buenos Aires proved to be a special case. There fear of crime has been used in an effort to strengthen the police and the government generally. Police violence in the capital itself has been a way not only to control people but to intimidate them into acquiescing in the corruption and violence of the police. In this way, the police perpetuate traditional authoritarian public attitudes; having seen the police be tough under authoritarian governments, the public expects them to be violent. If they do not see or hear of the police being violent, they think the police are not doing their job. And thus the cycle of official and private violence continues.

If Brazil and Jamaica show us how the lack of participation of citizens in the governmental process can contribute to a weak sense of solidarity and mutual rights, Mexico City, at least as it was until the nineties, reminds us that government legitimacy and a relatively pacified urban life are possible even without strong citizen participation. There the government has done its best to get control of the legitimate use of violence, especially in the Federal District. It has rigidly excluded any use of the military against the domestic population and has not used the "military" analogy for the police. It has succeeded as an authoritarian government sometimes through the appearance of increased citizen participation, and sometimes by corruption and cooptation and by offering benefits selectively. In Mexico City, these perquisites have included access to land, including technically "illegal" settlements, as well as access to health care and resources for community development.[327] At the same time, the government sought to discourage any alternative to its policies, through a quiet repression against those who could not be co-opted. The use of torture to solve even nonpolitical crimes is in part a product of this assertion of state power. To the populace, the police represent an order that is corrupt and capricious, in the sense that it may act against a person of any class. But the frequent use of deadly force against the underclass is missing.

The United States has enjoyed a good deal of success in pacifying its urban populations, although that trend has been weakening since the present massive fear of crime began some twenty-five years ago. As Roger Lane has put it, "The literally 'civilizing' institutions of the nineteenth century, from temperance societies to a variety of incarcerating institutions, worked to make the industrial city function smoothly as far as they did because they were going with the flow, reinforcing the felt needs of the new economic order, helping to create a new kind of mass social psychology."[328]

Violence has nevertheless always been close to the surface of consciousness in the United States. The current passionate resistance to government control of firearms is, quite precisely, an expression of protest against the government's attempt to monopolize the legitimate use of violence. The opponents of gun control believe that firearms must be retained not only as instruments of self-defense against invaders or assailants, but more importantly as a way of resisting the government. In a famous exchange, a spokesperson for the National Rifle Association argued at a hearing before Congress that the issue "is about all of our right to be able to protect ourselves against all of you guys up there."[329]

Our fantasies of independence and violent self-help, which are only slightly submerged by the pacifying influences of modern government, constantly show their vigor in popular films, such as the *Death Wish* series, in which a lone citizen metes out vengeance to violent criminals. Not surprisingly, such films convey a rather different meaning in countries like Brazil, where vigilantism and official violence are still a familiar presence. The extent to which the acts of violence depicted are fantasies is ambiguous in the United States and is even less clear to viewers abroad. Especially popular in Rio de Janeiro, for example, was a television series produced but scarcely noted in the United States, *Dark Justice,* in which at the beginning of each episode, one Nicholas Marshall, a criminal court judge, is seen reluctantly releasing a violent criminal on a legal technicality. The remainder of the episode is spent with the judge, riding a motorcycle and accompanied by a faithful detective staff, bringing the criminal to justice, usually in some violent way. I have heard Brazilians say that they need judges like our Nicholas Marshall.

While the examples drawn from popular entertainment and the debate about gun control are contemporary, it is clear that they are rooted in older attitudes in the United States. Vigilantism, even in cities such as Los Angeles, was with us at least until World War II. Before the changes wrought in municipal government by the influence of the Progressives, clientelism in politics was the norm in U.S. cities and participation was channeled by the machines. While these political characteristics undoubtedly encouraged official violence, the tendency was not exacerbated by landlessness, poverty, and debt to the extent it was elsewhere in the Americas.

Equally important in controlling police violence in U.S. cities has been the development of a strong sense of rights, a demand for equality and reliance on the system of law. As life in the cities became more orderly, citizens demanded order in their relations with the government. The social psychologist Tom Tyler has found that Americans are especially willing to comply with the orders of the authorities, however grudgingly, because we believe the authorities are at least minimally fair in the sense that they are unbiased and willing to permit participation.[330] The "rights revolution" in the United States since the 1950s can be seen as the end of a process in which the populace has ceded some of the control of violence to the government, in return for strong substantive and procedural rights. Interest-group politics in the United States reinforced the rights revolution; minority groups have protested police violence against their members as acts of discrimination. The relative strength of systems of police accountability and control in the United States is owing in large part to the constant vigilance of self-conscious minority groups.

While the development of suspects' legal rights has taken on a life of its own during the last thirty years, the sense of civil control in the cities has been diminishing, undermined by an increasingly violent atmosphere. The economic basis for the common bond of citizens in jobs and relative prosperity is disappearing, leaving in its wake inequality and conflict. The sense of participation through citizenship has been weakening, while a strong sense of individual rights has arisen in its place. Americans recognize that the rule of law is a source of and a component of their civilized life; the trouble is that civilized life seems to be slipping away.

A similar process can be seen elsewhere in the Americas, especially in the last decade, which has witnessed the passing of dictatorships and a rising interest in human rights. Some controls over official abuses have developed in all the cities studied, even while the fear that crime is out of control continues to grow.

The result of fear warring with a growing sense of rights is a crisis in the acceptance of the rule of law. In the punishment of criminals, hope for the correction of offenders has largely faded; a growing reliance on surveillance combined with retribution has taken root. Everywhere, citizens as well as law-enforcement agencies lament the ineffectiveness of the criminal justice system as a whole, complaining particularly about the courts and the penal system as a "revolving door," or words to that effect. The debate over the death penalty seems to express the conflict. In Latin America, where capital punishment has generally been abolished, it continues to have thousands of enthusiastic supporters among the populace. In the United States, we preserve our sense of revulsion against brutal and public punishment, at the same time that we practice the death penalty, by conducting our executions in secret and with the macabre pretence that our methods of execution cause no pain to the convict.

All this would seem to presage a further crisis, in the control of official violence. The waning confidence in the government's ability to control citizen violence leads to an increase in vigilantism and a corresponding sense of permission for the use of violence by the police. To put it simply, when people are fearful of violent crime and despairing of correcting offenders, the temptation to encourage summary punishment, even to the extent of eliminating the suspect, is correspondingly strong.

In the face of the crisis, police chiefs in the United States have held the line very well. Physical torture has been largely eliminated, and the use of deadly force has been greatly reduced over the last generation. Although vigilantism has been growing, the authorities continue to arrest and prosecute for criminal acts of self-help. Although the departments in Los Angeles have pushed a "war on crime," with accompanying violence, the police on the whole have become more, rather than less, protective of citizens' rights. *Blade Runner* is not yet.

In some places elsewhere in the Americas, the authorities have yielded to the temptation to try to control the streets directly and to circumvent the system of justice. That has been especially obvious in São Paulo and Jamaica in the recent past, as well as in Buenos Aires to a lesser extent. Nevertheless all these are in nations that are proud of their transition to democracy and where human rights is a field of political struggle. They all have a free press as well as a functioning criminal justice system that recognizes the rights of defendants; under the circumstances, the police cannot admit that they have taken upon themselves the administration of justice. The police maintain that the overwhelming majority of shootings by police are justifiable and in response to an armed assailant, and they officially deny the coercion of suspects. It is this contradiction that opens the way to accountability for the summary administration of punishment; if the police did not have to adhere to their claim, there would be no way to try to make them stop the abuses. The contradiction between the human rights standards and the actual conduct of the police has led in every city to a gradual, sometimes halting growth in accountability, under which abuses have declined.

Societies draw back from the vision of the mighty policeman as the people's avenger. As some citizens and officials have realized, excessive police violence does not have the effect of deterring violence among the population. The reformers in Brazil reiterate the old point that the use of torture serves to make the police more cruel and the victim more intransigent. The excessive use of deadly force, because it cannot eliminate violent crime, whets the appetite for more deadly force. Accepting the policeman as avenger does not strengthen the sense of security, because the power of the avenger is largely arbitrary. Such violence does not, at least in democratic polities under contemporary conditions, strengthen the authority of the state, because it is a manifestation of violence without law.

Rising economic pressures and the fear of crime, however, create a constant temptation to arbitrary violence as a supposed shortcut to order. Resistance to the temptation requires constant support from systems of control and accountability.

ACCOUNTABILITY, CONTROL, AND MANAGEMENT

In this book I have written of the way in which police work reproduces and represents the larger social order, and how tolerance of official violence reflects the relation between the government and its citizens. From this point of view, the effort at "improving accountability" for the police might seem futile. Society controls official abuse, or fails to, through institutions of accountability and management; those institutions can be expected to shape the police as the society wants them, and no other way. And it is true that the cities that least need them have the best systems of accountability; New York City has a disciplinary review board that is well organized and external to the police, while Los Angeles, which has a greater problem of institutionalized violence, has not had effective review of police misconduct.

The influence of institutions, nevertheless, is not simply reflexive. Just as the system of rights has taken on a life of its own that is not easily extinguished by the wave of fear of crime, so it is with systems of accountability. Prosecutors are sometimes ambitious and want to see their cases succeed even against police; courts are sometimes determined to protect structures of rights and to see to it that they are effective for suspects. Such officials wind up criticizing abuses by the police, however infrequently and reluctantly, because failure to do so is ultimately an abuse of their own office. City governments, furthermore, are answerable in limited ways to national governments, and they, in turn, however informally and irregularly, are called to account by the international community. When an institution of accountability is part of another polity, either the national government or an international body, it may be strongly critical of local abuses.

External Accountability

Institutions of accountability external to the police can have a real influence, then, especially in revealing and controlling police deviance that has developed as a consequence of police secretiveness and distance from the public. External controls are especially effective after the collapse of a repressive government. In Buenos Aires, for example, where the police have long hidden their violence through a system of corruption and have tried to justify some police violence as a legitimate response to crime, the prosecution of police for torture and assassinations through the criminal process has had a deterrent effect. In the end, however, as I pointed out in chapter III, criminal prosecution of police is a clumsy instrument. It cannot do much more than reaffirm broad norms that are applicable to everyone and make sure that they are applicable to the police, although in cities like São Paulo and Buenos Aires, that is in itself a major accomplishment.

Court processes have been used effectively, on the other hand, to increase the protection of suspects and discourage the coercion of confessions. In the United States, torture to extract confessions was largely stamped out by the courts, and a similar effort has been in progress in São Paulo and Buenos Aires. Detectives, after all, are always to some extent "judicial police," even when they are not labeled as such, in the sense that they collect evidence for presentation to the courts; the judges thus always have some potential control over investigations. While the courts cannot eliminate torture as a form of summary punishment or as an instrument of corruption, the process of eliminating coerced confessions from use at trials has been accompanied by a change in public consciousness through which all torture has become increasingly unacceptable and the discipline of police who mistreat suspects is made a little easier.

The device of judicial police, as it has been used in Mexico and Brazil, has not acted as an effective brake on police violence except when the courts have actually intervened to control the police. Nevertheless, in places like Argentina, where there is a unified police, a very small separate investigative body that would be actually attached to the judiciary and act to investigate official abuse could be a very useful device.

Civil remedies against the police have not been used very effectively in any of the places I studied. Civil damages claims for police abuses are used relatively little in the Latin American countries; although they are used somewhat more systematically in Jamaica, they still have not worked well as a means of accountability. Even in New York and Los Angeles, where large damages are awarded every year, the police departments and the city governments have largely failed to bring the results back to the police systematically as a deterrent. Throughout the Americas, tort claims have a potential for accountability that has scarcely begun to be realized.

Administrative discipline of police officers can be effective if police managers choose to make good use of it. The PM in Rio de Janeiro succeeded for a time in disciplining many police, while the PM in São Paulo permitted the cases to drag through a complex criminal process that was usually ineffective. In Mexico, officers in the capital have been disciplined under pressure from the federal government. Although disciplinary bodies may be somewhat more effective when their administration and investigation is separated from the police, discipline cannot be a great deal more effective than police management wants it to be so long as the decision to punish ultimately lies with police commanders. Indeed, discipline is most effective if it can be joined with management initiatives. It must deal jointly with corruption as well as violence if it is to break down the sense of impunity that surrounds police abuse.

Internal Management and External Oversight

The control of official violence presents a dilemma. If the monitoring influence comes from outside the police, it tends to rouse the opposition of police managers as well as the rank and file; without some cooperation from within, then, it is nearly impossible for the outsiders to investigate, and any policy recommendations they make are liable to be ignored. On the other hand, if the control is exclusively internal, it tends to become socialized to existing mores in the department and to be ineffective; this effect is especially strong in the United States, where there is very little lateral entry. Real accountability will have to combine internal and external controls.

The experience with the investigative commissions that have tried to reform local departments after periodic scandals—such as the Christopher and Kolts investigations in Los Angeles and the Mollen Commission in New York—and the experience with expert consultants—such as the Hirst consultants in Jamaica—suggest one part of a model. These bodies do not act like complaint review boards directly administering discipline in individual cases, but instead act as outside auditors or ombudsmen. They usually command information from within the department, often because as a practical matter it is politically inexpedient for officials to refuse to tell them what they want to know. They find out where the internal controls of the police have failed, broadly and as a matter of policy. Institutionally, the problem with investigative commissions is that they usually disappear after they finish their reports; similar bodies should instead be maintained as continuing auditors. They should have discretion to investigate a range of internal problems, including corruption as well as brutality, because corruption is so often used as a source of impunity for acts of violence. To be effective after the scandal passes, however, they need cooperation from inside the department, backed by a subpoena power; an inspector general or a similar officer must work within the department to see that recommendations are followed. The effective management of abuses requires a three-part system, including effective investigation of civilian complaints, an ombudsman who oversees the workings of the department and has power to collect evidence, and an internal inspector general who is committed to reform.[331]

The three-part system would require not only substantial funding but the complete cooperation of officials; such a system will be put in place only when the police as well as the rest of the government really wants to control violence and corruption. In many if not all cases, such a transformation is not at hand; police managers as well as the increasingly powerful rank-and-file organizations would oppose far-reaching reforms in accountability.

Even without broad change, there are relatively simple reforms in internal regulations that can control the worst instances of violence. For example, most police departments in the United States have established written regulations for the use of firearms. In crowd situations, the regulations should permit the use of firearms only upon command by a superior officer. Police departments should require a written report and an investigation every time a gun is fired, a form of regulation that has been in effect in New York for many years. This sort of bureaucratic control, while onerous and imperfect, has greatly reduced the number of shootings by police.[332] Police can be trained, moreover, to minimize situations in which they may have no choice but to use deadly force; they can learn to pause and call for backup, avoiding a confrontation in which there seems to be no choice but to shoot.

Regulations can be used to control less serious forms of violence. For example, the departments in Los Angeles now require written reports on the use of force, and a superior officer is in many cases required to report to the scene and investigate incidents involving bodily injury caused by police. These reports have to be tracked to determine whether certain officers or districts are using an unusual amount of violence. As this is written, the NYPD is reported to have outright rejected such a tracking system, proposed by its own corruption trouble-shooter.[333] Specific situations that commonly give rise to police violence can also be monitored and controlled. Vehicle pursuits, for example, which have frequently resulted in violence in Buenos Aires and São Paulo as well as in the United States, are being limited by many U.S. departments. Some departments completely forbid high-speed pursuits, relying instead on radios and helicopters to track vehicles; other departments require the approval of a superior officer or reason to believe that a violent crime has been committed before permitting a pursuit.[334]

Similarly, rules of procedure in court as well as police regulations can reduce the number of coerced confessions. The *Miranda* warnings required by the U.S. Supreme Court operate as regulations of the conduct of interrogations, widely understood and now accepted by police as well as by citizens. Mexico and Argentina, confronted with a long tradition of torture, have gone so far as to establish rules of procedure to exclude evidence of confessions taken solely by the police, without the presence of some other official in the criminal justice system. In São Paulo, judges have tried to take control of the interrogation process, requiring a court order and medical examinations for interrogations. All of these controls are fed by and in turn reinforce a public condemnation of the continued use of torture.

Community policing, which is being tried in New York as well as in many other cities, "emphasizes the establishment of working partnerships between police and communities to reduce crime and enhance security." Such police are supposed to try to solve the problems that the local community perceives to be critical. The PM in Rio de Janeiro, and lately in São Paulo, have taken action to introduce greater service through what the São Paulo PM calls "citizen police."

Community policing is a promising departure; certainly if the police can give an increased sense of security, as well as improve their understanding of and relations with the public, the endeavor is worthwhile. If they can exchange even a modicum of effective preventive policing based on the trust of the people for the control by intimidation that police have sometimes used, it is a clear gain.

Community policing is also an extremely difficult project. As the Los Angeles experience showed, community policing is in conflict with the habits of police work of the past generation, with its emphasis on response to reports of crime. Community policing is not popular with many police officers, who see it as too much like social work; in the end it may not prove popular with the public. We must recognize that this more humane approach will be accompanied by more surveillance of the community. If the community produces crime control in tandem with the police, the police must come to have a more intimate knowledge of the life of the community.

Generally speaking, as physically tough approaches to crime and punishment have been discredited, surveillance has increased. In penology, for example, when punitive "lock 'em up" policies fade, they are replaced by increased surveillance of offenders. As part of a similar process, any preventive policing that is more effective in suppressing and detecting crime will likely be accompanied by more oversight in public and probably even private places.[335]

We come full circle, at last, to reconsider a distinction made in the introduction. There I said that part of the project of this book was to study routine, or "low," policing of ordinary crime rather than "high" policing, found for example in political surveillance. In the end, however, routine policing cannot be distinguished from political policing, because both are means to control people. As routine policing moves closer to the community and becomes more understanding of it, then the high policing that is done primarily through surveillance will begin to collapse into routine policing.

Accountability to National Institutions

When local accountability fails, national governments can act to control local abuses. Mexico, which has a more centralized national government than any of the other countries, undertook review of human rights abuses in Mexico City as well as the rest of the country through the National Commission for Human Rights (CNDH). The CNDH effected a strong national system of accountability, stronger than any undertaken nationwide in the United States, Brazil, or Argentina. But the CNDH had the power only to investigate and recommend action—it could not order local officials to take action—and now even those powers are being handed over to decentralized local human rights commissions.

In the United States, as described in chapter III, the federal government has traditionally treated police violence as a local problem even when, as is usually the case, the police abuse constitutes a violation of the federal constitution. The federal government has rarely prosecuted such violations, the federal courts have usually refused on procedural and federalist grounds to enjoin them, and the government has not even kept systematic statistics about them. Provisions buried in the federal Crime Bill of 1994 offered an opportunity for change; the U.S. attorney general was directed to collect statistics on police abuses and at last was given the power to bring injunctive actions against them. While it seems unlikely that the federal government will want to exercise these powers and may actually repudiate them, they do point toward a model in which the federal government can set standards or guidelines and can monitor local police performance, making use of its funding powers—and in a few cases even of the powers of the courts—to ensure that the guidelines are met.

International Accountability

The international human rights standards concerning torture and the excessive use of force, including deadly force, are not many or complex; based on general provisions in the Universal Declaration of Human Rights and the Covenant on Civil and Political Rights, these standards are spelled out in the Convention against Torture and Other Cruel, Inhuman or Degrading Treatment or Punishment, the Code of Conduct for Law Enforcement Officials, and the Basic Principles on the Use of Force and Firearms by Law Enforcement Officials. In essence, the use of cruel or degrading police methods, as well as excessive force, including deadly force except as a means of last resort, are condemned.

There are agencies that administer international standards. For example, complaints can be made to the Inter-American Commission on Human Rights of the OAS; a case was presented to the Commission about the massacre in the Casa de Detenção in São Paulo, after it appeared that no effective action would be taken by the PM and state officials.[336] The U.N. Human Rights Commission has special *rapporteurs,* both for torture and for summary and extrajudicial executions, to whom complaints can be made, and who will press governments for explanations about individual cases. In some cases, individual complaints can be presented to the U.N. Committee on Human Rights.

The formal enforcement of international standards, however, is only the smallest part of the effectiveness of the strictures against torture and deadly force. Their authority grows out of the fact that the convention, code, and Principles largely embody accepted norms to which there is no dissent among the five nations in this study. Because none can admit to having deliberately violated them, the norms have a real force, especially against the background of dictatorships recently repudiated. For nations making the transition to democracy, adherence to law is an index of their legitimacy. The scandal caused in the press by reports of human rights abuses, together with pressure brought by foreign governments, the protests of U.N. officials, and the reports of nongovernmental organizations, tends to push the national governments toward at least a minimal control of abuses.

In the last analysis, the international norms have turned out to have a tremendous influence on the reform of police practices. In each case, the government claimed that it was adhering to the norms in substance, whether they were called by that name or not; pressure for reform is generated when officials deviate from the norms. In Argentina and Jamaica, the governments incorporated the Basic Principles on the Use of Force and Firearms into the domestic guidelines for the police. In the United States, the reliance on international norms has not been so direct; using analogous concepts under the U.S. Constitution, however, coerced confessions and deadly force have decreased over the last fifty years. In Mexico, the CNDH was created in large part because of protests about violations of international standards. And in Brazil scandal grew over torture and the abuse of deadly force because the nation claimed to have repudiated those methods through its new constitution and the international standards. In 1994, the state of São Paulo felt constrained to make a presentation to the U.N. Human Rights Commission showing that police violence had decreased substantially after the massacre at the state Casa de Detenção in the fall of 1992.[337] There is no doubt that international pressure and the corresponding pressure on São Paulo from the national government of Brazil would have increased if the level of violence had not dropped as it did in 1993.

International standards can increase their cutting edge through oversight of local police conduct by national authorities. The Basic Principles on the Use of Force and Firearms directs that "governments and law enforcement agencies shall ensure that an effective review process is available and that independent administrative or prosecutorial authorities are in a position to exercise jurisdiction in appropriate circumstances." The Convention against Torture requires nations that are parties to investigate and redress, on a national basis, incidents of cruel and degrading treatment and to train officers in proper methods of interrogation.[338] The experience in Mexico and the United States suggests that national governments should collect data from local governments and require regular reports concerning possible human rights abuses. The experience in Brazil suggests that, when local practice deviates far from international standards, a federal investigation may be necessary. The powers of the executive, as well as the courts in serious cases, should be used in all of the countries to establish and enforce minimum standards for the control of local police abuses.

ENDNOTES

The abbreviation "N/A," which appears in some tables in the text, means "not available."

Preface

[1] Paul Chevigny, *Police Power: Police Abuses in New York City* (New York: Pantheon, 1969).

[2] David Rieff, *Los Angeles: Capital of the Third World* (New York: Simon and Schuster, 1991), 133.

Introduction

[3] Paul Brodeur, "High Policing and Low Policing: Remarks About the Policing of Political Activities," *Social Problems* 30, no. 5 (1983): 507–20.

[4] Egon Bittner, *Aspects of Police Work* (Boston: Northeastern University Press, 1990) 22; Roger Cotterrell, *Sociology of Law* (London: Butterworth, 1992) 258–59. The phrase "tainted occupation" appears in Bittner, op. cit., 94.

[5] Richard Ericson, *Reproducing Order: A Study of Police Patrol Work* (Toronto: University of Toronto Press, 1982). Ericson argues principally that patrol is used to reproduce order; in this book I have included police investigative work in that function as well.

[6] See, for example, the survey of such studies in the United States, Roger Lane, "Urban Police and Crime in Nineteenth Century America" in Michael Tonry and Norval Morris *Modern Policing* (Chicago: University of Chicago Press, 1992). Outside the Americas, Ted Gurr, *Rogues, Rebels and Reformers: A Political History of Crime and Conflict* (Beverly Hills: Sage, 1976).

[7] The process of change in the use of deadly force in U.S. police departments is described in more detail in chapter IV.

[8] Quoted in Bittner, op. cit., 235.

[9] James Q. Wilson, *Varieties of Police Behavior: The Management of Law and Order in Eight Communities* (Cambridge Mass.: Harvard University Press, 1968).

[10] Bittner, op cit., 131.

[11] Paul Chevigny, *Police Power: Police Abuses in New York City* (New York: Pantheon, 1969).

[12] Elaine Scarry, *The Body in Pain* (New York: Oxford University Press, 1985); E. Staub, "The Psychology and Culture of Torture and Torturers," in Peter Suedfeld, ed., *Psychology and Torture* (New York: Hemisphere, 1990).

[13] Peter Spierenburg, *Spectacle of Suffering* (Cambridge: Cambridge University Press, 1984) 2. Spierenburg here draws on another author, Immink.

[14] Code of Conduct for Law Enforcement Officials, G.A. Res. 34/169, U.N.

Doc. A/34/46 (1979), Art. 3, commentary; Basic Principles on the Use of Force and Firearms by Law Enforcement Officials, U.N. Doc. E/AC.57/DEC/11/119 (1990); International Covenant on Civil and Political Rights, Arts. 6 and 7; Convention against Torture and Other Cruel, Inhuman or Degrading Treatment or Punishment, Art. 2 (hereafter usually referred to as "the Convention against Torture").

[15] The quotation is from Article 1 of the Convention against Torture and Other Forms of Cruel, Inhuman or Degrading Treatment or Punishment. Article 16 also requires state parties to prevent "other acts of cruel, inhuman or degrading treatment or punishment which do not amount to torture as defined in Article 1...."

[16] It is possible to take a count of newspaper stories about torture, which would give a minimum count. This has not been done for any city, so far as I know, and it is not clear how useful such a count would be. In Buenos Aires and São Paulo, as I recount in chapters I and II, there have sometimes been official tallies of how many complaints have been made, but those tallies do not purport to sum all the actual cases.

[17] I do not mean to suggest that the idea of counting shootings by police is original with me. At the conference in Bahia in 1988 "Mortes anunciadas: A (des)proteçao da vida na America Latina," a count of shootings in several countries was made, mostly from newspaper stories. And such counts have been reported for United States cities; see, for example, William Geller and Michael Scott, *Deadly Force: What We Know* (Washington, D.C.: Police Executive Research Forum, 1992). But an international comparison in which the figures are put in a social context has not been carried out before, so far as I know.

[18] In theory, the figures could be much improved. It would be useful, for example, to have a count of all the times police fired their weapons, since many such firings are potential shootings of others. Except in New York City, however, such a count seems to be out of the question. The most significant statistical relation might be the number of "shootings per officer," as compared with the number of arrests per officer for "violent felonies." This relation was used by James Fyfe, in "Blind Justice: Police Shootings in Memphis," *Journal of Criminal Law and Criminology* 73; 707 (1982), to give a very accurate picture of the relative danger to officers in comparison to the use of deadly force in New York and Memphis. I have not used this ratio because in some cases I do not have figures on shootings (as distinct from killings) and more important, because the definition of "violent felony" is variable and the figures may well be unreliable.

[19] I use the term *government* to refer to any kind of organized authority related to the state, because so much of the violence is caused at a municipal rather than at a centralized state level.

[20] Norbert Elias, *The Civilizing Process*, vol. 2 (Oxford: Oxford University Press, 1982; first published in German in 1939); David Garland, *Punishment and Modern Society* (Chicago: University of Chicago Press, 1990) chap. 10.

[21] Benjamin Franklin, "Inquiry into the Effects of Public Punishments upon Criminals and upon Society" (Philadelphia: Joseph James, 1787). The more general theme is treated in Peter Spierenburg, *The Spectacle of Suf-*

fering (Cambridge: Cambridge University Press, 1984) as well as David Garland, op. cit.

22 Ted Gurr, *Rogues, Rebels and Reformers: A Political History of Urban Crime and Conflict* (Beverly Hills: Sage, 1976); Anthony Giddens, *The Nation-State and Violence* (Berkeley: University of California Press, 1987) chap. 7.

23 Compare Max Weber, *Max Weber on Law and Economy in Society* Max Rheinstein, ed., (New York: Simon and Schuster, 1967) with works cited in the foregoing note.

24 Giddens, op. cit., chap. 8. Michel Foucault, *Discipline and Punish* (New York: Pantheon, 1977).

25 NAACP, *Thirty Years of Lynching in the United States, 1889–1918* (New York, 1919; reprint 1967). Generally, Richard M. Brown, *Strain of Violence* (New York: Oxford University Press, 1975).

26 Wilbur R. Miller, *Cops and Bobbies: Police Authority in New York and London, 1830–1870* (Chicago: University of Chicago Press, 1977), 16–23.

27 Thomas Holloway, *Policing Rio de Janeiro* (Stanford, Calif.: Stanford University Press, 1993).

28 David Rock, *Authoritarian Argentina* (Berkeley and Los Angeles: University of California Press, 1993).

29 Twenty years ago Ernest Duff and John McCamant undertook to account for relative violence and repression in Latin America by a model that drew upon the gap between social mobilization, including urbanization and communications, and social welfare. Duff and McCamant, *Violence and Repression in Latin America* (New York: Free Press, 1976). I think these factors are useful, and I have tried to draw upon them myself; Chevigny, "Police Deadly Force as Social Control: Jamaica, Argentina and Brazil," *Criminal Law Forum* 1: 389 (1990). But one cannot be sure that the same mix of factors can be used twenty years later, or that they could be used in the United States; in any case reliable and comparable figures for the urban areas to fill out the formulas for social welfare and social mobilization are not available.

30 U.S. Foreign Assistance Act, sec. 660, 22 USCA sec. 2420. On U.S. support of police operations in Latin America, see A. J. Langguth, *Hidden Terrors* (New York: Pantheon, 1978); Martha Huggins, "U.S.-Supported State Terror: A History of Police Training in Latin-America," *Crime and Social Justice* 27/28 (1987): 149–171; Ethan Nadelmann, *Cops Across Borders* (University Park, Penn.: Penn State University Press, 1993), 111–124. For the episode in Mexico, see chapter VIII.

31 David Garland, *Punishment and Modern Society*, 8.

32 Louise Shelley, *Policing Soviet Society* (London: Routledge, forthcoming).

33 The Human Rights Watch/America reports are, in chronological order: "Human Rights in Jamaica" (1986); "Police Abuses in Brazil" (1987); "Police Violence in Argentina" (1991); "Human Rights in Jamaica" (1993); "Urban Police Violence in Brazil" (1993). In the chapters that follow, I use the form "we" when I write about information that was received by a team making a report, and "I" when the information was received by me acting alone.

Prelude: Los Angeles and New York in the Americas

[34] A. Nossiter, "Police in New Orleans: Film Noir in Real Life," *New York Times*, Dec. 19, 1994, p. A14; R. Bragg, "New Orleans is Hopeful About Police Overhaul," *New York Times*, Jan. 29, 1995, p. A14.

[35] The official name of the Christopher Commission report is the Independent Commission on the Los Angeles Police Department, *Report* (1991). The report on the sheriff is James G. Kolts, *Los Angeles County Sheriff's Department* (1992). There are also unusually complete historical materials about the LAPD, discussed in the next chapter.

[36] Paul Chevigny, *Police Power: Police Abuses in New York City* (New York: Pantheon, 1969).

[37] The report of the Mollen Commission is Commission to Investigate Allegations of Police Corruption and the Anti-Corruption Procedures of the Police Department *Report* (New York, July 1994).

[38] C. Krauss, "Top Police Corruption Fighter Forced Out," *New York Times*, Jan. 28, 1995, p. 23.

Chapter I: Los Angeles: City and County

[39] Mobile digital terminal transmission made by a member of the Los Angeles city police, collected by the Independent Commission on the Los Angeles Police Department, *Report* (1991), 52 (hereafter, "Christopher Commission").

[40] Malcolm Sparrow, Mark Moore, David Kennedy, *Beyond 911* (New York: Basic, 1990), 60.

[41] August Vollmer, *The Police and Modern Society* (1936), quoted in J. G. Woods, *The Progressives and the Police: Urban Reform and Professionalization in the Los Angeles Police* (Ph.D. Diss., University of California, Berkeley, 1973), 44.

[42] On the semimilitary style and organization of the LAPD, see Egon Bittner, *Aspects of Police Work* (Boston: Northeastern University Press, 1990) 362–63. On civil service status and control of discipline, Woods, *Progressives and the Police*, 496; James Fyfe and Jerome Skolnick, *Above the Law* (New York: Free Press, 1993) 20–22. On the Los Angeles Police Commission, Craig Uchida, *Controlling Police Use of Deadly Force: Organizational Change in Los Angeles* (Ph.D. Diss., SUNY Albany, 1982), chap. 4; Christopher Commission, chap. 10.

[43] On Parker's politics, Woods, *Progressives and the Police*, 454–58; on the trial of the officer, Hannon, for advocating civil rights, id., 481–83. The term "cossackism," id., 243. On the contrast between punishments, for Parker's era, id., 497; for Gates's era, Christopher Commission, 165–68. The phrase "hardnosed, proactive," id., 98.

[44] The Larez case is *Larez v. City of Los Angeles*, 946 F.2d 630 (9th Cir., 1991); Gates comment, Hoffman, "The Feds, Lies and Videotape: The Need for an Effective Federal Role in Controlling Police Abuse in Urban America," *Southern California Law Review* 66 (1993):1453, 1510 (hereafter, Hoffman, op. cit.). For the shooting of drug users, see R. Ostrow, "Casual Drug Users Should Be Shot, Gates Says," *Los Angeles Times*, Sept. 6, 1990, p. A1.

45 On the ethnic makeup of the region, James G. Kolts, *Los Angeles County Sheriff's Department* (Los Angeles, 1992), 7 (hereafter, "Kolts Report"). On economic disparity, Hoffman, op. cit., 1465; the quotation about South Central Los Angeles, id., 1464. On the politics of the downtown elite, Mike Davis, *City of Quartz* (New York: Verso, 1990), chap. 2. On vigilantism and the police, Woods, *Progressives and the Police,* 290; the "White Spot," id., 424.

46 David Rieff, *Los Angeles: Capital of the Third World* (New York: Simon and Schuster, 1991). Pretext stops by LAPD, Hoffman, op. cit., 1477; Jeremiah Randle affidavit, dated July 2, 1991, in "Declarations in Support of Plaintiffs' Motion for Preliminary Injunction and Exhibits Thereto," in *Thomas v. County of Los Angeles* Case 90–5217 TJH (U.S. Dist. Ct., Cent. Dist. Calif.) (hereafter, "Thomas papers").

47 Davis, *City of Quartz,* 267–292; Hoffman, op. cit., 1475–76.

48 "Vietnam here" quotation, Davis, *City of Quartz,* 268. Quotations about shooting drug users, Ostrow, op. cit., p. A1. Material about gangs, Hoffman, op. cit., 1468. The Lynwood statement, affidavit of George Denny, dated June 5, 1991, in Thomas papers.

49 Kolts report 7; Christopher Commission, 21–22 and chap. 10.

50 Christopher Commission, 166; Kolts report, 65.

51 Christopher Commission, 57–58.

52 Hoffman, op. cit., 1489 n. 145, 1498; Amnesty International, "USA: Police Brutality in Los Angeles, California" (AI Index AMR 51/76/92, June 1992), 16 (hereafter, "AI LA report").

53 Christopher Commission, 128–29; Kolts report, chap. 19.

54 The transmissions from the mobile digital terminals were transcribed by the Christopher Commission, which monitored thousands of them in addition to the Rodney King transmissions. Those quoted here occur at pp. 14 and 72, respectively. The verb "tased" comes from the use of the taser, a nonlethal weapon that fires a barbed dart attached to wires that deliver a charge to the body of the person "tased." Quotation concerning "contempt of cop" from Kolts report, 319. Affidavit of Demetrio Carillo, dated May 31, 1991, in Thomas papers. Mr. Carillo was acquitted of the obstructing charge.

55 For the use of dogs, Kolts report, chap. 5; Christopher Commission, 77; Hoffman, op. cit., 1474 n. 77; AI LA report, 39–46; the quotation from Hubert Williams appears in Fyfe and Skolnick, *Above the Law,* 226.

56 On the use of chokeholds, Fyfe and Skolnick, *Above the Law,* 42.

57 "Who's boss" quotation, Kolts report, 319. Dalton Avenue raid, Hoffman, op. cit., 1475 n. 85, 1499. The city has paid some $4 million in damages for the Dalton Avenue raid. Comments concerning the prone-out position, Christopher Commission, 75–76. Lynwood quotation, affidavit of Mary Charles, dated June 13, 1991, Thomas papers.

58 The figures on shootings and arrests in relation to the size of the LAPD are from Anthony Pate and Edwin Hamilton, *The Big Six: Policing America's Largest Cities* (Washington, D.C.: Police Foundation, 1991), 129, 138. Policies on the use of deadly force from AI LA report, 28. Shootings by the LAPD from J. Mitchell, "Officer Involved Shootings at 10-Year High,"

Los Angeles Times, Jan. 28, 1993, p. B1; by the LASD, from LASD Semi-annual Report by M. J. Bobb, October 1993, 11. General homicides from Hoffman, op. cit., 1467, 1487. One reason the figures for 1992 are high for shootings by the LAPD is that nine people were shot in the riot in the spring of 1992. It should be noted that the LAPD and the LASD do not account for all the police shootings in the county; many towns have their own police. I know of no way to determine the total of police shootings in the county; even if the number of police killings by the LAPD and the LASD were doubled for 1992, from 43 to 86 (which is probably too high as an estimate for the county as a whole), they would still make only a small percentage of all county homicides.

59 The *Daily News* articles take up most of the issue of October 7, 1990; the front-page story is D. Parrish and B. Barrett, "The Sheriff's Shootings; Minorities Are a Majority." Hyong Po Lee's case appears in id., under the heading "Case Studies: Wounded or Killed When Deputies Opened Fire at Cars," and also in AI LA report, 29–30. Archambault's shootings are described in the same issue of the *Daily News,* same authors, "Deputy Accused of Firing at Men on Ground, Planting Weapons"; his acts are described, and the performance evaluation given, anonymously as "Deputy D" in Kolts report, 164–65. Pascual Solis case, also in AI LA report, 30–31. Testimony of Ernest Machuca in Thomas reply papers.

60 Mr. Freed's comment is quoted in William Geller, *Deadly Force: What We Know* (Washington, D.C.: Police Executive Research Forum, 1992), 331 n. 57; the McDonald's case is described in detail in Fyfe and Skolnick, *Above the Law,* 146–64; the quotation from Gates, id., 164. A representative of the LAPD told me in 1993 that in the McDonald's case, the SIS people thought they did not have enough evidence to arrest the perpetrators before they went in the place; the judge in the civil case based on the shootings specifically ruled that there was enough evidence to arrest.

61 Kolts report, chaps. 7, 8; Christopher Commission, chap. 9. Quotation from sheriff, Parrish and Barrett, "Investigation of Deputies Called an Illusion" *Los Angeles Daily News,* Oct. 7, 1990. The Amnesty International report appears in AI LA report, 32–33.

62 On Operation Rollout, Christopher Commission, 155, 162; Kolts report, chap. 8. The Kolts report at p. 110 notes that the investigations by sheriff's detectives in cases of nondeadly force were "uniformly thorough and fair," suggesting that sometimes there were grounds for prosecution but that the district attorney declined to prosecute.

63 Christopher Commission, chap. 3; Kolts report, chap. 9.

64 On the code of silence, Christopher Commission, 169–71; Kolts report, 117. On the prevalence of lying, and failure to act against it, Christopher Commission, 167; Kolts report, 62. The judge in the Dalton Avenue vandalism case is quoted, Christopher Commission, 170. The account of the FTO training deputies to lie, Kolts report, 259. On cover charges, for the LAPD, Fyfe and Skolnick, *Above the Law,* 5; for the LASD, Kolts report, 57, 110. For Carrillo, see n. 54 above.

65 Christopher Commission, 56; Kolts report, 26. The damages are only a fraction of the costs; the governments must pay their own lawyers, wit-

nesses, court staff, and, if the defendants lose, the fees and costs of the plaintiffs' lawyers.

⁶⁶ Concerning the effect of civil litigation, Christopher Commission, 55–65; Kolts report, chap. 4. Quotations in order from Christopher Commission, 55; Kolts report, 25, 31, 150. The opinions of Block and Gates, Hoffman, op. cit., 1510 n. 237. The other case where punitive damages were assessed against Gates was the Larez case, in which an apartment was wrecked. See n. 44 above.

⁶⁷ Fyfe and Skolnick *Above the Law,* 205–207; the Gates quotation is at p. 106. See also Hoffman, op.cit., 1510. The comparative figures on crime in relation to population, Pate and Hamilton, *Big Six* 115–120.

⁶⁸ D. Dietz, "Departing McNamara as Controversial as Ever," *San Francisco Chronicle,* Apr. 6, 1991, p. A3.

⁶⁹ The LAPD itself had the job of reporting on its compliance with the Christopher Commission recommendations, while the Kolts staff, led by Merrick Bobb, reported on the compliance of the LASD. At the end of 1994, "frustrated by the pace of reforms," the Police Commission took over the monitoring function from the LAPD. J. Newton, "Panel Takes Over Monitoring LAPD Reforms," *Los Angeles Times,* Dec. 21, 1994, p. A1.

⁷⁰ The changes in the departments are described in "LAPD Status Report on Christopher Commission Recommendations," December 1992; "LASD Semiannual Report by Special Counsel Merrick J. Bobb," October 1993 and April 1994. Punishment by the LASD for shootings, Kolts report, 138. Prosecution for beating the Salvadoran, Hoffman op cit., 1485 n. 134. Charter Amendment F to the City Charter of Los Angeles, see Fyfe and Skolnick, *Above the Law,* 21.

Chapter II: New York City and Its Police

⁷¹ The character of New York City government is sketched well in Jewel Bellush and Dick Netzer, eds., *Urban Politics, New York Style* (Armonk, New York: Sharpe, 1990). Statistics on inequality appear in the introduction, at 11. The classic account of the pluralistic style of party government before the sixties is Wallace Sayre and Herbert Kaufman, *Governing New York City: Politics in the Metropolis* (New York: Norton, 1965). The phrase "cosmopolitan constituency," coined by Andrew Hacker, is used in John Mollenkopf and Manuel Castells, eds., *Dual City: Restructuring New York* (New York: Russell Sage, 1991), 169. For the experience of the New York bureaucracy, see C. Brecher and R. Horton "The Public Sector," in id., 103–127; B. Blank, "Bureaucracy: Power in the Details," in Bellush and Netzer, op. cit., 107ff.; Paul Chevigny, *Gigs: Jazz and the Cabaret Laws in New York City* (New York: Routledge, 1991). The changes in the economy are discussed in R. Harris, "The Geography of Employment and Residence in New York Since 1950," in Mollenkopf and Castells, op. cit., 129–152. Contemporary city government is also sketched in the essays in that book as well as the companion volume, *Power, Culture and Place: Essays on New York City* (New York: Sage, 1988). For crime, Anthony Pate and Edwin Hamilton, *Big Six* (Washington, D.C.: Police Foundation, 1991), 115ff.

⁷² See Asher Arian, et al., *Changing New York City Politics* (New York: Routledge, 1991), chap. 8; Mollenkopf and Castells, op. cit., table 6.3 (p. 168). The underlying economic similarity of New York and Los Angeles is argued by E. Soja, "Poles Apart: Urban Restructuring in New York and Los Angeles," in id., 361–76.

⁷³ The Goetz case is *People v. Goetz*, 68 NY 2d 96 (1986). On the violence by private guards, Editorial, "Policing the Private Police," *New York Times*, June 22, 1991, p. A22. On Crown Heights, Richard Girgenti, *Report to the Governor on the Disturbances in Crown Heights* (Albany: NYS Div. of Criminal Justice Services, 1993). There seems to be no evidence that the failure of control in the disturbance was deliberate. On the later beatings, see R. McFadden, "New Bias Case Fuels Dispute with Dinkins" *New York Times*, Dec. 21, 1992, p. B1. The attackers did claim they were making a citizen's arrest and the victim resisted. Neither victim seems to have been charged with any crime, however.

⁷⁴ The taser comparison with the use of firearms comes from "Final Report of the Firearms Policy Review Committee" (Glover report), NYPD, 1990. The comparison between the LAPD and NYPD use of the taser is also reflected in William Geller and Michael Scott, *Deadly Force: What We Know* (Washington, D.C.: Police Executive Research Forum, 1992) 384–88.

⁷⁵ C. Krauss, "Poll Finds a Lack of Faith in the Police," *New York Times*, June 19, 1994, p. A1.

⁷⁶ This account is from the affidavit of Ronald Bedford Narr, dated Dec. 10, 1990, filed in support of motion for contempt in the case of *Black v. Codd*, 73 Civ. 5283 (JMC), Federal Dist. Ct., Southern Dist. of N.Y. While I was employed at the New York Civil Liberties Union in the sixties and seventies, we found the practice of "bystander arrests" so prevalent that we filed the *Black* lawsuit to enjoin it. After the NYPD entered into a consent decree, I heard little of the practice until it sprang up again in the eighties and the New York Civil Liberties Union reactivated the case. It is discussed further in the next chapter.

⁷⁷ Reports on the demonstration, C. Manegold, "Rally Puts Police Under New Scrutiny," *New York Times*, Sept. 27, 1992, Metro, p. B35; G. James, "Police Department. Report Assails Officers in New York Rally," *New York Times*, Sept. 29, 1992, p. A1.

⁷⁸ T. Purdom, "Lessons of 60's Forgotten in Park Riot," *New York Times*, Aug. 11, 1988, p. B22.

⁷⁹ Howard Leary, "Law, Social Order and Use of Deadly Force," speech given at Georgetown University Law Center, Washington, D.C., Mar. 21, 1967, quoted in Paul Chevigny, *Police Power: Police Abuses in New York City* (New York: Pantheon, 1969), 238.

⁸⁰ The Firearms Discharge Review Board is described in NYPD Patrol Guide, 116-20; an annual report concerning deadly force is issued. One decision by the FDRB that a shot was not necessary, in 1980, is described in J. Barbanel, "New York Police Limit Fire, but Critics Say Not Enough," *New York Times*, Aug. 29, 1981, p. A1. The training is described in C. Nix, " A Yardstick of Behavior: Deadly Force," *New York Times*, May 27, 1987, p. B1; Geller and Scott, *Deadly Force*, Chap. 5 and pp. 412–13. The

Firearms Discharge Assault Reports of the NYPD state that there were fifty-six incidents in 1993 and sixty-two incidents in 1992 in which police were fired on and did not return fire.

[81] Figures on police shot and civilians shot from NYPD Firearms Discharge Assault annual reports. Civilians wounded include bystanders accidentally shot. General homicide figures from *Sourcebook of Criminal Justice Statistics* (U.S. Department of Justice, annual). The officer who shot the drug courier is mentioned in the report of the Commission to Investigate Allegations of Police Corruption and the Anti-Corruption Procedures of the Police Department (Mollen Commission) (New York City, July 7, 1994), p. 45.

[82] The civil case is *Bobsy Miller v. New York City*, 92 Civ. 4879 (Federal Dist. Ct., Eastern Dist. of N.Y.). The criminal case is *People v. Bobsy Miller*, Indictment # 10177/91 (Kings County Supreme Court). In the text, I have left out the fullest explanation for some of the facts. It is very unlikely that this was a case of mistaken identity by the police and that Miller was unarmed; the person who was shot on Flatbush Avenue had earlier shot Miller's brother, and it seems that Miller may have been out for revenge. It is not an uncontroverted fact that Ms. Zephyr had no interest in the case; there was a very weak claim that she was friendly with Mr. Miller. On the whole, however, she seems the most disinterested witness in the case.

[83] The criminal matter against the policeman is *People v. Sean Gelfand*, Indictment # 6165/92 (New York County Supreme Court). The civil claim is reported in R. Sullivan, "Settlement of Over $1.5 million Is Won by Cabby Shot by Officer," *New York Times*, June 2, 1994, p. B7.

[84] The case is *Gerard Papa and James Rampersant Jr. v. City of New York*. The jury awarded $76 million in compensatory and punitive damages, which the court reduced to $6 million. News stories are C. Wolff, "Jury Awards Two Men $76 million in Police Brutality Case," *New York Times*, Mar. 8, 1990, p. B1; "Brutality Victims Urge Plan Aimed at Police," *New York Times*, June 6, 1990, p. B2.

[85] According to the *New York Times*, nineteen officers were indicted for homicide in the decade 1981–91. J. McKinley, "Police Cleared Officers on Their Word," *New York Times*, Mar. 21, 1991, p. B6. The only officer convicted of an on-duty homicide in the last twenty years was Thomas Ryan, convicted in 1977. E. Sachar, "Few Cops Convicted—or Charged," *New York Times*, same date, p. A33. I have not been able to find a count of indictments for assault, but they are more common. Some of the problems with prosecutors and judges in such cases will be discussed in the next chapter.

[86] Craig Uchida, Lawrence Sherman, and James Fyfe, "Police Shootings and the Prosecutor in Los Angeles County: An Evaluation of Operation Rollout" (Washington, D.C.: Police Foundation, 1981); James Fyfe and Jerome Skolnick, *Above the Law* (New York: Free Press, 1993), 234–35.

[87] For the stun-gun case outcome, J. Fried, "Ex-officers Get 2 to 6 Years in Queens Stun Gun Torture," *New York Times*, July 18, 1986, p. B3; J. Fried, "$1 Million Is Awarded to 3 Men in New York City Stun-Gun Suits" *New York Times*, July 11, 1990, p. B5.

[88] The 1874 incident is recounted in James Richardson, *New York Police:*

Colonial Times to 1901 (New York: Oxford, 1970), 195–97. The 1967 incident is described in Chevigny, *Police Power,* 173–76.

[89] The quotation is from Robert Johnston Jr. to Comm. Ben Ward, "Tompkins Sq. Park Incident" (NYPD memo, Aug. 23, 1988). The account that follows draws on the memo together with "Report of the Civilian Complaint Review Board on the Disposition of Civilians' Complaints Arising from Police Department Action Occurring at Tompkins Sq. Park on August 6–7, 1988" (CCRB of the NYPD, April 1989); New York Civil Liberties Union, "Tompkins Square Park: The First 100 Days" (Nov. 19, 1988) and "Police Abuse: The Need for Civilian Oversight" (July 1990). Other sources are cited in succeeding notes.

[90] The banner, see R. McFadden, "27 Brutality Charges Now Filed in Clash," *New York Times,* Aug. 9, 1988, p. B4. The condominium, R. Giordano and M. Perez-Rivas, "Nonviolent Park Protest," *Newsday,* Aug. 15, 1988, p. 2.

[91] Henry Stern quoted in R. McFadden, "27 Brutality Charges Now Filed in Clash," *New York Times,* Aug. 9, 1988. For the young man with the bottles and the "light show," J. Hirsch, "Complaints Accuse Police of Wild, Random Brutality," *New York Times,* Aug. 12, 1988, p. B4.

[92] One version of the restaurant story, R. Giordano, "Civilians, Cop Assess Altercation," *Newsday,* Aug. 10, 1988, p. 7. The CCRB comments are in its report, p. 10.

[93] So far as I can tell, no guidelines were issued until 1993, after the police had been criticized for the opposite sin of being too inactive in the riot of 1991 in the Crown Heights neighborhood in Brooklyn. The guidelines are "Disorder Control Guidelines" (NYPD, 1993). The report on the Crown Heights incident is Richard Girgenti, *Report to the Governor on the Disturbances in Crown Heights.* (Albany: NYS Div. of Criminal Justice Service, 1993).

[94] D. Hevesi, "Rally in Tompkins Park to Protest Police Action," *New York Times,* Aug. 12, 1988, p. B4. The letter was sent early in the process, and it is not clear that it would have been sent if the merchants in the chamber of commerce had known how much criticism would be levelled against the department.

[95] Commission to Investigate Allegations of Police Corruption and the Anti-Corruption Procedures of the Police Department (Mollen Commission) *Report* (July 7, 1994). Quotations are, in order, at 21, 47, 48.

[96] Mollen Commission, chap. 4, esp. p. 81. A good explanation of this phenomenon is in Egon Bittner, *Aspects of Police Work* (Boston: Northeastern University Press, 1990) 143–44.

[97] The two quotations, in order, Mollen Commission, 47, 49. The topics of lying and brutality are treated at 36–50.

[98] Mollen Commission, 90–100. The testimony of the IAD inspector is set forth at p. 94.

Chapter III: New York and the United States: Accountability and Control

⁹⁹ Egon Bittner, *Aspects of Police Work* (Boston: Northeastern University Press, 1990), 131. Wayne Kerstetter, "Who Disciplines the Police? Who Should?," in William Geller, ed., *Police Leadership in America* (New York: Praeger, 1985), 151; Wesley Pomeroy, "Sources of Police Legitimacy and a Model for Police Misconduct Review: A Response to Wayne Kerstetter," id., 183. William Muir, *Police: Streetcorner Politicians* (Chicago: University of Chicago Press, 1977).

¹⁰⁰ For Los Angeles, Christopher Commission report (1991), 9–11 and chapter 9. For New York City, Mayor's Advisory Committee on Police Management and Personnel Policy, *Final Report* (1987) (hereafter, "Zuccotti Commission") vol. 2, chap. 5. For the present New York board, New York City Local Law No. 1, 1993. For the percentage of review boards of different types, see Samuel Walker and Vic Bumphus, "Civilian Review of Police: A National Survey of the 50 Largest Cities," *Criminal Justice Policy Focus* 91:3 (University of Nebraska at Omaha). As of January 1995, there were seventeen major cities with external review boards. Samuel Walker and Betsy Wright, "Citizen Review of the Police, 1994—A National Survey," *Fresh Perspectives* (January 1995) (Washington, D.C.: Police Executive Research Forum).

¹⁰¹ The passage that follows is from David Bayley, *Patterns of Policing* (New Brunswick, N.J.: Rutgers University Press, 1985), 177–78. The sheriff of Los Angeles County, quoted in chap. 1. L.A. Chief Edward Davis, quoted in Kerstetter, "Who Disciplines the Police?," 174.

¹⁰² Editorial, "Mr. Ward's Lesson for Chief Gates," *New York Times,* Mar. 16, 1991, p. A22.

¹⁰³ Kerstetter, "Who Disciplines the Police?," 173. Kerstetter states four dilemmas, the first being the subjective character of judgment in police actions, as noted in the text, together with lack of credibility of internal review, the public's failure to accept the fairness or unfairness of the procedure, and the "costs" or possible ill-effects of external review. The second two seem to me almost collapsed into the first; the last I have already discussed. Andrew Goldsmith, ed., *Complaints Against the Police: The Trend to External Review* (New York: Oxford University Press, 1991).

¹⁰⁴ Kerstetter, "Who Disciplines the Police?," 165. For proponents of civilian review, see, e.g., New York Civil Liberties Union, "Police Abuse: The Need for Civilian Review" (New York, June 1990); NAACP, *Beyond the Rodney King Story* (1993).

¹⁰⁵ For the percentage of complaints sustained under different sorts of boards, Douglas Perez, *Common Sense about Police Review* (Philadelphia: Temple University Press, 1994), 181. The substantiation rate is of very little more than symbolic significance because it is so easy to manipulate the figure; for example, if cases obviously without merit are eliminated in some way, such as at intake, the percent substantiated can be increased. NYPD Civilian Complaint Investigation Bureau, "Survey of Civilian Complaint Systems" (September 1992). The comparison of the

number of complaints in Los Angeles and New York, K. Bishop, "Police Attacks: Hard Crimes to Uncover, Let Alone Stop" *New York Times,* Mar. 24, 1991, p. E1. On the experience of the New York CCRB, NYPD/CCRB "Report" (October 1987–December 1989). I am using a somewhat simplified terminology in the text. Review boards commonly have more categories than merely substantiated or unsubstantiated, referring to proven or unproven; the boards also use terms like "exonerated," when they find the police acts justified, and "unfounded," for cases in which the complaint is shown to be without foundation.

[106] For the figures on the Tompkins Square affair, NYPD/CCRB "Report" (October 1987–December 1990). For the criticism of the investigation, New York Civil Liberties Union, "Police Abuse: The Need for Civilian Oversight" (June 1990). For the investigation of the 1992 City Hall demonstration, G. James, "Police Dept. Report Assails Officers in New York Rally," *New York Times,* Sept. 29, 1992, p. A1.

[107] The unwritten rule requiring corroboration for a complaint and the functionally high standard of proof are part of my experience, confirmed in Wayne Kerstetter and Barrik Van Winkle, "Evidence in Investigations of Police Use of Force in Chicago," (Chicago, American Bar Foundation Working Paper #9015, 1989). The newly appointed civilian members of the CCRB in New York complained about it in 1989. CCRB/NYPD "Report" (October 1987–December 1989), 13.

[108] David Bayley, preface to Andrew Goldsmith, ed., *Complaints Against the Police.* To similar effect, James Fyfe and Jerome Skolnick, *Above the Law* (New York: Free Press, 1993), chap. 10.

[109] Malcolm Sparrow, Marie Moore, and David Kennedy, *Beyond 911* (New York: Basic, 1990), 94.

[110] Members of the board in New York complained of the lack of coordination with investigations by Internal Affairs and with the results of disciplinary trials, CCRB/NYPD "Report" (October 1987–December 1989) and "Report" (January 1990–December 1991).

[111] As late as 1991, the CCRB was trying to get a role reporting "trends and patterns" to the NYPD. CCRB/NYPD "Report" (January 1990–December 1991), 19. For the case against bystander arrests, see n. 130 below.

[112] Goldsmith, ed., *Complaints Against the Police, x.*

[113] G. James, "Chief Timoney: Point Man in Reorganizing Police Department," *New York Times,* June 7, 1994, p. B4. For the stun-gun case, see chap. II.

[114] Craig Uchida, *Controlling Police Use of Deadly Force: Organizational Change in Los Angeles* (Ph.D. Diss., U.C. Berkeley, 1982), 53; Paul Chevigny, *Police Power: Police Abuses in New York City* (New York: Pantheon, 1969), 249–50.

[115] Wayne Schmidt, "Section 1983 and the Changing Face of Police Management," in Geller, ed., *Police Leadership in America* (New York: Praeger, 1985), 226-36; Candace McCoy, "Police Misconduct Lawsuits: What Impact Do They Really Have?," in James Fyfe, ed., *Police Management Today* (Washington, D.C.: Internet's City Management Association, 1985), 55 The Supreme Court cases are, respectively, *Tennessee v. Garner,* 471 U.S. 1 (1985): *City of Canton v. Harris,* 489 U.S. 378 (1989).

116 The figures include settlements and judgments after trial. Christopher Commission, 56; I was informed by the New York City comptroller that the term "police misconduct" includes false arrest as well as excessive force, but excludes ordinary negligence such as auto accidents. The figure for payments per officer was calculated by Americans for Effective Law Enforcement by dividing figures for the total paid (as reported in "Police Litigation Nationwide," *Los Angeles Times,* Mar. 29, 1991, p. A3) by the number of officers in 1990. The police budgets are drawn from Anthony Pate and Edwin Hamilton, *Big Six* (Washington, D.C.: Police Foundation, 1991). 66ff.; the budgets given there are for 1986. In 1990, they were even larger.

117 NYC Comptroller's Office, Bureau of Law and Adjustment, "Report on Police Monitoring of Lawsuits and Claims of Police Misconduct" (February 1992). For Los Angeles, Christopher Commission, 55–60; Kolts report, 63–68.

118 There is a history of administrative practice behind these words, both in New York City and Los Angeles. It is usual in police tort cases to sue the individual officers as well as the municipality. In Los Angeles and New York, the cities have a duty to indemnify employees for actions taken within the scope of their duties, California Government Code sec. 825; N.Y. General Municipal Law sec. 50-j; the city's lawyers thus represent the individuals as well as the municipality. In New York, when the city declines to represent an employee, that is a signal that the city's lawyers think that the employee may be at fault in a way that would prevent indemnification and that might create a conflict of interest. It is clear, I think, that these relations make the tort system less effective as an instrument for setting norms.

119 NYC Comptroller's Office, op. cit., 12.

120 The damage action is *Posr v. Doherty;* 944 F.2d 91 (2d Cir. 1991). Mr. Posr was originally names Charles Johnson; in the course of the litigation he changed his name to Posr, which is an acronym for Prisoner of Self Respect. In a similar action, after the City of Los Angeles paid the punitive damages for Daryl Gates in the McDonald's bandits case, lawyer Steven Yagman sued the city, alleging that it was fostering violence. A similar case brought in federal court in San Francisco in 1989 by the journalist Ruth Keady is discussed in Alison Patton, "The Endless Cycle of Abuse: Why 42 U.S.C. Sec. 1983 Is Ineffective in Deterring Police Brutality" *Hastings Law Journal* 44 (1993): 753, 769–70.

121 Anthony Pate and Lorie Fridell, *Police Use of Force: Official Reports, Citizen Complaints and Legal Consequences* (Washington, D.C.: Police Foundation, 1993), vol. 1, 146. To similar effect, see Patton, "Endless Cycle of Abuse."

122 "1993 Juries Show Doubts About Police," *National Law Journal,* Jan. 17, 1994, p. S17.

123 The subject of federal oversight of local police, or the lack of it, is surveyed in Paul Hoffman, "The Feds, Lies and Videotape: The Need for an Effective Federal Role in Controlling Police Abuse in Urban America," *Southern California Law Review,* 66 (1993): 1453; Human Rights Watch, "Police Brutality in the United States: A Policy Statement on the Need for Federal Oversight" (New York, July 1991).

[124] *Graham v. Connor,* 490 U.S. 386 (1989). The Racketeer Influenced and Corrupt Practices Act (RICO) is 18 USCA sec. 1961 et seq.

[125] Testimony of March 20, 1991, quoted in Human Rights Watch, "Police Brutality in the United States: A Policy Statement on the Need for Federal Oversight" (New York, July 1991), 4.

[126] The case discussing the requirement of specific intent is *Screws v. U.S.,* 325 U.S. 91 (1945). The decision has been severely criticised for establishing an unnecessarily high standard of intent; see, for example, F. Lawrence, "Civil Rights and Criminal Wrongs: The Mens Rea of Federal Civil Rights Crimes," *Tulane Law Review* 67 (1993): 2113.

[127] *Rizzo v. Goode,* 423 U.S. 362 (1976). The quotations appear, respectively at pp. 369, 375, 380. The unsuccessful case brought by the attorney general was *United States v. City of Philadelphia,* 644 F.2d 187 (3rd Cir. 1980). The formal name of the Crime Bill of 1994 is the "Violent Crime Control and Law Enforcement Act of 1994." The section conferring upon the attorney general the power to bring actions against police abuses is sec. 210401, discussed more fully below in the text.

[128] *City of Los Angeles v. Lyons,* 461 U.S. 95 (1983). Mr. Lyons claimed that he had not resisted arrest and that the chokehold was used in cases where there was no resistance. The written policy did not authorize the use of the chokehold in such cases, however; the holding apparently is that the city was not responsible for the abuse of the chokehold where the regulations did not authorize it.

[129] The bystander case in New York is *Black v. Codd,* (U.S. District Court, Southern District of N.Y.) 73 Civ. 5283 (JMC). The case against the sheriff's deputies in Los Angeles County is *Thomas v. County of Los Angeles,* 978 F. 2d 504 (9th Cir. 1992). The appeals court showed how reluctant the courts are to allow these cases by reversing the grant of a preliminary injunction, although the case was not dismissed.

[130] James Fyfe, "Blind Justice: Police Shootings in Memphis," *Journal of Crime and Criminology* 73 (1982): 707. The U. S. attorney general's press release of March 14, 1991, containing the request to the National Institute of Justice, is quoted in Human Rights Watch, "Police Brutality in the United States" (July 1991), 8.

[131] Violent Crime Control and Law Enforcement Act of 1994. The power of the Attorney General to bring actions is sect. 210401; the section concerning data collection is 210402. The latter section provides that the data cannot contain the names of police or of victims, which will at a minimum make it very difficult to check on the accuracy of the data. The material about "cops on the beat" appears in sect. 10003.

[132] "Basic Principles on the Use of Force and Firearms by Law Enforcement Officials" U.N. Doc. E/AC.57/DEC/11/119 (1990), appears e.g. in Cherif Bassiouni, *Protection of Human Rights in the Administration of Criminal Justice* (New York: Transnational, 1994), 258ff. The Convention against Torture and Other Cruel, Inhuman or Degrading Treatment or Punishment, U.N. Doc.E/CN.4/1984/72.

[133] The NYPD quotation is from NYPD, "Policing New York City in the 1990s: The Strategy for Community Policing" (January 1991), 3.

[134] S. Mastrofski and J. Greene, "Community Policing and the Rule of Law,"

in Craig Uchida and David Weisburd, *Police Innovation and Control of the Police* (New York: Springer-Verlag, 1993), 86.

¹³⁵ See, e.g. Uchida and Weisburd, op. cit.

Chapter IV: Past and Present:
The United States, Latin America, and the Caribbean

¹³⁶ The decentralization of U.S. police agencies, together with the Justice Department count, is described in David Bayley, "Comparative Organization of the Police in English-Speaking Countries" in Michael Tonry and Norval Morris, *Modern Policing: Crime and Justice, a Review of Research, Vol. 15* (Chicago: University of Chicago Press, 1992), 509–45 (hereafter, *Modern Policing*). The history, including the seizure by the states, and the opposition to federal and state control, is summarized in Robert Fogelson, *Big-City Police* (Cambridge, Mass.: Harvard University Press, 1977) chap. 1; concerning J. Edgar Hoover, p. 190. For a summary of cooperation between federal and local police, see William Geller and Norval Morris, "Relations between Federal and Local Police" in *Modern Policing*, 231–348. For possible changes due to federal legislation see the previous chapter of this book. Opinion of Clubber Williams, James F. Richardson, *The New York Police, Colonial Times to 1901* (New York: Oxford University Press, 1970), 190.

¹³⁷ Detection as a judicial function is discussed by Egon Bittner, *Aspects of Police Work* (Boston: Northeastern University Press, 1990), 116–17. The history of the absorption of independent detectives, David Johnson, *Policing the Urban Underworld* (Philadelphia: Temple University Press, 1979), chap. 2.

¹³⁸ For the Lexow Commission, Richardson, *New York Police*, 233. Generally on control of elections, Fogelson, *Big-City Police,* chap. 1.

¹³⁹ The L.A. politician was Wilbur LeGette, quoted in J. G. Woods, *The Progressives and the Police: Urban Reform and the Professionalization of the Los Angeles Police* (Phd. Diss. University of California, Berkeley, 1973), 315 (hereafter, Woods, *Progressives and the Police*). Bittner, *Aspects of Police Work*, 27. Concerning New York City, Lawrence Sherman, *Scandal and Reform* (Berkeley: University of California Press, 1978).

¹⁴⁰ Figures for New York from the NYPD; most of the criminal matters are said to be drug cases. The New Orleans murder case is reported in A. Nossiter, "Police in New Orleans: Film Noir in Real Life," *New York Times,* Dec. 19, 1994, p. A14.

¹⁴¹ On hiring gangs to enforce at elections and protect politicians, and protection of toughs from the law, Richardson, *New York Police*, 72–74; David Johnson, *Policing the Urban Underworld* (Philadelphia: Temple University Press, 1979), 173–75. Police participation in crime, Fogelson, *Big-City Police* 72–73; R. L. Smith, *The Tarnished Badge* (New York: Crowell, 1965). On judges corrupted to protect criminals, Richardson, op. cit., 74 (New York City); Johnson op. cit. 24 (Philadelphia); Woods, *Progressives and the Police,* 340 (Los Angeles). On corruption of prosecutors, Woods op. cit., 256, 338. On the change to the contemporary professional prosecutor, L. Fleischer, "Thomas E. Dewey and Earl Warren: The Rise of

the Twentieth-Century Urban Prosecutor" *California Western Law Review* 28 (1991): 1.

¹⁴² On the development of police out of the militia in the United States, see Richardson, *New York Police,* 8; Johnson, *Urban Underworld,* 14. On the military analogy, Fogelson, *Big-City Police* chap. 2; David Bayley, *Patterns of Policing* (New Brunswick: Rutgers University Press, 1985), 40–45. On the military origins of policing in Brazil, see Thomas Holloway, *Policing Rio de Janeiro* (Stanford, Calif.: Stanford University Press, 1993). On the flaws in the military analogy, Fogelson, op. cit.; James Fyfe and Jerome Skolnick, *Above the Law* (New York: Free Press, 1993), chap. 6.

¹⁴³ On salaries, historically, Fogelson, *Big-City Police,* 197; Richardson, *New York Police* 173; Johnson, *Urban Underworld* 101. At present, Skolnick and Fyfe, *Above the Law,* 93. On the success of the reforms, Fogelson, op. cit. chap. 7. On the prevalence of the "anticrime" model, Malcolm Sparrow, Mark Moore, and David Kennedy, *Beyond 911: A New Era for Policing* (New York: Basic Books, 1990).

¹⁴⁴ J. Q. Wilson crystallized this perception in *Varieties of Police Behavior* (Cambridge, Mass.: Harvard University Press, 1968). The styles he picked out he called watchman, service, and legalistic; the latter is similar to what I call "anticrime."

¹⁴⁵ Quoted in Richardson, *New York Police,* 186. All commentators remark on the corruption created by efforts to reform vice, and the resistance to it by much of the population. Fogelson, *Big City Police,* 108–11; Richardson, *New York Police,* 252; Woods, *Progressives and the Police,* 27, 30, 69.

¹⁴⁶ Critiques of the military analogy are legion; see note 7, supra. For the early military analogy as an image of a model "paramilitary bureaucracy," see Richardson, *New York Police,* 177. For the Pennsylvania State Police, see Thomas Reppetto, *Blue Parade* (New York: Free Press, 1978), chap. 4.

¹⁴⁷ Mark Moore, "Problem-Solving and Community Policing" in Tonry and Morris, *Modern Policing,* 99–158; abstract at p. 99.

¹⁴⁸ Chicago *Tribune,* Nov. 22, 1875, quoted in Reppetto, *Blue Parade,* 211.

¹⁴⁹ For Tompkins Square, Richardson, *New York Police,* 196; For Republic Steel, Fogelson, *Big-City Police,* 228.

¹⁵⁰ Eric Monkkonen, "History of Urban Police," in Tonry and Morris, *Modern Policing,* 556. For Los Angeles, Woods, *Progressives and the Police,* 228.

¹⁵¹ Wilbur Miller, *Cops and Bobbies: Police Authority in New York and London, 1830–1870* (Chicago: University of Chicago, 1977), 53, 146, quoting *New York Times,* Nov. 7, 1857, p. 4, and Nov. 18, 1858, p. 4, respectively. Further on public attitudes toward police use of firearms in the early days, Johnson, *Urban Underworld,* 139–41.

¹⁵² The story about the sailor and the patrolman Cairnes appears in Wilbur Miller, *Cops and Bobbies,* at p. 146. Comments about "delegated vigilantism" by the police, id. at pp. 16, 140–48. Comments about the criminal courts in New York after the Civil War, Richardson, *New York Police,* 157.

153 New York, Richardson, *New York Police,* 143; Los Angeles, 1927, Woods, *Progressives and the Police,* 246. The Gates remark is given the account most friendly to Gates, in Daryl Gates *Chief* (New York: Bantam, 1992), 286; see also chap. II supra.

154 Illinois Association for Criminal Justice, *Illinoise Crime Survey* (1929), 601–602, 610. Judging by the wording of the report, the first category does not include police killings. An article by D. Rousey, "Cops and Guns: Police Use of Deadly Force in 19th Century New Orleans," *American Journal of Legal History* 28 (1984): 41–66 makes a newspaper count, finding in the period 1863–89 that there were ten civilians and seven police personnel killed. It seems impossible at this distance in time to evaluate the accuracy of the news count. Police Foundation figures cited in William Geller and Michael Scott, *Deadly Force: What We Know* (Washington, D.C.: Police Executive Research Forum, 1992), 192.

155 The two cases are in Woods, *Progressives and the Police,* 251–52 and 357–61, respectively.

156 Woods, *Progressives and the Police,* 78, 118.

157 Woods, *Progressives and the Police,* 246; Richardson, *New York Police,* 158, 191; Johnson, *Urban Underworld,* 136, 145; the quotation appears on the latter page and is drawn from *New York Times,* July 18, 1866.

158 Richardson, *New York Police,* 189–93; 210. Woods, *Progressives and the Police,* 225, 288. The Chicago cases, Heirens and Degnan, in F. Inbau, et al., *Criminal Interrogation and Confessions* (Baltimore: Williams and Wilkins, 1987), 22; Leopold and Loeb in M. Haller, "Historical Roots of Police Behavior: Chicago, 1890–1925," *Law and Society Review* 10 (1976): 319.

159 On the early history of the venality of detectives, Johnson, *Urban Underworld,* chap. 2; on Byrnes and the New York detectives, Richardson, *New York Police,* 208–13. On Los Angles, Woods, *Progressives and the Police,* 225. On Detective Lucas and others in Los Angles, id., 260–61.

160 For August Vollmer, Woods, *Progressives and the Police,* 217. National Commission on Law Observance and Enforcement, *Report on Lawlessness in Law Enforcement* (Washington, D.C.: GPO, 1931). The routine use of torture is described in Haller, "Historical Roots of Police Behavior," 303–23.

161 For an account of the legal change in more detail, see Fyfe and Skolnick, *Above the Law,* chap. 3. The case is *Miranda v. Arizona,* 384 U.S. 436 (1966).

162 The material on the Chicago tortures is voluminous. See Amnesty International, "Allegations of Police Torture in Chicago, Illinois" (AMR/51/42/90, 1990). A good account is John Conroy, "House of Screams," *Chicago Weekly Reader,* Jan. 26, 1990. The Illinois Supreme Court case is *People v. Wilson,* 506 N.E.2d 571 (1987). The 1992 case is described in D. Nelson, "3 Teens Say Police Used Shock Torture," *Sun-Times,* July 19, 1992, p. 1.

163 A good account of the changes in regulations appears in Samuel Walker, *Taming the System: The Control of Discretion in Criminal Justice* (New York: Oxford University Press, 1993), chap. 2; the evaluation of Fyfe's work appears at p. 27. The article described is J. Fyfe, "Administrative Interventions on Police Shooting Discretion: An Empirical Examination"

Journal of Criminal Justice 7(1979):309–23; similar findings appear in L. Sherman, "Reducing Police Gun Use: Critical Events, Administrative Policy, and Organizational Change," in Maurice Punch, *Management and Control of Police Organizations* (Cambridge Mass.: MIT Press, 1983), 98–125. Fyfe's findings on Philadelphia, Fyfe and Skolnick, *Above the Law,* 139–42. Conclusions about the nation as a whole are in an exhaustive work, Geller and Scott, *Deadly Force.* The Supreme Court case is *Tennessee v. Garner,* 471 U.S. 1.

[164] The *Life* story is "Revolt in the Newark Ghetto" *Life,* July 28, 1967, pp. 16–28; there was later a question about the authenticity of some of the photos, but not the ones discussed here. The quotation concerning Memphis is from J. Fyfe, "Police Use of Deadly Force: Research and Reform," *Justice Quarterly* 5 (1988): 165–205 at 194.

[165] Gallup poll set out in S. Keeva, "Demanding More Justice," *ABA Journal,* Aug. 1994, p. 47.

[166] Fleischer, "Thomas E. Dewey and Earl Warren: The Rise of the Twentieth Century Urban Prosecutor," G. E. White, *Earl Warren: A Public Life* (New York: Oxford University Press, 1982), 33, 81–82.

[167] Steven Gregory, "Time to Make the Doughnuts: On the Politics of Subjugation in the Inner City," *Political and Legal Anthropology Review* 17 (1991): 43–54; E. Nieves, "Joy Rides Turn Deadly in New Jersey," *New York Times,* Sept. 21, 1993, p. B1; C. Strum, "Newark Officer Acquitted of Shooting Teen-Age Thief," *New York Times,* Dec. 7, 1993, p. B1.

[168] Willemse quotation, Richardson, *New York Police,* 190. The general recognition of the use of cover charges, NAACP, *Beyond the Rodney King Story,* 54–55. In *Police Power,* cover charges are in chap. 8. The code of silence has been mentioned and criticized so often that it would be difficult to make a bibliography for it at this point in time. Recent descriptions are: *Beyond the Rodney King Story,* 114–16; Fyfe and Skolnick, *Above the Law,* 108–12.

[169] *Webster v. City of Houston,* 689 F. 2d 1220 (5th Cir. 1982); rehearing en banc, 735 F. 2d 838 (1984); rehearing en banc, 739 F. 2d 993 (1984). Quotation from Chevigny, *Police Power,* 141.

[170] The literature on this problem is voluminous. In Jerome Skolnick, *Justice Without Trial* (New York: John Wiley, 1966), the defiant individual appears as the "symbolic assailant." In Albert Reiss, *Police and the Public* (New Haven, Conn.: Yale University Press, 1971), defiance is identified as one factor leading to violence. The pattern is described also in John Van Maanen, "The Asshole," in Peter Manning, and John Van Maanen, eds., *Policing: A View from the Street* (Santa Monica, Calif.: Goodyear, 1978), 221–38.

[171] Hans Toch, *Agents of Change: A Study in Police Reform* (New York: John Wiley, 1975), chap. 4.

[172] Sparrow, et al., *Beyond 911,* 133–34.

[173] The "unnecessary conversation" regulation, Sparrow, et al., *Beyond 911,* 37. The "bunker mentality" and secretiveness is well-described by Fyfe and Skolnick, *Above the Law,* chap. 5. The origins of the separation from the public, Richardson, *New York Police,* 191.

[174] For the United States, Stuart Scheingold, *Politics of Law and Order: Street Crime and Public Policy* (New York: Longman, 1984), chaps. 2 and 6; the increase in the belief that the courts are not harsh enough at p. 46. For some police attitudes, see for example, W. McDonald, "Prosecutors, Courts and Police: Some Constraints on the Police Chief Executive" in William Geller, ed., *Police Leadership in America* (New York: Praeger, 1985), 203–15. For other cities in this study, see the chapters that follow.

Chapter V: São Paulo

[175] The Brazilian Constitution of 1988, Art. 144, sec. 6, provides that the civil and military police are under the control of the state governors. The present PM of São Paulo was formed during the dictatorship out of two pro-tomilitary forces, a Força Publica and a Guarda Civil. H. Fernandez, *Forca e seguranca: a força pública do estado de S. Paulo* (São Paulo: Alfa Omega, 1974), 155; chap. 9. Thomas Holloway, *Policing Rio de Janeiro: Repression and Resistance in a 19th Century City* (Stanford, Calif.: Stanford University Press, 1993) chap. 7.

[176] Figures on PM from PM interviews; on civil police from civil police interviews.

[177] J. Lang, *Inside Development in Latin America* (Chapel Hill: University of North Carolina, 1988), 151; UNDP, *Human Development Report 1993* (New York: Oxford University Press, 1993), 170.

[178] For total population, Seção de Economia e Planejamento, Mun. de S. Paulo, 1990, p. 32; for the percentage of people called "miserable," Sistema Estadual de Analise de Dados, *São Paulo em Perspectiva* 4(1990):103. Compare the estimate of population cited in Teresa Caldeira, *City of Walls: Crime, Segregation and Citizenship in São Paulo* (Ph.D. Diss., University of California, Berkeley, 1992), 229. (hereafter, "City of Walls").

[179] The anthropologist Daniel Linger found, for example, that the police accounted for one quarter of all the homicides in the northeastern city of São Luis in 1984. "Essential Outlines of Crime and Madness: Man-Fights in São Luis," *Cultural Anthropology* 5, no. 1 (Feb. 1990): 62–77. See generally, Amnesty International, *Brazil: Torture and Extra-Judicial Execution* (New York: Amnesty International, 1990).

[180] In my conversations with officials of the PM in 1991 and 1992, I was repeatedly told that the police were only reacting to armed suspects; Paulo Pinheiro and his investigators at the Center for the Study of Violence at the University of São Paulo found that more than 70 percent of the cases between 1983 and 1987 were explained officially as "resistance" or "shoot-out," while others were labeled more vaguely. Pinheiro, et al., "Violencia fatal: conflitos policiais em São Paulo (81–89)," 95–112. Comparison with the dictatorship appears in Caldeira, *City of Walls*, 161.

[181] The figures for 1982–1989 appear in Paulo Pinheiro, et al., "Violencia fatal" *Revista USP* 9 (1991): 95–112, and are drawn from official figures. The figures for 1990–1992 are official figures of the PM of São Paulo. They sometimes vary slightly from newspaper accounts and even from different sources within the PM.

[182] Anuario Estadistico do Estado de São Paulo shows 4,749 homicides in the São Paulo metropolitan region in 1992; 5,634 in 1991. It is impossible to find out whether killings by police are included in this figure or not; so the proportion of all homicides constituted by police killings remains undetermined. Nevertheless, it is obviously a considerable proportion even if the police killings were added to these figures. For the deaths of police, Caldeira, *City of Walls*, 173, citing *Folha de São Paulo* Dec. 10, 1991. Caco Barcellos, *Rota 66: a história da polícia que mata* (São Paulo: O Globo, 1992), 259, reaches similar conclusions from his own data.

[183] Guaracy Mingardi, *Tiras, gansos e trutas: cotidiano e reforma na policia civil* (São Paulo: Scritta, 1992), 52.

[184] Forum Nacional, *A questão social no Brasil* (São Paulo: Nobel, 1991) 39; Comissão Justica e Paz, *São Paulo, trabalhar e vivir* (São Paulo: Brasiliense, 1989), chap. 8.

[185] Quotations respectively from Nancy Cardia, "Percepção de direitos humanos: ausência de cidadania e a exclusão moral" (São Paulo: Nucleo de Estudos da Violência, 1993), 32; Caldeira, *City of Walls*, 186.

[186] The phrase *homem cordial,* is drawn from Sergio Buarque de Holanda, *Raizes do Brazil* (Rio de Janeiro: José Olympio, 1969), chap. 5. The quotation is at p. 107 n. 157. A similar argument, using the dichotomy of "house" and "street" is made by Robert DaMatta, "As raizes da violência no Brasil" in M. C. Paoli, ed., *A violência brasileira* (São Paulo: Brasiliense, 1982); same author, *Carnivals, Rogues and Heroes* (South Bend, Ind.: Notre Dame University Press, 1991), 170.

[187] Roberto Kant de Lima, "Legal Theory and Judicial Practice: Paradoxes of Police Work in Rio de Janeiro City" (Ph.D. Diss., University of California, Berkeley, 1986), 122–23.

[188] DaMatta, *Carnivals, Rogues and Heroes*, 163; A. and E. Leeds, "Accounting for Behavioral Differences: Three Political Systems and the Responses of Squatters in Brazil, Peru, and Chile," in John Walton and L. Masotti, eds. *The City in Comparative Perspective* (New York: John Wiley, 1976), 192–248.

[189] Paulo S. Pinheiro, "Violência do estado e classes populares" *Dados* (Rio de Janeiro) 22 (1979), 5–24; quotation from Italian minister at p. 9. Slavery had been abolished in Brazil a little more than a decade before this remark. Thomas Skidmore, *Politics of Military Rule in Brazil, 1962–85* (New York: Oxford University Press, 1988), 126–27.

[190] Alfred Stepan, "The New Professionalism of Internal Warfare and Military Role Expansion," in Alfred Stepan, ed., *Authoritarian Brazil* (New Haven, Conn.: Yale University Press, 1973), 47–65. Joan Dassin, ed., *Torture in Brazil* (New York: Vintage, 1986).

[191] For the PM, see Heloisa Fernandez, "A organização da Rota e a violência policial no estado de São Paulo," conference paper, University of São Paulo, 1988; Pinheiro, "Police and Political Crisis: The Case of the Military Police" in Martha Huggins, ed., *Vigilantism and the State in Modern Latin America* (New York: Praeger, 1991), 167–88. For the civil police, see Caldeira, *City of Walls*, 171–72.

[192] Caldeira, *City of Walls*, 211.

[193] Mingardi, op. cit., 53.

[194] Mingardi, op cit., 57. I was given an account virtually the same in all respects in 1987 by a distinguished *delegado* who had been one of the reformers under Montoro.

[195] Figures from Guilherme Santana, 1987, set forth in "Police Abuses in Brazil" (New York: Americas Watch, 1987), 36. It is apparent from these figures that many cases carry over from year to year, since the number resolved is larger than the number opened. I have no data on what happened to "officers guilty" (*condenados*).

[196] See, for example, policeman quoted in Skidmore, *Politics of Military Rule,* 409 n. 151. Interview with Afanásio Jazadji by Bell Chevigny, July 1987.

[197] Forum Nacional, *A questão social no Brasil,* chap. 1. For the crime rate, see Caldeira, *City of Walls,* 130; chap. 2 passim.

[198] José de Souza Martins, "Lynchings—Life by a Thread: Street Justice in Brazil, 1979–1988," in Huggins, ed., *Vigilantism and the State in Modern Latin America,* 25. To the same effect, based on similar evidence, see in the same volume, M. V. Benevides and R-M F. Ferreira, "Popular Responses and Urban Violence: Lynching in Brazil," 33–46.

[199] "Urban Police Violence in Brazil" (New York: Americas Watch, 1993); "Final Justice: Police and Death Squad Homicides of Adolescents in Brazil" (New York: Americas Watch, 1994); "Public Opinion on Human Rights in Greater São Paulo," report by IBOPE, 1990. Claim by Fleury, reported in V. Salaro, "Fim dos Justiceiros em São Paulo?" *Metro News* (São Paulo) May 16, 1988, p. 17.

[200] Heloisa Fernandes, "Authoritarian Society: Breeding Ground for *Justiceiros,*" in Huggins, op. cit., 67.

[201] Alba Zaluar, "Condominio do diabo: as classes populares urbanas e a lógica do ferro e do fumo," in Paulo S. Pinheiro, ed., *Crime violência e poder* (São Paulo: Brasiliense, 1983) 249–77. To the same effect, R. Shirley, "A Brief Survey of Law in Brazil," *NS: The Canadian Journal of Latin American and Caribbean Studies* 13, no. 23 (1987): 1–13. The quotation is from IBASE, "A gente enterra o morto, silencia e se conforma" (Rio de Janeiro: IBASE, 1990), 17.

[202] A. L. Paixão, "Segurança privada, direitos humanos, e democracia," *Novos Estudos CEPRAP* 31 (1991): 131–41. Compare Clifford Shearing, "The Relation between Public and Private Policing," in Michael Tonry and Norval Morris, eds., *Modern Policing* (Chicago: University of Chicago Press, 1992).

[203] Cardia, "Percepção de direitos humanos," 27.

[204] Statement dated July 17, 1992, São Paulo OAB, office of human rights, binder "Depoimentos tomados e não autuados." The idea was apparently not original with the São Paulo civil police; an Amnesty International investigator saw a club similarly decorated in Pernambuco in 1988. "Brazil: Torture and Extrajudicial Execution in Urban Brazil" (New York: Amnesty International, 1990), 2.

[205] "Jornalismo policial radiofônico: A questão da violência," *Principios de Justica e Paz* (São Paulo) 1, no. 1 (1985): 16.

[206] "Não dá para dar botão de rosa para marginal," *Folha de S. Paulo,* July 7,

1991, p. 4-1. The minister repeated the phrase in an interview in August 1992 at the Center for the Study of Violence at USP. The word *marginal,* which is constantly used in Brazil, is sometimes translated as "outlaw," but it suggests also that those at the margin are to be identified with crime.

207 Sérgio Adorno, "Criminal Violence in Modern Brazilian Society: The Case of the State of S. Paulo" (São Paulo Center for the Study of Violence, 1992).

208 Barcellos, *Rota 66,* 249, 258–59.

209 São Paulo Military Tribunal, case # 36587/89.

210 Eloi Pietá, "Notícias de crimes na polícia militar," Aug. 29, 1991, on file at the office of Human Rights in the São Paulo bar association.

211 This account adapted from "Final Justice" (New York: Human Rights Watch, 1994), 48; I heard an incomplete account from a prosecutor in 1992, before the case had been reinvestigated, which was in all respects consistent.

212 This pattern is noted by Eloi Pietá in his report, op. cit., and also by Barcellos, *Rota 66,* 113, 151.

213 For the state of the spirit, S. Sanvito, "A defesa da Rota por seu chefe," *Estado de São Paulo,* Aug. 3, 1983, p. 13. For the PM protest, A. Braido, "Soldados reclamam uma PM 'mais democratica'," *Folha de S. Paulo,* Apr. 17, 1983.

214 Fernandes, "A organização da Rota e a violência policial no estado de São Paulo."

215 Barcellos, *Rota 66,* 161.

216 Quoted in Americas Watch, "Urban Police Violence in Brazil," 11. Persons in the São Paulo state administration who were in a position to know stated to me that they believed the document was genuine and was consistent with other acts by the commander.

217 "Pressionado, Pimentel ameaça 'tirar a focinheira da policia'," *Folha de S. Paulo,* June 2, 1983. See also Caldeira, *City of Walls,* 214–17.

218 "Fleury manda a Rota dar duro nos bandidos," *Diario Popular* Dec. 2, 1991, p. 3. The "boldly" phrase is quoted by Caldeira, *City of Walls,* 218.

219 For the secretary of public security, "Secretário desmente temer 'convulsão social'," *Folha de S. Paulo,* Aug. 3, 1983, p. 13. For the ROTA, "Rota, a mistica, os métodos e as mortes," *Folha de S. Paulo,* Oct. 10, 1982, quoted in Caldeira, *City of Walls,* 214.

220 Blitzes are described in "Police Abuses in Brazil" (New York: Americas Watch, 1987), 24.

221 A. Lazzarini, "A Segurança publica e o aperfeiçoamento da polícia no Brasil" (Encontro dos Comandantes Gerais da Polícias Militares, Sept. 26–27, 1991, São Paulo).

222 Constitution of 1988, Art. 5, secs. LVI and LXIII; Codigo de Processo Penal Cap. IV and V. It also appears that the provision criminalizing torture in the 1988 constitution has never been put into a statute providing a set of penalties against torture.

223 IBOPE public opinion poll on human rights, São Paulo, 1990.

224 A contrast with the situation in Rio de Janeiro strengthens the impression that a widespread change in public attitudes, more than a particular set of

institutional changes, is at work. Rio does not appear to have had activist administrative judges like those in São Paulo; instead the reform was effected through the disciplinary office of the civil police and the state attorney general's Advisor for Human Rights and Collective Interests, an office that takes complaints from the public, investigates them, and sends them on to the office of the prosecutor. The investigating lawyer often has gone to the scene of the abuse to put a stop to it. In 1991, Governor Brizola established a special police center to investigate torture and the abuse of authority in the state. Thus torture was reduced using a different institutional mechanism from that in São Paulo, but with similar results.

[225] Administrative dismissals sometimes seem to be politically motivated. In 1987, after PMs killed Fernando Ramos da Silva, he turned out to have been the boy who played the protagonist in the film *Pixote* years before. Some of the perpetrators were dismissed from the PM and commented to Caco Barcellos, "We were only dismissed because the guy was famous, on account of the film he made." Barcellos, *Rota 66,* 243. The *Pixote* case is also described in Americas Watch, "Police Abuses in Brazil" 52–53.

[226] Official analysis by the Military Tribunal, state of São Paulo; also, "Justiça militar, saturada," *Folha de S. Paulo,* Apr. 20, 1992.

[227] Case #21029/83, São Paulo Military Tribunal. This case has been described several times, Americas Watch, "Police Abuse in Brazil," 48; Americas Watch, "Urban Police Violence in Brazil," 10; Americas Watch, "Final Justice," 58.

[228] R. Lombardi, "Rota e acusada de ameaçar juiz e promotores," *Estado de São Paulo,* Dec. 17, 1993, p. C7; "Depoimento da Dra. Stella Kuhlmann e do Dr. Marco Antonio Ferreira Lima ao Conselho Estadual de Defesa do Direitos da Pessoa Humana em 19 de Novembro de 1993."

[229] This case, which was reported to us by Col. Celso Guimarães of the Rio PM, is detailed in Americas Watch, "Urban Police Violence in Brazil," 18.

[230] J. Brooke, "Brazilian Justice and the Culture of Impunity," *New York Times,* Aug. 29, 1993, p. E7; "PMs vendiam armas para traficantes," *O Globo,* Sept. 9, 1993; W. Schomberg, "Brazil Slum Massacre Puts Death Squad in the Dock," Reuters, Oct. 21, 1993; "The Killings in Candelaria and Vigario Geral: The Urgent Need to Police the Brazilian Police," (New York: Americas Watch, 1993). The resistance to reform in Rio is recounted in Americas Watch, "Final Justice," 72–79.

[231] In 1986, at the Presidente Venceslau prison, the PM killed thirteen unarmed prisoners; in 1987, at the state penitentiary, they killed twenty-nine, many after the prison had been retaken. On the prison killings in 1986 and 1987, Amnesty International, "Brazil: Torture and Extrajudicial Executions," 14–15; Ordem dos Advogados do Brasil, São Paulo, Commissão dos Direitos Humanos, "Relatório dos fatos ocorridos na penitenciaria do Estado de São Paulo," July-August 1987. For the 1992 events, J. Brooke, "Brazil's Police Enforce a Law: Death," *New York Times,* Nov. 4, 1992, p. A22; Americas Watch, "Brazil: Prison Massacre in São Paulo," Oct. 21, 1992.

[232] Americas Watch, "Urban Police Violence in Brazil," 15. As the number of killings by the PM dropped, the general homicide rate began to rise. Some police suggested that the change showed that the earlier killings had been

an effective deterrent. As this is written, it has been suggested to me that the number of unexplained homicides might in some measure be due to killings by the police for which the police are no longer in a position to take credit. The evidence is extremely sketchy at this point, and it is impossible to make a reliable assertion.

[233] "Comandante da Rota afasta 38 sargentos," *Diário Popular,* Aug 7, 1993, p. 13; K. Ellison, "Killer Cops Get Lesson in Humanity," *Miami Herald,* Sept. 24, 1993, p. 1; report prepared by the secretary of justice of the state of São Paulo, Brazil, for the 50th Session of the Commission on Human Rights of the United Nations (Geneva, 1994); S. de Freitas, "Ministro anuncia pacote antiviolência," *Folha de S.Paulo,* Mar. 29, 1994, p. 3-3. Concerning the threat to Caco Barcellos, I was told personally by Barcellos; see also "Relato devastador," *Veja SP,* Oct. 21, 1992, p. 16.

Chapter VI: Buenos Aires: City and Province

[234] Former member of the federal court of appeals, quoted in "Policías duros," *Clarín,* November 24, 1991.

[235] On the economic and political history of Argentina in this century, see Juan Corradi, *The Fitful Republic* (Boulder, Colo.: Westview, 1985), 32–39; Carlos Waisman, *Reversal of Development in Argentina* (Princeton, N.J.: Princeton University Press, 1987), chap. 8.

[236] On the politics of Argentina, see A. Garro, "Nine Years of Transition to Democracy in Argentina: Partial Failure or Qualified Success?" *Columbia Journal of Transnational Law* 30 (1992): Corradi, op. cit. On the relative prosperity of Argentina, see Garro, id., and UNDP *Human Development Report 1993* (New York: Oxford University Press, 1993). Population figures from *The World Almanac, 1994.*

[237] Americas Watch, "Police Violence in Argentina" (New York: Americas Watch, 1991), 7 (hereafter "Americas Watch 1991").

[238] Rodríguez Molas, *Historia de la tortura y el orden represivo en la Argentina* (Buenos Aires: Eudeba, 1985), 1:103. The quotation is from R. Walsh, "La Secta del Gatillo Alegre," *CGT* (journal of the CGT, Buenos Aires), May 9, 1968.

[239] The material concerning Etchecolatz is drawn from M. C. Caiati, "Hace dos décadas Rodolfo Walsh ya había denunciado a un feroz represor, aúnque no llegará a conocer su nombre: Miguel Etchecolatz," *Nuestra Presencia,* July 3, 1987 (Buenos Aires), p. 9. The best description of the nationalist ideology and its antiliberal roots is David Rock, *Authoritarian Argentina* (Berkeley and Los Angeles: University of California Press, 1993); quotations about the mission of the military are at p. 98. The material concerning the son of Leopoldo Lugones appears in Rodriguez Molas, *Historia,* 2:87–92, drawn from M. Onrubia, *Los Torturados* (Buenos Aires, 1931).

[240] See, for example, the editorial, "Seguridad pública" *Clarín,* Mar. 25, 1992; "En la última década se triplicaron las causas por abuso de armas" and "Las empresas de seguridad consolidan la conformación de guetos," *La Maga,* Dec. 15, 1992; R. Giordano, "Lluvia negra," *Noticias,* Apr. 15, 1990.

[241] Reprinted in Rodríguez Molas, *Historia,* 2:295–96 from *La Nación,* Mar. 30, 1985.

[242] The foregoing paragraph is based on A. Garro, "Nine Years of Transition" 38–40. The data from the Dirección Nacional de Derechos Humanos is in Ministerio del Interior, DNDH, "Informe: Investigación sobre aplicación Arts. 144, 144bis y 144ter del código penal (apremios ilegales)" (Buenos Aires, 1991); Americas Watch 1991 at p. 20 mistakenly gives the figure as 678, not 698, apparently a misprint. The later report of the Dirección Nacional de Derechos Humanos is mentioned in "Excepciones" *Página 12,* May 14, 1994.

[243] Representative of the numerous news reports is "Caso Nuñez: acusan a más policías" *Clarín,* Apr. 16, 1994.

[244] The reforms are described in Garro, "Nine Years of Transition," 39, 43 n. 135.

[245] Parts of the case are reported in the press, "Cuatro policías detenidos por homicidio simple en José C. Paz," *Página 12,* Feb. 3, 1988; "Macondo en José C. Paz," *Página 12,* Mar. 2, 1988; "Policías con prisión preventiva por un cuadruple homicidio," *Clarín,* Mar. 6, 1988. The case is summarized in Americas Watch, 1991, pp. 34–35. The quotation in the text is from the "Macondo" story.

[246] The decision is Stipelman et al., #21.832, Sala 6a, Camara Nac. de Apelaciones en lo Criminal y Correccional, March 26, 1992. News reports are "Los condenados" *Página 12,* Mar. 31, 1992; "Perpetua para 3 policías que mataron a sangre fría a un joven de 20 años." *Clarín,* Mar. 31, 1992.

[247] The material on the Ingeniero Budge case is voluminous, and some of it is summarized in Americas Watch 1991 pp. 31–34. In Argentina, the adjective *negro* is often a term of disparagement, but it refers generally to persons of lower status and not to persons of the Negro race. The figures on the changes in Comisaria 42 and Lanus were assembled by CELS and are reported in Americas Watch 1991 at p. 18.

[248] The figures for police killings were collected by CELS from newspaper accounts and are reported in somewhat different form in Americas Watch 1991, p. 12. The figure for 1991 is from "Informe sobre violencia policial, Año 1991 y 1er semestre 1992" (Buenos Aires: CELS, 1992). The actual number of killings by police is probably undercounted, since some killings may not be reported. I do not report figures on civilians wounded because, although CELS collects such data from the newspapers, it is impossible to say whether or not the papers may fail to report a larger proportion of the nonfatal shootings than of the fatal shootings; thus the two figures cannot be reliably compared. The figures for general homicides, including accidents, for 1988–90, were collected from the morgue and are reported in Americas Watch 1991, p. 14. For the figures for intentional homicides, 1990 and 1991, see "Hubo 85 asesinatos en Capital, el 40% cometido por menores de 25 años," *Clarín,* Sept. 3, 1992. It is always possible that the latter figures have been manipulated in some way to make them smaller, but there is nothing in the circumstances of the study to suggest such a manipulation. It is virtually certain that homicides by police are not included in the latter report.

[249] The CELS public opinion study is in "Informe sobre violencia policial,

Año 1991 y 1er semestre 1992" (Buenos Aires: CELS, 1992) and is summarized in "El miedo a los uniformados, según una encuesta" *La Maga,* Dec. 9, 1992, p. 2. For the decline in the crime rate, see "Según un informe oficial, descendió el nivel de delincuencia," *Clarín,* Dec. 12, 1993.

[250] E. Videla, "No podemos poner a toda la policía bajo sospecha" *Página 12,* Feb. 9, 1994, p. 14.

[251] "Budge fue un enfrentamiento," *Página 12,* Aug. 7, 1991, p. 28; "La autopsia reveló que la Policía mato a quemarropa a cuatro chicos en Pacheco," *Clarín,* Feb. 27, 1992.

[252] "Acciones de la Divisiín Robos y Hurtos," CELS, May 13, 1991; "Ratoneras: Tras un nutrido tiroteo," *El Porteño,* June 1991.

[253] "Significativas cifras sobre el uso de la tortura," *Crónica,* Jan. 23, 1991.

[254] "Ring of Agents Never Ended 'Dirty War,' Argentina Says," *Miami Herald,* Nov. 27, 1991, p. 1A; N. Nash, "Argentina Finds a Kidnapping Ring of Policemen," *New York Times,* Dec. 8, 1991, p. A12. The conviction for shooting the man, Bulgheroni, for the traffic infraction, is described in "La coima o la vida," *Página 12,* May 18, 1993.

[255] E. Tenenbaum, "A veces torturar esta bien" *Página 12,* Jan. 2, 1994, p. 2.

[256] The press on Patti's case was extensive. It is summarized in Americas Watch 1991 at pp. 22–24 and in Americas Watch, *Truth and Partial Justice in Argentina: An Update* (New York: Americas Watch, 1991). The quotation from Patti appears in "Me voy a presentar a la justicia, pero no ante ese juez," *Clarín,* Oct. 4, 1990; the quotation from Menem, from "Argentine police 'Torturer' Enjoys Status of a Hero," *London Times,* Oct. 14, 1990.

[257] Garro, "Nine Years of Transition," 74.

[258] E. R. Zaffaroni, "Right to Life and Latin-American Penal Systems" *Annals of the American Association of Political and Social Sciences* 506 (November 1989): 64.

[259] "Menem pidió mano dura contra el delito," *Clarín,* Mar. 25, 1994, p. 10; "Menem decidió crear una supersecretaría de seguridad...," *Clarín,* May 12, 1994, p. 2.

[260] Concerning the Commission of Relatives and dismissals of policemen, J. Gociol, "Algunas de las cincuenta muertes que permanecen impunes," *La Maga,* Dec. 9, 1992, p. 3; U.S. State Department, *Country Reports on Human Rights Practices for 1992,* (Washington, D.C.: GPO, 1993) 323. For the conviction of torture and murder, "Cadena perpetua para 2 policías que torturaron y mataron a un detenido," *Clarín,* May 14, 1994, p. 38.

Chapter VII: Jamaica

[261] Desmond Dekker, "Shanty Town (007)" © 1968 Beverly's Records Ltd. Used by permission. All rights reserved.

[262] Population and other statistics drawn from *The World Almanac and Book of Facts, 1994* (New York: World Almanac, 1994) and "Doing Business in Jamaica" (Price Waterhouse, 1985). Provisions of the governmental structure from Jamaica's constitution of 1962.

[263] M. J. Hirst, *Review of the Jamaica Constabulary Force* (Kingston: mimeo, 1991) secs. 3.4.10, 3.4.11 (hereafter, "Hirst report").

[264] The quotation is from Obika Gray, *Radicalism and Social Change in Jamaica* (Knoxville: University of Tennessee Press, 1991) 116. Ideas in the foregoing paragraphs are drawn from Gray as well as from Terry Lacey, *Violence and Politics in Jamaica* (Totowa, N.J.: Frank Cass, 1977), and Diane Austin, *Urban Life in Kingston, Jamaica* (London: Gordon and Breach, 1981). The "semimilitary" characterization appears in the Hirst report, sec. 2.2.4.

[265] DeLisle Worrell, *Small Island Economies: Structure and Performance in the English-speaking Caribbean Since 1970* (New York: Praeger, 1987), 3, 114.

[266] Gray, *Radicalism and Social Change*, 117.

[267] Lacey, *Violence and Politics*, 55; see also Anthony Payne, *Politics in Jamaica* (New York: St. Martin's, 1988), 19; Gray, *Radicalism and Social Change*, 9.

[268] Concerning the rise in crime, see Klaus Albuquerque, "A Comparative Analysis of Violent Crime in the Caribbean," *Social and Economic Studies* 33 (1984): 93–129; H. Ellis, "Crime and Control in the English-Speaking Caribbean," in Hans-Gunther Heiland, et al., eds., *Crime and Control in Comparative Perspectives* (Berlin and New York: de Gruyter, 1991), 133–61. Concerning the prevalence of violence, Lacey, *Violence and Politics in Jamaica*.

[269] Lacey, *Violence and Politics*, 138. The narrative here concerning the repressive policies in the sixties is based on Lacey, chap. 7, and Gray, *Radicalism and Social Change*, 116–24.

[270] The same pattern of repression has appeared elsewhere in the Caribbean; for example, in Trinidad, political protest at the end of the sixties was treated as though it were a revolutionary threat, by repressive legislation, a declaration of a state of emergency, and violent police tactics. In Guyana, it resulted in the tactics of dictatorship. Cynthia Mahabir, *Crime and Nation-Building in the Caribbean* (Cambridge, Mass.: Schenkman, 1985); Percy Hintzen, *The Costs of Regime Survival: Racial Mobilization, Elite Domination and Control of the State in Guyana and Trinidad* (Cambridge: Cambridge University Press, 1989).

[271] Lacey, *Violence and Politics*, 71. Reference to the *Gleaner* editorial appears at p. 132. Lynching and self-help are discussed at pp. 74–81, and the politicization of the police in chap. 7, "Police and Politics."

[272] Lacey, *Violence and Politics*, 71–74. Of course, we do not know what proportion of shooting incidents, either by police or civilians, was not reported in the press. Nevertheless, the principal newspaper, the *Gleaner*, is a chief source of information for the island, and it is likely that the trends are accurately reported by Lacey.

[273] Payne, *Politics in Jamaica*; R. Looney, *Jamaican Economy in the 1980's: Economic Decline and Structrual Readjustment* (Boulder, Colo.: Westview, 1987).

[274] Dudley Allen, "Crime and Treatment in Jamaica," in Rosemary Brana-Shute and Gary Brana-Shute, *Crime and Punishment in the Caribbean* (Gainesville: University of Florida Press, 1980).

275 Public opinion poll reported, K. Freed, "Violence Mars J'can Paradise," *Sunday Herald,* Nov. 29, 1992, p. 6A. Story on lynching, "Market Gunman Beaten to Death," *Gleaner,* July 3, 1986, p. 3. Statistics on lynching from E. George Green, private communication.

276 The story about Manley, "'You Damn Well Have to Smile'—Manley," *Middlesex News,* June, 1989, p. 7. Number of security guards, Carl Stone, "Assessing Americas Watch," *Gleaner,* Oct. 15, 1986. Some security guards do not work full time, and there is some overlap with the police, who often "moonlight" as guards.

277 Quotation from the Hirst report, sec. 7.9.8. For the John Headley case, "Death in Ramble Lock-up—Witnesses forced to sign paper," *Weekly Gleaner,* Nov. 16, 1992, p. 2A.

278 Civilians killed by police, 1983–85, culled by the Jamaica Council for Human Rights from reports in the *Gleaner;* all other figures from the Jamaican government. The figure of 20* police killed in 1984 includes seven auxiliaries; it is not clear whether other years include auxiliaries. The record concerning police use of deadly force in the eighties and nineties is unusually complete because the Jamaica Council for Human Rights clipped the newspapers and kept a tally of the number of persons killed each year by the police. After Americas Watch made a field report in 1986 (in which I participated) on the human rights situation generally in Jamaica, we were able to get statistics from the government itself.

279 The Jamaican constitution provides in section 14 for a right to life, adding in subsection 2 that

> a person shall not be regarded as having been deprived of his life in contravention of this section if he dies as a result of the use of force to such extent as is reasonably justifiable in the circumstances of the case
>
> (a) for the defense of any person from violence or for the defense of property;
>
> (b) in order to effect a lawful arrest or to prevent the escape of a person lawfully detained....

It is not clear what "reasonably justifiable" force would be, but this passage would appear to contemplate the use of deadly force against unarmed persons fleeing from arrest. Nevertheless, the authorities rarely admit that a person shot was unarmed.

280 Patrick Locke case, G. Sinclair, "Paralyzed Man Still Waiting to Collect $1.7m Award," *Gleaner,* May 12, 1992, p. 1. The rooftop cases, "Paraplegic Wins Lawsuit," *Weekly Gleaner,* Aug. 12, 1991; "Cop on Another Murder Charge," *Star,* July 7, 1992. The Sidney Francis case, Carl Stone, "Crude Crowd Control," *Weekly Gleaner,* Aug. 5, 1991, p. 28; "Cops Charged for Murder," *Weekly Gleaner,* Sept. 23, 1991. Eddie Hayle case from statements of six witnesses, files of Jamaica Council on Human Rights. The case appears in Americas Watch, *Human Rights in Jamaica* (New York: Americas Watch, 1986) 19, 24, 62. The shooting of the youth in the foot is from the files of the Jamaica Council for Human Rights and is reported in the Americas Watch follow-up report, "Human Rights in Jamaica" (New York: Americas Watch, 1993), 8.

[281] More detailed accounts of cases involving Gardner and Laing appear in Americas Watch, "Human Rights in Jamaica" (1986 and 1993).

[282] M. Cargill, "Letter to Americas Watch," *Gleaner*, Oct. 19, 1986.

[283] Carl Stone, "Reassessing Americas Watch," *Gleaner*, Oct. 15, 1986, p. 8.

[284] Carl Stone, *Political Opinions of the Jamaican People (1976–81)* (Kingston, Jamaica: Blackett, 1982), 68.

[285] C. Stone, "The Police and the Public," *Weekly Gleaner*, Sept. 9, 1991, p. 22; "Jamaican Police 'Brutal, Corrupt'—Commissioner Condemns Police Indiscipline," *Weekly Gleaner*, Aug. 19, 1991; "Too Many Questionable Police Killings—Says Knight," *Weekly Gleaner*, May 29, 1992. Stories about public protest: "Residents Block Road to Protest Killing by Police," *Star*, June 15, 1992, p. 1; "Four Meet Violent Deaths," *Gleaner*, July 26, 1992, p. 39; "Retaliation for Police Shooting," *Gleaner*, July 22, 1992, p. 1; "Killing Sparks Protest," *Gleaner*, July 2, 1992, p. 25; Editorial, "Investigating the Police," *Herald*, July 31, 1992, p. 9.

[286] The figures on the number of prosecutions for homicide were supplied to me by the Ministry of National Security and Justice. The Headley prosecution as well as the sum paid in damages in 1991 are mentioned in U.S. State Department, *Country Reports on Human Rights Practices for 1993* (Washington, D.C.: GPO, 1994), 484. The Patrick Locke case, G. Sinclair, "Paralyzed Man Still Waiting to Collect $1.7m Award," *Gleaner*, May 12, 1992, p. 1; roof shooting case, "More Money for Man Shot by Cop," *Weekly Gleaner*, Nov. 24, 1992, p. 1. Quotation from Hirst report, sec. 6.3.54.

[287] The Hirst report considers the management and personnel problems of the JCF in chaps. 3 and 4; accountability in chap. 6. Recommendations appear at p. 112 and generally in chap. 9. Some of the issues have also been dealt with by Anthony Harriott, "Vigilante Justice or Police Reform: Problems of Crime Management in Jamaica," paper presented at seminar in honor of Prof. Carl Stone, University of the West Indies, Jamaica, November 1992.

[288] Office of the Police Public Complaints Authority, Jamaica, "Annual Report 1993/94."

[289] "Cop on Another Murder Charge," *Star*, July 7, 1992.

[290] "Police Recover Gun That Killed Trinity's Wife," *Gleaner*, July 19, 1992, p. 3A. It is not clear what difference the disappearance of the gun could have made to the homicide prosecution, since Gardner admitted he shot his wife, claiming it was an accident. It is possible that at the time the gun disappeared, however, it might have seemed more important.

[291] "Suspected Thief Shot 6 Times by Policemen," *Weekly Gleaner*, Mar. 18, 1991.

[292] Louise Shelley, *Policing Soviet Society* (London: Routledge, forthcoming).

[293] Carl Stone, "Poor PJ Patterson," *Gleaner*, May 18, 1992. The article was written shortly after the LAPD officers who beat Rodney King were acquitted in state court and before they were tried in federal court. Cases of civil disturbances in response to perceived prejudiced acts by police in Jamaica, "Retaliation for Police Slaying?," *Gleaner*, July 22, 1992, p. 1. "Partiality in Pt. Maria Shooting Angers Citizens," *Middlesex News*, October 1989, p. 1.

Chapter VIII: Mexico City, the Federal District

[294] The results of the Bahia conference have not been published. The puzzlement is reflected, however, in Raúl Zaffaroni's short piece that grew out of the conference, E. R. Zaffaroni, "Right to Life and Latin-American Penal Systems," *Annals of the American Association of Political and Social Sciences* 506 (November 1989): 57.

[295] Table 3 in George Grayson, ed., *Prospects for Democracy in Mexico* (New Brunswick, N.J.: Transaction, 1990), 267.

[296] Sidney Weintraub, "Structural Reforms," 149–60 and David Simcox, "Demography, Development and Migration," 205–18, both in Grayson, ed., *Prospects for Democracy in Mexico*. Population figures from *Macrópolis* (Mexico City) Oct. 29, 1992, p. 16. Data on poverty and housing in Mexico City from Peter Ward, *Mexico City* (Boston: G. K. Hall, 1990), 21, 186.

[297] Both quotations from Pablo González Casanova, *Democracy in Mexico* (New York: Oxford University Press, 1970), 68 and 33–34, respectively. On the strength and centralization of the state, see also Stephen Morris, *Corruption and Politics in Contemporary Mexico* (Tuscaloosa: University of Alabama, 1991), 24–25. For the place of the army, see also Roderic Camp, "The Military," in Grayson, ed., *Prospects for Democracy*, 85–91.

[298] The "peace and order" phrase is from Morris, op. cit., 35. For the control of government units, González Casanova, op. cit., chap. 1.

[299] M.D. Baer, "The Press," in Grayson, ed., *Prospects for Democracy*, 105–8; U.S. State Department *Country Reports on Human Rights Practices for 1992* (Washington, D.C.: GPO, 1993), 445.

[300] Morris, *Corruption and Politics*, passim and esp. 43. J. Bailey, "The Bureaucracy," in Grayson, ed., *Prospects for Democracy*, 26–32.

[301] "Seguridad en el DF," *Macrópolis*, Oct. 29, 1992, pp. 15–27.

[302] Camp, "The Military," 86.

[303] Grayson, ed., *Prospects for Democracy*, 175.

[304] For the effects of corruption, D. Aponte, "La corrupción obstaculiza el desarrollo de AL," *La Jornada*, May 2, 1993, p. 43. For the end of exceptionalism, S. Aguayo Quezada, "La agonía de la excepcionalidad mexicana," *La Jornada*, June 26, 1993, p. 5.

[305] There is a series of stories in the newspaper *El Financiero* (Aug. 28, 1993, n.p.), concerning the auxiliary police. The stories appear to be promotion of services to industry. Among them are "Se Moderniza la Policía Auxiliar del DF" and "Una Policía Auxiliar Acorde a Cada Epoca de la Ciudad de Mexico."

[306] The informal official history is Alesandro Iñigo, *Bitacora de un Policía 1500–1982* (Depto. del D.F., 1985), ch. 14. For Durazo's administration, see Jonathan Kandell, *El Capital* (New York: Random House, 1988), 544–49.

[307] The facts of the case are recounted in G. Castillo García, "La ciudadania en constante peligro, ahora le tocó el turno al reportero Rafael Luviano," *7Cambio*, January 1993, p. 16; R. Ramirez Heredia, "Y si no fuera peri-

odista?," id., p. 22. The final results I was told orally by Luviano's office.

[308] Comisión de Seguridad Pública y Protección Civil, ARDF, "Relación de denuncias presentadas por ciudadanos en contra de elementos de secretaría general de protección y vialidad," December 1992, pp. 11–12.

[309] "Protestan Policías ante Camacho Solís en la Ceremonía Oficial del DDF al Príncipe Carlos," *El Financiero,* Feb. 16, 1993; F. Sanchez y E. Estrada, "Tiene remedio la policía capitalina?," *Contenido,* August 1992, pp. 46–54.

[310] H. González, "Investiga la Controlaría el Desorden Adminsitrativa y Operativa en la Policía Durante la Gestión de Tapia Aceves," *El Financiero,* Mar. 24, 1993, p. 38.

[311] The Quijano case is reported as follows: Amnesty International, *Mexico: Torture with Impunity* (New York: Amnesty International, Index AMR 41/04/91), 42; and "Mexico: The Persistence of Torture and Impunity" (London AI Index AMR 41/01/93) 18. Americas Watch, *Human Rights in Mexico: A Policy of Impunity* (NY:Americas Watch, 1990), 14; and "Unceasing Abuses: Human Rights in Mexico One Year After the Introduction of Reform" (New York: Americas Watch, 1991), 12–13 (hereafter, "Americas Watch 1991" and "Americas Watch 1993," respectively). U.S. State Department, *Country Reports on Human Rights Practices for 1992* (Washington, D.C.: GPO, 1993), 441. The killing of people in autos, Americas Watch 1991, p. 17; Minnesota Advocates for Human Rights, "Paper Protection: Human Rights Violations and the Mexican Criminal Justice System" (Minneapolis, 1990), 12; the story about the invasion of Ceballos, Durango, id. at pp. 13–14.

[312] The quotation from Coello Trejo, former head of the narcotics police, is from Amnesty International 1991, p. 42. The quotation of the U.S. official is from M. Miller, "Mexico Has New General in the War on Narcotics," *Los Angeles Times,* Nov. 13, 1990; quoted in Americas Watch 1991, p. 33.

[313] Mexican officials were implicated in the torture-murder of the U.S. DEA agent Enrique Camarena in 1985, which resulted, among other cases, in the abduction by U.S. officials of a defendant from Mexico and the decision of the U.S. Supreme Court in the case of *U.S. v. Alvarez-Machaín,* 112 S. Ct. 857 (1992).

[314] This case is discussed in Americas Watch 1991, p. 28; Amnesty International 1991, pp. 10–11; Comisión Mexicana de Defensa y Promoción de los Derechos Humanos, *Informe sobre los Derechos Humanos en México* (Mexico City, 1992) 64–65; the CNDH informed me of further results.

[315] This account is based on CNDH Recommendation #15/91, *CNDH Gaceta,* Apr. 15, 1991; Amnesty International 1991, pp. 14–16. Where the two accounts differ, I have relied on the CNDH.

[316] U.S. State Department, *Country Reports on Human Rights for 1993* (Washington, D.C.: GPO, 1994), 490.

[317] For procedure with respect to confessions before 1991, Minnesota Advocates for Human Rights, "Paper Protection: Human Rights Violations and the Mexican Criminal Justice System" (Minneapolis, 1990); Sarre Iguíniz, at that time a lawyer in Aguascalientes, is quoted at p. 15. I also rely on Americas Watch 1990, p. 11.

[318] The case is CNDH Recommendation #12/92; the final outcome for the complainant and the accused officials was obtained from the CNDH also.

[319] The change in the code of criminal procedure appears as the Decreto de 22 de diciembre de 1990 in *Diario Oficial,* Jan. 8, 1991; La ley federal para prevenir y sancionar la tortura in *Diario Oficial,* Dec. 27, 1991.

[320] CNDH case #122/92/DF/CO2148 and Acordo, Jan. 19, 1993.

[321] Concerning the failure to prosecute and the promotion in the Quijano case, Americas Watch, 1991, p. 13; Amnesty International 1993, pp. 17–18. Concerning the Buendía and Corona prosecutions, U.S. State Department, *Country Reports on Human Rights Practices for 1993* (Washington, D.C.: GPO, 1994), 490.

[322] As of 1993, Amnesty International identified only one torture victim who had been compensated, Amnesty International 1993, p. 15. Rafael Luviano was compensated for the loss of his eye, but that was a matter of executive discretion. It only emphasizes the fact that compensation ought to be regularized. The U.N. Convention against Torture and the International Covenant on Civil and Political Rights, which Mexico has ratified, require compensation to victims of abuse.

[323] A. Urrutia, "Fueron sancionadas el año pasado, 404 Agentes Judiciales: Cabrera," *La Jornada,* Jan. 7, 1993, p. 48; S. Guerrero Chipres, "531 policías Consignados en el Sexenio," *El Financiero,* Feb. 3, 1993.

[324] As a matter of logic, it is impossible to exclude the possibility of many secret killings, not admitted by the police. Certainly there were hundreds of political disappearances in the last twenty years, all over the country, for which no official body has accepted responsibility, although the CNDH has tried to investigate them, see e.g., U.S. State Department *Country Reports on Human Rights Practices for 1993,* 491; Americas Watch, 1991, pp. 35–38. *Madrinas* and other police auxiliaries may have committed other crimes for which the authors are unknown. But so far as I know there are few complaints attributing street killings to the police.

Chapter IX: Conclusion

[325] The argument is made more extensively in the introduction. The literature is surveyed, for example, in David Garland, *Punishment and Modern Society* (Chicago: University of Chicago Press, 1990), chap. 10; Roger Lane, "Urban Police and Crime in Nineteenth Century America," in Michael Tonry and N. Morris, eds., *Modern Policing* (Chicago: University of Chicago Press, 1992), 1–50.

[326] Teresa Caldeira, "Violence, the Unbounded Body, and the Disregard for Rights: Limits of Democratization in Brazilian Society" (paper delivered at LASA, March 1994), 39.

[327] Peter Ward, *Mexico City: The Production and Reproduction of an Urban Environment* (Boston: G. K. Hall, 1990), chap. 6.

[328] Lane, "Urban Police and Crime," 34–35.

[329] P. Weiss, "A Hoplophobe among the Gunnies" *New York Times Magazine,* Sept. 11, 1994, p. 84. See also Gary Kleck, *Point Blank* (New York: De Gruyter, 1991). While it is true that the ideology opposing firearms

control is strongest in rural areas of the United States, it is by no means absent in the cities.

330 Tom Tyler, *Why People Obey the Law* (New Haven, Conn.: Yale Uuniversity Press, 1990).

331 The three-part proposal was suggested by passages in M. J. Hirst, "Review of the Jamaica Constabulary" (Jamaica, 1991) and in Wayne Kerstetter, "Who Disciplines the Police? Who Should?," in William Geller, ed., *Police Leadership in America* (New York: Praeger, 1985).

332 When in *Tennessee v. Garner*, 471 U.S. 1 (1985), the U.S. Supreme Court announced a rule limiting the use of deadly force to situations in which the suspect poses a threat of violence, many police departments already had rules which limited the use of deadly force as much or more than the decision.

333 W. Rashbaum and J. Forero, "Top Cop Nixed Brutality Unit Idea: Sources," *NY Newsday,* April 10, 1995, p. A8.

334 S. Walker, "Historical Roots of the Legal Control of Police Behavior," in Craig Uchida and David Weisburd, *Police Innovation and Control of the Police* (New York: Springer-Verlag, 1993); S. Mydans, "Alarmed by Deaths in Car Chases, Police Curb High-Speed Pursuits," *New York Times,* Dec. 26, 1992, p. A1.

335 Diana Gordon, *The Justice Juggernaut: Fighting Street Crime, Controlling Citizens* (New Brunswick, N.J.: Rutgers University Press, 1990); Michel Foucault, *Discipline and Punish* (New York: Pantheon, 1977). The phrase describing community policing is from M. Moore, "Problem-solving and Community Policing," in Tonry and Morris, *Modern Policing,* 99. The phrase from São Paulo appears in V. Quadros, "São Paulo muda orientaçao da PM," *Jornal do Brasil,* Jan. 21, 1994.

336 Complaints to the Inter-American Commission are not presented under the United Nations standards, but technically under analogous provisions of the OAS Charter and the American Convention on Human Rights. T. Buergenthal, "The Inter-American System for the Protection of Human Rights," in Theodor Meron, *Human Rights in International Law* (New York: Oxford University Press, 1985).

337 "Report Prepared by the Secretary of Justice of the State of São Paulo, Brazil, for the 50th Session of the Commission on Human Rights of the United Nations" (Geneva, 1994)

338 Code of Conduct for Law Enforcement Officials, U.N. Doc. A/34/36 (1979); Basic Principles on the Use of Force and Firearms by Law Enforcement Officials, U.N. Doc. E/AC.57/DEC/11/119 (1990). The quotation is from Art. 22.

INDEX

D